MY FIRST 79 YEARS

MY
79
FIRST · YEARS

ISAAC STERN
written with
CHAIM POTOK

DA CAPO PRESS

A CIP record for this book is available from the Library of Congress.

First Da Capo Press Edition 2000
ISBN 0-306-81006-9

Published by Da Capo Press
A Member of the Perseus Books Group
http://www.dacapopress.com

1 2 3 4 5 6 7 8 9 10—04 03 02 01 00

*To my adorable and supportive wife, Linda,
who had no idea what she was getting into,
and to my deeply loved, extraordinary children, Shira, Michael, and David, who could
have told her!*

—*Isaac Stern*

Acknowledgments

WITHOUT the help, thoughtfulness, and advice of the persons and institutions listed below, this book would have been more boring than necessary.

Bach, Beethoven, Brahms, Mendelssohn, Mozart, Schubert, Tchaikovsky, and Guarneri del Gesù, among many others.

The Archives of Leonard Bernstein, Carnegie Hall, the Chicago Symphony, the Los Angeles Philharmonic, the New York Philharmonic, and the Israel Philharmonic.

Amberson, Inc., Joan Benny Blumofe, Jacques Boubli, Laura Case, Allen Damerell, Joan Davidson, Roméo Enriquez, Sam Guy, Eva Hornyak, Gino Francesconi, Peter Gelb, Bob Gottlieb, Marta Istomin, Lee Lamont, Bella Linden, Anthea Lingeman, Rita Madrigal, Nancie Monteux-Barendse, William S. Moorhead III, Rene Morel, the New York Public Library, Lynne Normandia, Lionel Rudko, the San Francisco Conservatory of Music, the San Francisco Symphony, Walter Scheuer, Ken Schneider, Henry Shweid, Teri Stein, David Stern, Michael Stern, Shira Stern, Linda Reynolds Stern, and Roman Terleckyj.

MY FIRST *79* YEARS

*T*O BE a musician in the service of music is not a job; it is a way of life.

Two things are necessary for a life in music: a clear idea of what you want to be, and the arrogance to pursue it. You can't walk onstage and say to the public, "Excuse me, I'm here." You must believe in yourself and make immediately clear to everyone, "I'm going to play. *Listen!*"

For me, the art of making music is a highly personal affair that involves the performer, the instrument, and the public. It's all too easy to be ignorant, or feign ignorance, of basic rules of music, and to say or think, "This is the way I feel, I will do whatever I like, I don't need to recognize the boundaries of good taste or know the historical development of musical composition or have some rudimentary idea of the history of musical performance." But to abide by the strict disciplines of music and, accepting those limitations, develop an individual voice; to become perceptive and honest; and above all, to recognize how to convince the listener—not go to the listener, but bring the listener to you—*that* is the mark of musical artistry.

Certainly, there are enormously original performers who see possibilities beyond the academic limitations of a few black spots on lined white paper, but their individuality comes out of deep knowledge and consciousness of the origins of musical creativity and the wondrous potentials of sound and imaginative phrasing that make an individual performance so arresting and so true. This only proves what is, for me, a basic truth: there are many ways to play music beautifully and with originality. That is why the same piece of music in the hands of many great artists can sound so different and yet remain faithful to all the possibilities, all the variants, that are true to the imagination of the creative spirit who wrote the music. This is the wonder of being a musician: the demanding, lifelong search for more and better ways to play a given piece of music beautifully. It is why no one artist can ever give the definitive performance.

All my formative years as an artist were spent in America, at a time when there was an ingathering of musical influences from virtually every country of Europe—an amalgam of cultures meeting and making music in the United States. The people with whom I studied in San Francisco and New York came from the European experience. European musicians had an enormous influence on string, wind, and brass playing in America. The American sound today is a variegated, colorful hybrid grown from the best seeds of Europe. Had there not been an America to run to, none of this unique musical strength could have developed as it did.

I think of the good fortune, the marvelous concatenation of circumstances, that enabled me to grow up and play with really great European musical figures, starting with Pierre Monteux, then Otto Klemperer and Frederick Stock, and later on with Eugene Ormandy, Charles Munch, George Szell, Fritz Reiner, William Steinberg, Thomas Beecham, and so many, many others. I have been privileged to play with famous conductors and some not internationally known, faithful and constant friends with whom I have enjoyed making music and who are part of my musical consciousness.

Of immense importance to me was my familiarity in my early days with the violin playing of Fritz Kreisler, Jascha Heifetz, Jan Kubelik, Bronislaw Huberman, Nathan Milstein, David Oistrakh, and Joseph Szigeti. Someone said of Szigeti that he looked as though he'd learned to play the violin in a telephone booth; he was so *awkward*. But he was one of the most profound musicians I have ever known, and a very good friend. I often visited with him in Switzerland, where he had his home. He was always very nervous onstage. I remember a performance he gave at Carnegie Hall in the mid-forties. In the opening work, he was ill at ease and not quite with it. Then he played the Brahms G Major Sonata, one of the most seraphic, poignant, soul-searching works in all the violin literature—music you don't perform, you live through. You try to show to what degree it is the essence of living, an appreciation for the act of life. Szigeti hit his stride and took off. I believe the pianist was Nikita Magaloff; the pianist is always so vitally important in such music. It was one of the most ennobling performances I have ever heard. Nobody in the hall breathed. You were not listening to a performance of someone standing on the stage at Carnegie Hall; you were surrounded by a golden aura of music.

It's moments like these that define for me why one is a musician and what one tries to achieve when performing. While you're doing it, you're also a little way outside yourself, watching and listening to yourself. You're physically savoring it; you're psychologically rolling in it. You're enjoying doing it; you're enjoying being it; you're enjoying every part of it. You're lifted up to a level far beyond words. You're at one with something that is more than you are. In the final analysis, that's what music is all about.

It is this passion for music—how it was brought to realization in me, and my lifelong effort to share it with others—that I'm trying to convey in these pages.

ONE

*E*ARLY ONE October morning in 1937 I boarded a double-decker bus at 72nd Street in Manhattan and disappeared. I was seventeen years old.

For the next six hours, no one knew where I was: not my mother, whom I had left at our apartment without informing her that I was going out, nor our friends. The bus traveled up and down the length of Manhattan, from Washington Square to Washington Heights and back again, and I rode and rode, entirely unaware of what I was doing.

I sat on the top deck, gazing out at the streets but not taking in what my eyes were seeing. I had to face a critical moment in my life, and I needed to be alone. My head was filled with the reviews of my debut performance at Town Hall on the evening of October 10. The reviews, I thought, were disastrous.

One critic, writing that I had "sailed into Tartini's 'Devil's Trill' Sonata with the greatest aplomb, revealing a big, beautiful tone of the G string and a pleasant one on the others," added a tart comment about my "generally erratic understanding of the structure and the musical content of the ancient and honorable composition." About my playing of the Glazunov Concerto in A Minor, that same critic wrote that "the work brought no new elements from the violinist's equipment to the surface" and alluded to "a few technical smears."

Another critic began his review with these condescending words: "From that far away land of violinistic prodigies, movie 'yes-men' and sunshine, California, there comes yet another violinist"; and then went on to mention, as if in passing, that I had "definite possibilities." A third wrote, "His tone is good, especially in the lower part of the scale," but added, concerning my technique, "it can scarcely be called transcendent."

I remember yet another critic mentioning that violinists seemed to be "as prevalent in California as oranges," and while conceding that "his talent is indubitable," nevertheless concluded that "one was not wholly convinced that he has actually traversed the Great Divide that separates the promising player from the artist."

I had hoped that my Town Hall debut would be the moment of breakthrough for me, the beginning of a career as a solo concert violinist. Instead, the New York critics were telling me to go home and practice some more, to learn how to ride the horse better. And, riding that bus, I was asking myself repeatedly: Should I keep on trying to become a concert violinist, or should I take one of the many jobs I had been offered by symphony orchestras in New York for more money than I had ever dreamed of making, money that would have meant security for my family?

The hours went by. I didn't know it at the time, but there was a huge panic developing over my disappearance. My mother was telephoning friends to find out where I was. She called the concert manager's office and was beginning to consider calling the police.

In the meantime, I was riding back and forth, trying to decide. My mind was churning. I sat there, letting it churn.

I had come for that Town Hall performance from San Francisco, where I grew up and still lived with my parents and my younger sister, Eva. My father, Solomon—a dour man, then in his mid-forties—was born in Kiev. There are pictures of him as a dashing young man with a goatee, wearing high boots and an open silk shirt and holding an easel and a paintbrush. He came from the upper-middle class, as did my mother, Clara, who was seven years younger than he. Her birthplace was Kreminiecz, a town on the Russian-Polish border. My parents told me that they and their families, who had been there for at least a generation or two, always considered the town Russian. And during the week of my birth, my mother had received a scholarship to study singing at the conservatory in St. Petersburg, which was then headed by the famous composer

Alexander Glazunov. In order to study in St. Petersburg at that time, she'd had to wear a yellow star, a rule for Jews living outside what was called the Pale. During the turbulent years of 1918–1920, following the Bolshevik Revolution, Kreminiecz changed hands about every two weeks. I was born there on July 21, 1920. It was the Polish two-week period.

In the midst of the Russian Civil War and shortly after the failed Bolshevik invasion of Poland, my father obtained a Polish passport and a visa to the United States. The passport showed his profession to be artist-painter, and his domicile Kreminiecz. After months of travel through Siberia and across the Pacific, we arrived in San Francisco, where my mother's older brother had settled some years before. I was ten months old.

My parents' language was Russian; neither spoke English. They knew a little Yiddish, but it was not a language we used in the house. It's a very expressive language, with many untranslatable phrases, and my parents would use it only to heighten or color certain comments. There was no hint, in anything my parents said, of their having lived anything remotely resembling a traditional Jewish life in Kreminiecz. I doubt that my father ever had a bar mitzvah, and he felt no inclination to insist that I should, so I didn't. The traditional Jewish home— challah every Friday night, candles, prayers—did not exist for us. Religion played no part in my family's life.

Politics, yes—we were refugees from Russia. My parents were well educated, and naturally liberal. I was impressed then, and still am, by the truth that you can take a Russian out of Russia but you can never take Russia out of a Russian. My parents had nothing to do with Soviet life or the Communist cause. There were long political discussions between them and with other Russian émigrés; they were part of a large group of people to whom everything Russian was familiar and necessary.

My father wasn't trained in a profession. As an artist of sorts, he knew a little bit about paints, so he became a house painter and was quite ill in later life with lead poisoning. He loved stewed prunes and hot chocolate, and he drank coffee; no, he drank sugar with a touch of coffee in it. A normal breakfast for him consisted of eggs, sausage, hotcakes, cheeses—which might have contributed to the ulcers he developed. During the Depression years, he started going from house to house, selling MJB coffee. Occasionally during the worst times of the Depression, when we didn't have enough money for food, we received the day's version of food stamps: boxes of cans without labels, whose contents we never knew until we opened them.

We moved a number of times during our early years in San Francisco. The two houses I remember best were the Buchanan Street house and the one at 383 29th Avenue. The house on Buchanan Street had a long series of steps that went up to the front door; it was situated on one of those typically steep San Francisco hills that always scare anyone who has never lived in a city like that. The 29th Avenue house, pale yellow or dirty white, was located in the Sunset district, about five blocks from the bay, and two or three miles from the Pacific Ocean and the beach, where there was a seal house and seal rocks and an enormous building, Fleischaker Pool, that had three or four pools, some with salt water and some heated—quite an exciting structure and for many years a great meeting place. Nearby was the Palace of Fine Arts, built for the 1915 World's Fair.

That was the normal topography of my life. As a child, I would go with my parents and sister, and with cousins and uncles and aunts, for Sunday picnics in Golden Gate Park, one of the largest and most beautiful urban parks in the country, and I remember all our drives through it. There was the area for buffalo, and the large aquarium, and a Japanese teahouse and garden with its little bridges, and Kezar Stadium, home of the San Francisco Seals, the double-A farm team of the New York Yankees, where Joe DiMaggio and Dom DiMaggio played and were trained by the famous batting coach Lefty O'Doul. I saw my first football games in that stadium. The city was also the cultural center of California, for everything except movies. There were theaters, the Geary and the Curran, and the Opera House and the Veterans Auditorium, a huge public library, and beautiful stores . In those days, no lady went downtown without wearing a hat and white gloves. There were few high-rise buildings. To this day, I remember the sound of the foghorn and the rich sea scent of the fog as it rolled into the Bay Area from the Pacific. There were only ferries then to take you across the bay to Oakland and the trains, and to Marin County. The ferries left from the Ferry Building on the Embarcadero, the dock area, where all the ships came in and were loaded and unloaded. In Chinatown, the largest in the world outside China, the street signs were all in Chinese; the district had its own telephone central, in Chinese. The Fillmore area, thick with drugs and rock music during the sixties, was the Jewish shopping district when I lived in San Francisco. There were stores where you bought herring and pickles and lox and rye bread. Fillmore and Divisadero Streets were like the lower East Side in New York. That was the world I grew up in.

I remember that my mother sometimes sang and my father played the piano. When I was six, I started piano lessons, shortly before my sister, Eva, was born. At that time, we were living on a street about three blocks from the northern side of Golden Gate Park. Across the street from us lived a family named Koblick, with whom my parents were friendly. They had a son named Nathan. When I was eight years old, Nathan was already playing the violin.

I've often said that I didn't return home from a concert one day and plead for a violin. Nor did I begin, at the age of five or six, to pick out melodies on the piano. None of that; nothing so mysterious, so romantic. My friend Nathan Koblick was playing the violin; therefore I wanted to play the violin. I can't recall what Nathan looked like as a child. The adult Nathan was tall, gaunt, with a long nose and a pained, sardonic expression on his face. He was, for a time, an insurance salesman and, later, a good tutti violinist with the San Francisco Symphony.

I don't remember how I acquired my first violin; probably my family got it for me. It was a little fiddle. I had one teacher for a while, then another, and another. Those teachers—none of them particularly effective—found that I was progressing beyond their capacity to teach me, at a faster pace than they could handle. I insisted on continuing with the violin, not because I thought I was musical but because Nathan Koblick was still playing. My parents must have turned to some friends for advice. Suddenly, for a reason not clear to me, I was enrolled in the Sunday school of San Francisco's prominent Reform synagogue, Temple Emanu-El. I proved to be a very apt student, learning to read Hebrew in a short time and becoming the best Hebrew reader in my class. That I understood not a single word of what I was reading was another matter.

The cantor at the temple was a man named Reuben Rinder. He was a very good cantor of the old school, and he loved music. One day there was some occasion when I played the violin in the temple. Cantor Rinder chanced to hear me and suddenly realized he was hearing talent. He knew my family had no money for lessons; there was hardly any money then for us to live on. And so he spoke about me to a certain maiden lady.

I can only conjecture about all the connections that were taking place, none of which I understood at the time. Temple Emanu-El was founded in 1850 by German Jews. The building where I attended Sunday school had been built in 1925 by people of wealth and influence, people who knew music and the arts, who were supporters of the San Francisco Symphony, the San Francisco Opera, and the San Francisco Conservatory of Music. One of those supporters was a woman named Lutie D. Goldstein.

She was a little pigeon of a lady. High-heeled, but sensible high heels, not spike heels. Long skirt, white gloves, little black hat, sometimes with a veil; an elfin face, always with a ready smile. She had no family except for a sister. They were the only children of a man who had made a large fortune in produce, in central California. The two sisters lived not in a house but, I seem to remember, in the Mark Hopkins Hotel. I do remember that Lutie Goldstein rode around in a chauffeur-driven Cadillac. Such high class! She was among the group of people to whom the conservatory, the symphony, and the opera always went for support. Cantor Rinder suggested that I play for her. And she adopted me, financially and personally, if not legally. It was she who brought me to the attention of the conservatory and for many years supported me in my musical studies.

The heads of the conservatory at that time were Lilian Hodgehead and Ada Clement, two women who were determined to encourage culture and musical education in San Francisco. The conservatory was then situated in a ramshackle building on California Street, but it did have a faculty. The first decent music teacher I had was a man named Robert Pollak. There is a photograph of Mr. Pollak and his class, with me in there and my friend Miriam Solovieff, who now lives in Paris. She was six; I was eight. We remain friends to this day. I have another photograph of Mr. Pollak, this one of him alone, dated 1930, on which these words appear above his signature: "To my beloved pupil Isaac Stern—May he watch every day over the treasure nature has given him."

After Robert Pollak, my teacher was Nathan Abas. By then I was the concertmaster of the conservatory orchestra. The criterion for the choice of a concertmaster was talent: who played best and could lead a group of players. I remember playing with Ernst Bloch, the famous Swiss composer, who was head of the school at the time and conducted the orchestra. One of the pieces he conducted, with me as concertmaster, was his Concerto Grosso. I wore short pants, and when I sat, my feet didn't reach the floor.

Music was a natural part of my parents' life, not an acquired social function. They would scrape together money to go to concerts; they owned a crank-up Victrola, with one of those arms that came down and had a bamboo stylus at the end that wore out after half-a-dozen plays. There were recordings by Stokowski and Toscanini in the house. It became quickly apparent to the people at the conservatory that I was an exceptional talent, and as soon as my parents realized it, there was suddenly pressure on me to study. They desperately wanted me to be a musician, a good musician. Of course, they cared about the element of success that came with being an accomplished performer, but that was not the driving force for them. What they wanted most was that my abilities be realized. My father took a great interest in my work, and my mother even more so. She was home all the time, and she kept me to the practicing grind when my tendency was to be elsewhere.

One day when I was ten years old, I suddenly discovered that I could do things on my own with the violin, things no one had taught me— move the bow in certain new ways; feel my fingers on the strings; bring forth shades of sound. I do not believe in moments that come out of nowhere. As I see it, what happens is an accumulation of experiences that blossom into a sudden sense of self and the ability to actually do something on one's own. These moments differ from child to child;

they depend so much on what the child has been exposed to. In my case, suddenly one day I became my own master. I *wanted* to play; I *wanted* to learn how to play better. I wanted to do it because I was beginning to revel in my own abilities. That was when things changed for me; when I began to discover what I could already do and to sense the possibilities of how much more I might be able to do. Never again did I need to be urged to practice.

At about that time, someone on the San Francisco Board of Education suddenly woke up and asked why I wasn't attending public school. I had been taken out of school by my parents at the age of eight because they had decided my time would be better spent practicing the violin than going to school. From time to time, I had what might laughingly be called tutors; they helped me read certain things, taught me the rudiments of mathematics. I was receiving no formal schooling, and the Board of Education decided I should be tested to find out how backward I was. They gave me the Stanford-Binet intelligence test, which was supposed to measure what the mental acuity of a child was at a given age. I took it for age ten, and it turned out that I had the capacity of a sixteen-year-old. The Board of Education told me that I was all right on my own, I should go on doing what I was doing, but I wonder about how much I missed by never having gone to high school and college. All my life I have learned from talking with people, from arguing, and from listening to others trying to convince me how wrong I was about some matter. I've made a profession of informal education.

Some months later, I gave my debut recital, in Sorosis Hall on Sutter Street. On the printed invitation, the San Francisco Conservatory of Music announced that "Isaac Stern, 10 year old student of Nathan Abas, would give a violin recital, with Miss Dora Blaney at the piano," on Tuesday, April 28, 1931. The music critic for the *San Francisco Chronicle* was present at the concert. In the review the following day, there was a comment about "a boy violinist of exceptional talent" and his excellent technical control of the instrument.

Around that time, I went to hear the pianist Ruth Slenczynska. Her father was there, and, informed that I was a young, promising violinist, he turned to me and said, "Show me your hands." Dutifully, I put out my hands. He took one look and said, "No good, you'll never be a fiddle player."

There is a picture of me, taken one year later, when I was eleven. I'm holding a violin. The picture, which appeared in the San Francisco *Call-Bulletin,* carried below it a statement that "Isaac Stern, talented 11 year old violinist, pupil of Nathan Abas, will give a recital at the Community Playhouse next Thursday night." At that recital, I played Tartini's G Minor Sonata, Bloch's *Abodah,* Schubert's *Ave Maria,* the slow movement of Lalo's *Symphonie Espagnole,* Wieniawski's *Scherzo-Tarantelle,* and other pieces. The music critic of the *Chronicle,* Alexander Fried, wrote that the violin recital "proved that he belongs to the higher order of precocious talents," and singled out my playing of a Tartini sonata, where, he commented, "his musical insight, nurtured by a distinctive schooling, was especially apparent." That was the very same Tartini piece I played six years later in my Town Hall debut—to considerably less praise from the New York critic Samuel Chotzinoff.

It was Lutie Goldstein who backed the idea of sending me to New York to study with Louis Persinger; she paid for the trip, the rented apartment, and the lessons. Louis Persinger had been Yehudi Menuhin's teacher in San Francisco and had since moved to New York, where he was one of that city's leading music professors. Someone had come up with the idea of having me play for him. I was almost thirteen; studying with Persinger seemed the next logical step for me. A letter went out to him, recommending that he take me as his student, and he replied affirmatively. My parents were informed; there were discussions; my parents, in turn, informed me. I was to travel to New York with my mother; we would live there for six months; I would study with Louis Persinger; my father and sister would remain in San Francisco and manage on their own. No one asked me what I wanted. "This is what we suggest will be good for Isaac," people said. And Isaac went along with it.

And so one day I found myself on the ferry to Oakland, together with my mother and Lutie Goldstein. In Oakland, my mother and I said our goodbyes to my benefactor and boarded the transcontinental train to Chicago. We must have had sleeping accommodations of some kind; I don't remember nights of sitting up. In Chicago, we took the Broadway Limited to New York. The trains crossed the country in the impossibly quick time of three days. I carried with me a fiddle I had borrowed from someone in San Francisco, a fiddle of now forgotten name and origin.

Louis Persinger turned out to be a warm, friendly man in his mid-fifties, dressed casually in a jacket and sport shirt. He was short and stocky, with hair around the perimeter of his head and more than slightly bald on top. Always with a chuckle in his voice, and his face wreathed in smiles. We met in his studio; I don't remember where it was located. Nor am I able to recall what I played for him. I do remember his playing the piano, and then picking up his violin and strumming the accompaniment, pizzicato, with the instrument tucked under his arm.

In the months that followed our first meeting, I went to him at least once a week. The time between lessons I spent with my mother in our apartment, practicing, always practicing. I was constantly astonished by Persinger's ability to play by heart the piano parts of any of the compositions I prepared for my lessons. He was a sweet, gentle, amiable man, not at all strict or demanding—and, in retrospect, I'm not sure that amiability was what I then needed from a teacher. As a child, I had only been taught some of the more rudimentary exercises of the *Carl Flesch Book of Scales and Etudes*. Flesch presented a series of scales, first single notes, then thirds, sixths, octaves, fingered octaves, and tenths; a method that trained a lot of people very well—the kind of training I never received. It was a piece of artillery I didn't have; I had to develop my own artillery as time went on.

The money given us by Lutie Goldstein, a few thousand dollars, ran out, and I returned with my mother to San Francisco. I was by then no longer at the conservatory; I had left about a year before. People began to look around for another teacher for me. Again, Lutie Goldstein entered the picture. She knew that the San Francisco Symphony Orchestra had just engaged a new concertmaster, a violinist named Naoum Blinder. When Blinder arrived, in 1931, the orchestra was on strike, and it remained on strike for a year. The conductor was Issay

Dobrowen, who went off soon after the strike began and was replaced by Pierre Monteux, in 1932 or 1933. Monteux, one of the truly great conductors of our time, was the first great conductor whom I met and with whom I played.

Naoum Blinder had escaped from the Soviet Union with his wife and young daughter years before: he went to Japan on a concert tour and never returned to Russia. Eventually he came to New York to teach at the Institute of Musical Art, which later became the Juilliard School. His daughter, who was my age, had died suddenly in New York.

When he arrived in San Francisco to assume the role of concert-master of the orchestra, Blinder found himself in a phantom position because of the strike. It was arranged for me to play for him, and he took me on as his student in 1932. He was my first true teacher; my only real teacher, as a matter of fact. I studied with him for five years, until I was seventeen, and haven't studied violin with anyone else since.

Blinder was very special for me. He influenced the way I've felt about music-making and music-teaching throughout the rest of my life. He was not a classically trained musician; he didn't have the background in harmony and theory of the German instrumentalists who studied in Berlin in the twenties and early thirties. Nor was his training that of the Carl Flesch method or the Russian school, where violin playing became ingrained by repetition and endless exercises of scales and études. He lived in a hectic time and had a more intuitive approach to music. His teacher had been a man named Adolph Brodsky, with whom he studied in Manchester, England. Before that, in Odessa, he had studied with Pyotr Stolyarsky, who had taught Milstein, Oistrakh, and others. It was Brodsky who had played the world premiere of the Tchaikovsky Violin Concerto, so there was a direct line, a connection, from Blinder to that concerto.

He knew the standard literature of the violin and some chamber music, and learned a great deal more in San Francisco. He was the most intuitively gifted musician one can imagine, one who thought of the violin in terms of beauty and songfulness. Through him I learned some things that became my strengths, and did not learn some other things, which became my weaknesses. Most important, he taught me to listen, to think for myself. He taught me to become my own person, not an imitation of him, not merely his disciple, and I've found that to be one of the most valuable things I ever learned in music.

He didn't, on the other hand, insist, as did other great teachers, on daily exercises and on constant practicing of scales. I would use the scales in the Beethoven concerto or the chords in a Bach sonata to train myself to think harmonically. I played scales from various compositions, always changing the fingerings to suit the musical direction of that scale. Great violinists like Heifetz and Milstein, a generation older than I, shared that tradition of rock-solid grounding in the basic training of the hands and the bow arm; it gave them ease in performance and continuing strength in their later years. The same is true of others approximately my age, like Arthur Grumiaux, the great Belgian violinist, and the Russian Leonid Kogan; and, closer to our time, Gidon Kremer; and today, performers like Itzhak Perlman, Pinchas Zukerman, Anne-Sophie Mutter. I envy the basic building-block training that all these superb artists experienced, and which gave them such a Gibraltar-like base on which to build. I remember that Heifetz, probably the greatest exponent of classical violin playing, would always ask violin students who gathered the courage to play for him, and somehow managed not to drop their instruments out of sheer fright, to do scales in odd keys—not only C major, D major, or A major, but also F-sharp minor or E-flat major, in scales, arpeggios, octaves—to test whether they had learned the proper, basic skills, a first necessity for violin study.

As I didn't have that training from Naoum Blinder, or from any of the teachers who had preceded him, I had to learn some of these basics on my own. I was fortunate to have had a natural facility for the instrument and a good ear for the underlying harmonies of whatever I was playing, whether it was a fast virtuoso piece or a slow, beautiful melody. And the cooperation between what my ear wanted to hear and what my hands wanted to do gave me a measure of the freedom I hear in some of my early recordings. As I developed and began a full-fledged concert career, I learned how to think about a new work and to train my hands as I practiced it; how to compensate for the physical difficulties and find ways to make the music simple and seemingly inevitable.

Today I am not completely convinced that I was gifted enough to do anything my ear and imagination demanded without having gone through the mill of endless basic preparation and mindless repetition that the other kind of training demanded. Yet that pitiless method of physical training by rote forced the fingers to play in preset patterns rather than encouraging a flexibility to change those patterns. I felt then, and still do, that the composer's musical directions to any series of notes always held primacy over playing the notes simply through some ingrained habit, but I know that many intelligent, gifted, and capable colleagues will disagree with me. At any rate, I had to discover for myself how to overcome numerous physical and technical problems; how to respond to the increasing difficulties I faced as I learned more and more literature for the violin and my repertoire began to grow. Those were among the things that Naoum Blinder thought it best to have me teach myself.

He was a tall, portly gentleman who always dressed in shirt and tie and generally wore a jacket and a vest with a gold chain and a gold watch. I have the watch to this day; his widow gave it to me. He had many students. As the concertmaster, he became *the* teacher of the area; young people came to him from everywhere. He was never dogmatic, never rude, never caustic. He spoke with an inherent dignity. His was a kind of benign strength. He didn't stamp out a student's personal approach to music so that one recognized the teacher, not the student. In time, his students constituted half the violin section of the orchestra. He was an astonishingly strong personality, without any trace of the egotistical about him. He encouraged me to follow my instincts and would stop me only when he felt I was doing something wrong. In other words, he let me develop my own voice on my instrument. His way of teaching became the forming ethic of my whole musical life. He taught me how to teach myself, and for that I will always be grateful. He was the single most important factor in my development.

We were very close. Later, when I came back as a successful traveling fiddler, I was allowed to call him Nousha. In a way, he adopted me and my future career as a memorial to his dead daughter—though I understood that only years later, of course. When success came and the touring began, if I was anywhere near San Francisco I would go see him and play for him, and we would talk about music. We were good friends until his death, in 1965; and I remained close to his wife, Genia, until her death, in 1989.

Naoum Blinder and Pierre Monteux became very close, and their wives took to each other like sisters. The women looked much alike: squarish from the neck down to the ankles, with thickness to match. They were determinedly gracious, very careful to associate with the highest social elements in the city while making sure that their husbands were part of those elements. And they were both very good housekeepers.

Blinder organized a string quartet, first with Willem Dehe as cellist and later with his own brother, Boris, who had become the first cellist of the San Francisco Symphony Orchestra. I would listen to them play. Through him I got to know all the first-chair players of the symphony. At thirteen, I began to play chamber music once or twice every week with the best musicians in the city, who adopted me as their mascot. I played with Herman Reinberg, cello; Willem Dehe, cello; Al White, viola; Mafalda Guarnaldi, violin; Lev Schorr, pianist; and Frank Hauser, a pupil of Blinder's who in time replaced him as the concertmaster.

I remember Dr. Leo Eloesser, a leading surgeon, who was the unofficial physician of the orchestra, the doctor of virtually every one of its players. He was a short man with a birdlike neck who favored starched, inch-high collars, looked like a young man who had suddenly grown old, and played the viola horrifically. During the Spanish Civil War, he organized and paid for a field hospital and went over to Spain to care for wounded Loyalist troops. An exceptional human being. We would play chamber music in his apartment, which was near Lombard Street, or in Herman Reinberg's home on Maple Street. We played trios, quartets, sextets. You put music on the stand, and you played another couple of quartets. There was a hunger for music and food. We were nourished by both.

I was the new kid on the block, yet the men with whom I played treated me as an equal. They were in their thirties, forties, fifties; we were a generation or two apart; but I was accepted as a colleague. There was not the slightest hint of condescension from them. I was very careful not to make serious mistakes, because I knew I would never get away with them. Whenever they would hear me doing something wrong, they would lay into me like nothing you ever saw. They were without pity—something for which I am everlastingly thankful. From them I learned how central chamber music was to the life of a musician.

Because I was a fresh talent and Blinder's student, I was taken by one person or another to every concert that came to town. And I was allowed to go to all the rehearsals of the orchestra, including those for the opera. When I was fifteen, I heard the Wagner *Ring* cycle for the first time, with the famous Wagnerian conductor Artur Bodanzky and a cast that included such "local" singers as Lauritz Melchior, Kirsten Flagstad, Elisabeth Rethberg, Lotte Lehmann, and the great bass-baritone Friedrich Schorr. Great artists and great performances that left behind lasting impressions.

Watching Monteux rehearse and conduct, I began to learn repertoire simply by listening. And I was also listening to records at home on our Victrola. I heard my first recording of Brahms' Symphony No. 4 with Stokowski; to this day, I can remember listening to the last movement, the passacaglia, with the soaring flute solo played, I believe, by William Kincaid.

At fifteen, I heard for the first time performances of all the Beethoven and Bartók quartets, played by the Budapest String Quartet. They appeared at Mills College, in Berkeley, across the bay from San Francisco, where the composer Darius Milhaud was in residence at the time. Alexander (Sasha) Schneider, the quartet's second violin, and I played some tennis and, despite that, became very close friends, and when I moved to New York in 1940, he became my closest friend, both musically and personally, until his death in 1993. His thoughts and attitudes about life and music exerted a profound influence upon me. He was my severest and most unrelenting critic, loudly telling me the "troot," and also my greatest musical champion.

What a revelation it was to hear the entire cycle of Béla Bartók's six quartets! It led me to learn the twentieth-century language of Bartók's music, which was based on the great past of Mozart, Beethoven, and Brahms.

During those teenage years, I heard Rachmaninoff give an all-Beethoven-sonata program; I heard Artur Schnabel; I heard Fritz Kreisler and Jascha Heifetz. Music, all kinds of music, was my whole life. It was not just playing the fiddle; it was *being a musician.* It was talking, doing, living music. San Francisco's rich musical life was my training ground. It formed me.

It has taken this long look back for me to realize what a fortunate youthful life I had. One could enjoy the outdoors all year long in San Francisco; one listened constantly to music; one ate fairly decently. I still remember when we lived on Buchanan Street, a block or two from Union Street. My "teenage period" revolved around two friends, both also pupils of Blinder: Nathan Ross, a Canadian to whom my parents had rented a room in our house, and Henry Shweid. Nathan would do his practicing in his room and I in mine. We'd take a break and go out and play tennis on a nearby public court; my life-long passion for tennis was born on that court. Then, when we got thirsty, we'd go to a store and buy a watermelon, cut off the ends, slice it in half, and eat the whole thing. There was a fabulous ice-cream parlor on the corner of Union and Van Ness. Henry Shweid and I would slip away from practicing and get the greatest milk shakes God ever invented. Eight inches tall, and so thick that when you put a spoon in, it stood straight up. That was a real milk shake! My mother kept wondering why I wasn't losing weight.

In those years, there was, at least for me, no "dating," as the term is understood today. I remember one of Blinder's students, a girl, coming to me one day in a diaphanous dress and asking me to "listen to her play." I listened, and that was it. I didn't know what else to do. My teenage life was music.

I had a tutor for a while, and I began to read seriously. Between all the sessions with the violin were the books of Arthur Conan Doyle, Agatha Christie, Joseph Conrad, John Dos Passos, and first readings of Shakespeare. One book that made a great impression upon me was *Man, the Unknown,* by Alexis Carrel. It made me aware of the awesome power of the human mind.

There were always people around the table in our house, my parents' friends and members of the family. All kinds of grown-up conversations took place. I learned from them what was going on politically. We read the morning *Chronicle* and *Examiner* and the afternoon *Daily News*. As far as I can recall, there were no Russian or Jewish newspapers in our house. The language of the house was English, with some occasional Russian. My sister, Eva, seven years younger than I, was going to school all through those years and was involved in her studies.

And, of course, there were the movies. To go to a movie, you traveled downtown to the Golden Gate Theater on Market Street, the city's major downtown thoroughfare. Those were the halcyon days of the movies, with orchestras in the pit. I especially loved the Westerns and the romantic comedies with Carole Lombard.

In February 1935, I made my recital debut at the Veterans Auditorium. I played the Bach Double Violin Concerto, with my teacher, Naoum Blinder. A woman named Betty Alexander, the first pianist I worked with professionally, was our accompanist. I remember also playing the Ernst Concerto, a fiendishly difficult work, which I haven't had the courage to play ever since. The critics were favorable. A year later, I played for the first time with the San Francisco Symphony Orchestra at the Civic Auditorium, a huge convention space one block south of City Hall. It was the Saint-Saëns B Minor Concerto; the orchestra was conducted by Willem Vandenberg, then the assistant conductor and first cellist. The critic of the San Francisco *Chronicle*, Alfred Frankenstein, wrote, "There is nothing of the boy prodigy about his playing anymore."

In March 1937, I played my first really professional concert, with Pierre Monteux conducting. It was on a Friday afternoon, one of a series of concerts broadcast live coast to coast, sponsored by the Junior Chamber of Commerce of San Francisco. Suddenly the country heard this young kid out of the West playing the Brahms Violin Concerto. Apparently it went quite well, because there was a ripple effect. That concert was the immediate launching point for my first tour, to the Pacific Northwest, on which I played concerts and recitals in Vancouver, B.C., Portland, and eastern Washington State.

Betty Alexander was once more my pianist. A gracious, quiet person, who seemed to me much older than what she was in fact: in her late forties. She wore her blond hair pulled back and was always beautifully dressed in what could be described more or less as English country style: light tweeds and sensible shoes. She was very well educated and extraordinarily gentle, but firmly helpful when necessary. She lived in San Francisco on Lombard Street, a steep, serpentine, narrow thoroughfare that at the time had only a few houses on it. Hers was the third from the top, and we rehearsed there often. She had a gentleman friend, the pianist Henri Deering, who lived in Carmel, and sometimes I would visit and work with her there.

In the summer of 1937, I played the Saint-Saëns Violin Concerto at what was then called the Rosebowl Concerts, in Portland, Oregon. The conductor was Basil Cameron. Before the concert he carefully instructed me about doing something special onstage at the end of the second movement when the orchestra would be playing *plik plik plik plik,* and then the harp would go *pyappyappyappyappyap,* and I would play *papapapopopop* harmonics together with the flute, all very dainty. Basil Cameron said to me, "You know, Isaac, let me tell you how to make a success today and in your future years. When you come to this part, look up toward the heavens as if you were playing to the angels, and the whole audience will applaud." I don't recall if I looked up appropriately, but I do remember the advice.

By the time I was seventeen, I had appeared in many places in and around San Francisco, and people were beginning to say, "This is really talent, he should go to New York and make his debut." That was the start of the idea of my playing in New York, the dream for every musical family. You went there to prove your worth. It was too early for me to play Carnegie Hall, with its 2,800 seats, but the second venue, Town Hall, was beautiful and acoustically wonderful. It had about 1,500 seats.

Lutie Goldstein went to a local violin expert and asked him for a good violin, a really fine violin, for Isaac Stern to play, and he sold her a Giovanni Baptista Guadagnini for $6,500. She then gave it to me as a gift. Someone arranged with a New York management company to rent the hall, print the tickets, handle the advertising, contact the critics. For the second time, my mother and I traveled to New York, sponsored by Lutie Goldstein.

There was a sense of destiny about that trip, especially on the part of my parents. From the time I was ten, they had shaped their lives to the needs of their wunderkind, and they hoped with all their hearts for my success. Menuhin was by then world-famous, and he was only four years older than I. Two other prodigies had emerged from San Francisco: the pianist Ruth Slenczynska and the violinist Ruggiero Ricci. All of San Francisco saw me as an equally magical talent. Friends from the orchestra accompanied me on the ferry to see me off. Now came the necessary moment of self-realization on the stage of Town Hall.

People in San Francisco wrote letters to their friends in New York, asking them to attend the concert. Many people were pushing tickets. Critics were called and cajoled into attending, which may account, in part, for their grudging reaction. Lots of free tickets were given out to create an audience.

The hall was by no means full. I wore a dark suit, a white shirt, a dark tie. I remember very little about the hours before the concert. My accompanist was Arpád Sándor. We rehearsed, and I played the concert. Bach. Wieniawski. Tartini. Nováček. Glazunov. Szymanowski. An enormous program. A friend of mine said later, "Isaac, what were you trying to do, play the whole violin repertoire in one concert?"

I have no clear memory of the audience. I probably did then what I've always done: play the violin and, once in a while, cast a glance at the audience. Once it becomes fixed in my mind that there are live people out there, I can close my eyes and just play, because I know the audience is there and listening. I've always had to have a vision of faces around me when I play.

After the concert, people started coming backstage. My mother. Friends. Later, we went out and ate. There was an excellent restaurant around the corner from the hall, a German sauerkraut, sauerbraten, and beer restaurant. I needed to eat.

The reviews started coming in the next day. That was a time when you were reviewed immediately after a performance. I went out early the next morning and bought the papers and read the reviews with my mother in our apartment. We were so bitterly disappointed. I was the

Great White Hope of San Francisco's music world. Everything had come so easily to me until then; I'd been so lauded for my playing and had simply taken it for granted that Town Hall would be a continuation of my successes. Instead, as I kept reminding myself on the upper deck of that bus riding up and down Manhattan, I was being patted on the head by some of New York's most eminent critics and told that I hadn't yet crossed the "Great Divide" into the lofty realm of the artist; that my playing was "erratic"; that I ought to go back to San Francisco, to the "land of violinistic prodigies, movie 'yes-men' and sunshine," and practice some more. Each of the three New York radio symphony orchestras had offered me the position of concertmaster—that meant money for the family instead of a continued struggle for income, security instead of uncertainty, stability instead of a life of never-ending travel. And if I went back to San Francisco, spent another year or two practicing and practicing, and then returned to Town Hall, how could I be certain that I would succeed even then?

Back and forth on that Manhattan bus, my head and heart churning, while my frantic mother kept telephoning to find someone who might know where I was. I recall finally saying to myself, "What the hell." I had invested so much of my life in music, I couldn't quit now. I would keep trying. I would give the career another year, another two years. I would go back to San Francisco and practice, practice, practice, and play. And I would return to Town Hall for a second chance.

TWO

*I*N SAN FRANCISCO, my Town Hall debut had been reported as an unqualified triumph. No one seemed to be taking it as a possible deathblow to my career; they were all reading the favorable sections of the reviews and glossing over the doubts and slights.

"A highly critical audience acclaimed him as a genius of rare talent" was how the *Examiner* saw it. New York irony and condescension seemed entirely lost on the *Daily News*, which, reporting the remark in the New York *Sun* about violinists being as prevalent in California as oranges, handled it as straightforward praise and added:

> But of the many reports reaching San Francisco of the splendid success achieved by Isaac Stern in New York, none is so treasured by Naoum Blinder as the following letter from Louis Persinger, with whom Isaac had studied during a brief sojourn in New York before beginning work with Mr. Blinder.
>
> Mr. Persinger wrote Mr. Blinder as follows:
>
> "No doubt you have had ample reports of the splendid success Isaac Stern had at his recital here, but I wanted to put in a word of congratulation for the remarkable way he has developed since I last heard him play.
>
> "I attended the recital, of course, and one of the things which impressed me most in Isaac's playing was his musical APPROACH to each of the works performed. The SPIRIT, I mean, whether the work required brilliancy, poetry, intensity, musical simplicity, or a hundred other things. . . .

The boy certainly showed a musical SOUL, and the audience was quick to recognize his worth and gave him a genuine ovation."

The *Daily News* article concluded by noting that "the words in capitals are Mr. Persinger's."

But the San Francisco newspapers could not diminish the disappointment I felt at the New York reviews. As soon as I arrived back home, I began to work like a madman, a very young man utterly possessed. I was getting some dates for concerts—enough to begin to realize what it meant to travel, to play, to practice, to perform. I played in Seattle, Portland, Vancouver. Once or twice, early on, my mother came with me; mostly I traveled alone or with Betty Alexander.

I remember taking the train to play a concert somewhere in Oregon or British Columbia. I entered the dining car and saw an incredibly beautiful woman, with whom I fell instantly in love. She wore slacks and a sweater, out of which rose an exquisite, unbelievable, swan-like neck. She had big black eyes and was sitting demurely, eating breakfast. She looked like nothing I had ever seen before in my life. It was Vivien Leigh. I didn't dare speak to her. I never saw her in person again.

When I wasn't touring, I worked, with Blinder and on my own, to hone my skills. I had to take my natural instincts and bind them together into stronger and stronger equipment, into greater and greater facility. I had to learn the works more profoundly; I had to practice them more; I had to get them really grooved into my swing—to use a sports term. And it was the same with playing the fiddle. You practiced and played until everything physical became almost automatic. I played in homes and temples, at festivals and celebrations—any place where I might practice, in front of an audience, the program I had to present in New York. I taught my hands and fingers to recognize what they were doing and what they were supposed to feel like while they were doing it, to feel where they were going and what they were supposed to feel like when they got to where I had to go.

From very early on, I could speak expressively with music without being told how. I don't know why, but music has always been more or less an open book to me. That was my talent. I spoke then in the language and timbre of a teenager, but it was musical. Now I was putting luster on the control of sound, becoming more aware of the varieties of musical expression.

What I remember most of all from that time is the higher level of concentration at which I functioned. It wasn't a matter of practicing longer hours, but of concentrating, of learning to do in three hours what would normally take me twelve. I didn't agree with everything the New York critics had said, but I knew I had certain weaknesses, and they had to do with concentration. And so I worked on that, in an entirely self-driven way. Perhaps the word "driven" is too strong. Eager, desirous, anticipatory—those are closer to my feelings that year. I had tasted the edge of something in New York. I wanted the whole meal. I needed to prove myself in Town Hall.

It seemed to me that the challenge of returning to Town Hall for a second chance implied an obvious need this time for professional advice, for someone who would know how to organize the event. I needed a good personal manager.

For about two years I had been managed by a red-faced, red-haired, hard-drinking young Irishman named Wilfrid Davis, who was connected in some way with San Francisco's musical life and took it upon himself to organize my life. Davis told a manager named Paul Stoes about me. Stoes had an office in New York and represented two major attractions: the Vienna Boys' Choir and the Don Cossack Chorus. He traveled a good deal. On the advice of Wilfrid Davis, he heard me play in San Francisco and took me on.

He was originally from Texas, blond and of a political persuasion that made Attila the Hun seem like a liberal. A more hard-drinking, foulmouthed reactionary I have never known. But he loved music and quickly came to feel a deep affection for me. He loved the fiddle and had been unsuccessful in his attempt at a musical career. I think he may have found in me a projection of his hopes for himself.

As I remember those events, I think how fortunate I was in my youthful years to come across people who formed personal associations with me not only because I played the fiddle but because I was me. Naoum Blinder for one, Paul Stoes for another. Both believed deeply in me. It was Stoes who arranged my second appearance in Town Hall. He managed the concert: "Paul Stoes Presents Isaac Stern."

And so, once again, less than two years later, I traveled with my mother to New York. This time, I was able to pay some of the expenses from my own meager earnings as a touring fiddler; the expenses I could not cover were (of course!) taken up by Lutie Goldstein.

The second concert took place on a Saturday afternoon in February 1939. I didn't feel the same sense of exultation that I had the first time. My accompanist was Wolfgang Rebner. Once again, the rehearsals. Once again, the black suit, the white shirt, the black tie. Once again, the vision of the audience inside my closed eyes as I played. Once again, my mother and friends and well-wishers backstage afterward. Once again, a late meal in the nearby German restaurant. Once again, going out in the early morning for the reviews.

This time they were positive, glowing. No reticence, no backhanded praise, no condescension. It was like night and day. The *Times* referred to me as a fiddler who was technically "well-equipped," with a "round and luscious" tone and a bow that was "beautifully controlled." And the *Herald Tribune* critic wrote, "Mr. Stern should be included among the most important violinists now to be heard."

It was a different world. I was suddenly accepted. I had been given the key to a musical career.

My mother and I returned to San Francisco. By the time we arrived, everyone in the music world of the city knew what had transpired in New York, and there was happiness on all sides. There must have been a party with my friends from the orchestra, though I don't remember it. I am certain there was a party at home, eating, drinking, dancing— it was, after all, a Russian house. Naoum Blinder was delighted and proud. And Paul Stoes was booking concerts for me.

That second Town Hall appearance was the real beginning of my professional life.

THREE

*A*ND SO IT began—the slow, steady struggle to build a career. I entered the University of the Real World. The years 1926 to 1939 had been my elementary school, high school, and college. The years 1939 to 1943 were my graduate school. Universities at best teach one how to learn. I had already learned that. Now I was beginning to put the learning to professional use.

Paul Stoes was trying to arrange concerts for me on the West Coast and in other parts of the country. He would call orchestra conductors, tell them my repertoire, the concerti that I knew at the time, inform them of my reviews, and ask if they would engage me. My fee was a few hundred dollars, no more. I took whatever concerts came my way.

The West Coast was my training ground for a life of travel. I learned to be thankful for small favors: when, for example, I could get a lower instead of an upper berth on a train. If I traveled with Betty Alexander, naturally she would take the lower berth—and I would climb up and try to figure out how to get out of my clothes, put on pajamas, and settle in with an eight-inch clearance over my head and a fiddle case in the berth with me. The fiddle was the $6,500 Guadagnini given me by Lutie Goldstein. Giovanni Baptista Guadagnini, who lived from 1711 to 1786, had been a notch or two below Stradivari and Guarneri in the echelon of quality fiddle makers. My Guadagnini was the very center of my world, and I held on to it tightly wherever I went. And I went any place people wanted to hear me play.

Wherever I played, the reviews were excellent. At times, in later years, when I exhibited a certain arrogant nonchalance in playing, the reviewers commented on it. But there was nothing I could learn from them; they simply didn't know enough. All they could tell me was their reaction to a given performance. In the whole course of my career, very few critics have intelligently or usefully informed me about anything. Still, during those early years—how I reveled in the good reviews.

At times I traveled by bus from town to town and stayed in hotels that cost $2 a night. On occasion I rode with Paul Stoes in his Buick to audition for conductors. We would drive from one city to another. The Buick wasn't exactly well sprung—I remember the noise the rumble seat made when we needed to go across railroad tracks.

It was through Stoes that, some years later, I met Fritz Kreisler and played for him and came to know him. The two of us, Stoes and I, went to Philadelphia to hear Kreisler play, and then walked with him from the concert hall to his hotel, a block away. The audience followed in the street, applauding Kreisler, who, after changing in his room, took us to a German restaurant, where he happily ate—because his wife, Harriet, wasn't there—real (not mock) turtle soup, lobster, steak, desserts, each with the proper wine, all the time explaining why this wine went with that course, the vintage, the cost, while also expounding on the joys of living and the relationship between music and literature. An extraordinarily cultured man, he radiated Viennese gemütlichkeit. One can hear it in his playing; in any Kreisler recording, there is a golden, honeyed quality to his sound. He used only about 70 percent of his bow, rarely touching the top or bottom 15 percent. And he didn't like to use the fourth finger, often managing to get around it. Stoes had met him, may even have been a road manager for him at one time. I played for him, and he was very encouraging. I still remember how he would walk out on the stage, twitch his mustache and throw back the little velvet lapel protector he wore on his tailcoat, then gaze benignly at the audience as a grandfather might look at his family—and begin to play. He was a very special man.

That first year of touring, 1938–1939, I think I had all of about seven concerts. Wherever people were willing to pay me, I went, mostly in small cities like Santa Barbara, Palo Alto, Fresno.

In those days, there were two major concert organizations and one great independent. One of the majors was Community Concerts, a subsidiary of the Columbia Radio Network; it booked the concerts for about 1,500 small towns. The second organization was NCAC, the

National Concert and Artist Corporation, a subsidiary of NBC radio. Under the name Civic Concerts, it booked artists for about 900 cities.

In addition to those two organizations, there was one great lone impresario, Sol Hurok, who represented performers of the highest stature, like Arthur Rubinstein, Marian Anderson, Jan Peerce, and Roberta Peters.

NCAC was run by George Engles and Marks Levine. Levine, whom everyone called Max, was a hard-boiled, hard-bitten New Yorker who spoke in clipped accents and had the warmth of a slightly gelatinous iceberg. Engles and Levine decided to merge with Hurok: NCAC needed Hurok's very special group of artists, who were among the most famous and successful at that time; and Hurok needed more exposure, which the long reach of NCAC could give him. The merger took place in early 1940.

Sometime later that year, the merged organizations of NCAC and Hurok made an offer to buy out Paul Stoes: they wanted the Don Cossack Chorus and the Vienna Boys' Choir, both still managed by him. Stoes had grown somewhat weary of the precariousness of his position as an impresario who was able to offer only two major attractions, and so he agreed to the merger and folded his management into NCAC, which already had under its aegis the major artists managed by Sol Hurok, in a subsidiary known as the Hurok Division. Stoes made the merger contingent on one condition: that NCAC take me as well.

There then followed a discussion as to who would take on this young fiddler from California, NCAC or Hurok? Hurok was not entirely enthusiastic about having a virtually unknown musician join his august group of artists, but he agreed to take me on. Stoes worked as a traveling road man for NCAC, selling concerts and series around the country and, at the same time, overseeing the details of my growing career.

Hurok always claimed to have "discovered" me. In actual fact, I was pushed on him by Paul Stoes. Neither NCAC nor Hurok wanted me. I was an unknown quantity, a struggling young artist—gifted, yes, but so many are gifted. NCAC and Hurok wanted artists who were already successful. But Stoes made the deal, and that was how I began with Sol Hurok.

At first, Hurok booked me by attaching me to his star attractions.

For all intents and purposes, he was saying to the concert organizers who came to him, "I'll give you a pound of Arthur Rubinstein or Marian Anderson if you'll take three ounces of Isaac Stern." That was the way one started!

I began to meet many musicians and conductors, but I was still in the farm league, double and triple A. One of the experiences I remember from about that time was a rehearsal of the Tchaikovsky Violin Concerto with the New York Philharmonic Orchestra, Artur Rodzinski conducting. The concerto takes about forty minutes, but I got only eighteen minutes of rehearsal time from the conductor. That was how they sometimes treated a new kid, as if to say, "He's lucky to be here at all. We'll let him do what he can at the performance, and we'll meet him at the end."

The audiences in the small towns got to hear some of the best talent, artists they would never have heard had they not been brought in by Civic or Community Concerts. In a tour of about twenty-five concerts a year, I would play about seven of them in towns smaller than Dubuque, Iowa. Those were the years I learned how to be with people, and as I have always been naturally gregarious, people became my friends, true friends. I would meet them, in the coming years, each time I returned to play in their towns. A network of friends.

Only once in all those early years did I encounter an overt act of anti-Semitism. In 1939, my family moved from San Francisco to New York and rented an apartment at 865 West End Avenue. During that summer my parents and sister and I took a motor trip to upstate New York; my father was having a problem with his lungs, and we thought the fresh air would do him good. We stopped at a hotel somewhere in the Lake Saranac region and asked for rooms, and were told by the clerk that the hotel didn't take Jews. I have no memory of how I felt or of any conversation with my mother and father about that rebuff. I remember clearly that we were in a hotel in the Catskill Mountains of New York in September 1939 when we heard over the radio that Germany had invaded Poland, and the Second World War began.

That was when I became really conscious of Europe. My parents, of course, were constantly aware of the situation there, but the invasion of Poland caused me to focus on this place called Europe and this problem called Nazism; forced me to realize that there was an England, a Russia. Remember, this was before 1941; America was determinedly neutral, even isolationist, at the time.

Both my mother and my father had family in Europe, in the town of Kreminiecz, where my parents had lived before they emigrated with me to the United States. They heard from no one during the war, but toward the end heard a rumor, never really verified, that their families had been among a large group of Jews herded together in a barn and burned alive. Not one of my mother's or my father's relatives overseas survived the war.

In the fall of 1941, my parents and sister returned to San Francisco, and I remained behind in New York. By then, living in New York had become very important to me—the career was beginning to take off—and I moved into the apartment of Herb and Elsie Katzman, whom I had met at the Town Hall concerts. They lived on Central Park West and 66th Street. Herb Katzman had a very successful clothing business in midtown Manhattan, and was an amateur fiddle player. Often, in the evening, he would have some of the leading musicians in the city come over, and they would all play quartets. I remember that, years later, I once brought Jack Benny over, and he played, too. Herb and Elsie—"Hey, Hoib, who are we having ovah for dinnah tonight, Hoib?"—became my surrogate father and mother after my parents left New York.

Herb Katzman was an inveterate gambler, and introduced me to the world of horse racing. He would bet fifty or one hundred dollars, and sometimes I would add on two or three dollars. It was very impressive, his gambling, his easy way with money. He was in his mid-fifties, and his wife was small, perky, with a high-pitched voice and carefully coiffed hair, a sort of blonde. I met so many people through them. And the music was continuous. I would play in their apartment; I would go on a tour and play; I would return to the apartment and play. There were music stands in the living room, always with music on them. Herb had files of quartet music in the apartment. He and Elsie loved music, they loved people, they loved to invite friends for food and music. And I am certain that they loved me, too.

I lived with them for more than a year. It was in that apartment that a girlfriend of a friend of mine, all of thirty-five, completed the one thing missing from my overall education by initiating me, with great warmth and tenderness, into that mysterious rite of passage involving the opposite sex. Oh joy! I think my playing took on a new patina!

New York was now my base for tours. By then there were commercial airplanes you could take on a regular basis; the DC-3 got you across the country, with only six stops, in the astonishing time, as I remember it, of fourteen hours. If a town was on the concert circuit, sooner or later I played there.

Those years in the University of Real Life were an extraordinary education for me. I learned how to travel in all sorts of circumstances. I learned how to practice anywhere: on trains, in hotel rooms, in local auditoriums. I learned what it meant to be onstage. I learned to overcome my fears. Before every performance, there was always the keen edge of excitement; with the start of the performance, I would lose myself in the music. I honed my craft.

MY ACCOMPANIST at the concerts I played in New York and Palo Alto in early 1940 was a pianist named Leopold Mittman. He and another pianist, Alexander Zakin, had been students together during the thirties at the Berlin Hochschule für Musik. They formed what was then a popular musical group called the Four Piano Quartet, which traveled around and, amazingly, actually managed to find four pianos wherever they went. Mittman and Zakin left Germany in the late thirties, about three steps ahead of the Nazis, and eventually found their way to America, where they began independent lives as musicians. Mittman was my accompanist until the end of 1940; he dropped me when he got a better offer from Mischa Elman. Zakin then became my accompanist, a relationship that lasted thirty-three years.

In the winter season of 1940–1941, I was on my third national tour, fulfilling thirty engagements, some with orchestra, some in solo recital. Syracuse. New Orleans. New York. San Francisco. Utica. Immediately after my appearance with the New Orleans Symphony, the conductor signed me up again for the following year. To be asked back immediately was one of the more important signs of a rising career.

In mid-1941, around the time of my twenty-first birthday, I went back to San Francisco to fill out an application for my personal citizenship papers. Even though I had received derivative citizenship when my father became a citizen in 1927, I felt the need to have my own papers, in my own name, when I reached twenty-one. I then left San Francisco in late fall for an eastern tour, and returned in December to spend some time with my parents. I remember that I was at home on December 7, 1941, listening to Arthur Rubinstein playing with the New York Philharmonic on their usual Sunday radio broadcast, when the program was suddenly interrupted by the announcement of the surprise attack on Pearl Harbor. The next day, America declared war against Japan. Then Germany declared war against America.

I don't recall any particular conversations with my parents or friends about the Japanese bombing; we all shared anger at the attack and great willingness to have the United States take up arms in self-defense. I think anyone who was alive at that time will remember the sudden news of the attack and President Roosevelt's speech to Congress the next day, the speech that referred to the day of the attack as "a date which will live in infamy." I can still hear the sound of his voice, the way he phrased the words, his sorrow and anger at what had happened at Pearl Harbor.

Our entry into the war had no immediate effect on my career. I have no recollection of any perceptible difference in audience moods after Pearl Harbor. I do know from my own experience that music proved to be a haven of quiet and rest after the daily reports of battles and lists of casualties and the need to do war work at the highest possible speed. Music became a necessary island of peace that, if only briefly, took people away from the enormous strains that were part of everyone's wartime consciousness.

During the early weeks of 1942, I played in Phoenix; I played my return engagement with the New Orleans Symphony; I played in San Francisco; San Angelo, Texas; Minot, North Dakota. Whenever I could fit it into my travel schedule, I played for troops at bases and in hospitals. Remote towns, big cities; small halls, large auditoriums; recitals with Zakin, concerts with well-known conductors. My career was slowly growing.

By early 1942, it was already apparent that I would soon have to face the next enormous challenge to my career: the debut in Carnegie Hall.

I NEEDED a new place to live. With all my affection for the Katzmans, I felt I had outgrown them; it had all become too familial; I was too much a part of their lives. To prepare properly for the Carnegie Hall debut, I needed to have my own working and thinking time.

Among the many people I had met in New York was a man named Hy Goldsmith, who was a professor of physics at City College. He was fifteen or twenty years older than I, a shy, gentle, self-effacing soul and a brilliant scientist who had never bothered to get a Ph.D. He had an enormous passion for music and possessed an encyclopedic knowledge of music in general and chamber music in particular. He knew from memory more scores than most musicians did, and could give you the opus numbers and K listings of all the Beethoven and Mozart quartets. In early 1942, when I told him about the Carnegie Hall debut and asked if he knew of a place where I could live and practice, he invited me to move in with him.

Hy had a rather incredible apartment on West 72nd Street, in the Oliver Cromwell Hotel. The apartment was next to the water tower. I remember you had to take the elevator to the 30th floor and then walk up two flights to get to his apartment, which was over the elevator shaft. The apartment was enormous, about fifty feet long and thirty-five feet wide, with a small diagonal stage in one corner of the room, on which there was a piano. The place had once been a ballroom! There was also a small kitchen and a bathroom all done in black marble; anytime you washed, it left stains.

The year or so that I lived in that apartment was one of the most important periods of my life, a mind-enhancing time. Hy Goldsmith would leave to teach at City College, and I would have the apartment to myself. All day long, I practiced, and practiced, and practiced.

Some evenings after Hy returned from teaching, musicians would start coming over. They were among the best musicians in town: young pianists studying for their solo careers, or starting their solo careers, as I had started mine on the violin; and players with the radio orchestras, which were really first-class: NBC, Blue and Red, and CBS. We'd start playing chamber music about eight in the evening. By ten, everyone would be a little tired, and we'd break for sandwiches from the local deli—a mountain of food. By the time we were through eating, other musicians who had finished their various jobs would be coming in, and we would form new groups. We bathed in music. We didn't play for social or career reasons but for the sheer joy of making music, of being able to explore the literature together. The neighbors didn't hear us because we were so high up. We could have fired rockets there and no one would have known. We'd play until one in the morning. Then more food and something to drink. Beer and sodas, occasionally some wine. When the other musicians left, I'd stay up and play sonatas with a gifted pianist friend of mine, Sidney Foster. Eventually I'd go to bed.

Hy Goldsmith, who was convinced of my possibilities in music, wanted to make sure that I was ready to play Carnegie Hall. On some nights when no musicians had been invited over and no chamber music was being played and he'd stayed up late working, he would wake me and say, "Get up and play this work, play it right now!" He'd make me get up and dress and take the fiddle and play. In the middle of the night! He figured if I could do it under those circumstances, I wouldn't be fazed by Carnegie Hall.

I was touring at the time: Cincinnati, El Paso, Texarkana, Pittsburgh. I would return to the apartment—and to more music. It was a period of unending music-making. Chamber music, chamber music, chamber music—part of the blood of my life, as a person, as a musician. To this day, it remains the bedrock of my musicianship.

When I got on the stage of Carnegie Hall to play that concert, I was really ready. The debut took place on January 8, 1943: "S. Hurok Presents Isaac Stern, Violinist." I selected pieces that would serve as the necessary reaffirmation of the reason I was a musician, pieces that would prove to myself and to others that I had the right to be there. Compositions by Mozart, Bach, Szymanowski, Brahms, Wieniawski. Alexander Zakin was at the piano. I played almost defiantly, to demonstrate my skills, to show them all what I was capable of doing with the fiddle. The sheer concentration!

Irving Kolodin, music critic of the New York *Sun*, seemed to sense the defiance. "The program . . . [Stern] played last night," he wrote in his review, "would have appalled most of the case-hardened virtuosi . . . but Mr. Stern survived the challenge he set for himself with imposing dexterity and musical resourcefulness." The critic for the New York *Herald Tribune* referred to me as "a musician of fine sensibility and superb technique." One year later almost to the day, on January 12, I played again at Carnegie Hall. Virgil Thomson, writing for the *Herald Tribune,* was full of praise: "Isaac Stern . . . is one of the world's master fiddle players."

The second Carnegie Hall concert catapulted me into major recognition. It was my musical coming-of-age, my professional bar mitzvah. I was twenty-four.

HY GOLDSMITH moved to Chicago, where he took part in the development of the atomic bomb. When I would be in Chicago to play a concert, there would often be an evening of chamber music with local musicians. I would play, and Hy and other scientists would on occasion be present: many scientists are music lovers; there is a correlation between mathematics, music, and science.

Major secret work on the atomic bomb was then being done in Chicago beneath Stagg Stadium. I was once asked by Hy and some other scientists if I would participate in an experiment that would help establish reaction time at certain heights and depths. There is a film somewhere that shows me in a sealed area with all sorts of wires attached to me. I was handed a fiddle and told to play something. I played the presto of the G Minor Solo Sonata by Bach, as the pressure and the oxygen levels in the room went from very much below sea level to very much above. The scientists monitored the reactions of my trained hands to the various atmospheres. That film was never shown to me and remains a secret to this day.

Hy Goldsmith became the editor of the *Bulletin for Atomic Scientists;* I remember helping him prepare his application and curriculum vitae for that position. He was destined to do great things in physics. But one summer, two or three years after the war, while vacationing in upstate New York or Vermont with his sister's family, he went for a walk along a stream and slipped. His head struck a rock, and he died instantly.

FOUR

HE ORDER to Report for Induction was mailed on June 14, 1943, to the address in San Francisco where my parents and sister lived.

GREETINGS:

Having submitted yourself to a local board composed of your neighbors for the purpose of determining your availability for training and service in the armed forces of the United States, you are hereby notified that you have been selected for training and service in the Armed Forces.

It ordered me to report to my local draft board at 428 Market Street, San Francisco, on June 24. I requested, and was granted, a stay. The second Order to Report for Induction was mailed to me on September 25. Earlier that year, I had played nineteen concerts; I was scheduled to play an additional seventeen concerts by year's end, and sixteen more by the following summer. I returned to San Francisco and reported to the local draft board on October 6, as ordered.

The physical examination revealed that I had very flat feet. The doctor who performed the examination asked about the scar at the base of my spine. I explained that in my early teens I had suffered from a pilonidal cyst at the end of my spinal column, just below the coccyx. It was very big, but not serious—a vestigial remainder, I was told, and at that time believed, of what used to be a tail. They operated and, I was later informed, removed so much flesh you could bury your hand in up to your wrist. I learned how to sleep on my stomach.

Reasonable medical facts—the flat feet and the spinal surgery—

caused me to be considered physically unfit by the examining physician. I was rejected from service in the Armed Forces of the United States and classified 4-F.

I returned to New York and spent the following months fulfilling my concert obligations. There is a story by Guy de Maupassant about a man who juggled clubs in front of a statue of the Virgin Mary because it was the only way he knew how to pray. The thing I did best was play the fiddle; I thought I might do something for the war effort through music. I played at Stage-Door Canteens in New York, Philadelphia, and San Francisco. During a six-day period in San Francisco, Zakin and I played at six different camps and hospitals all around the area. We'd come into the wards wheeling a little piano for Zakin, play about five selections, and move on—twenty to thirty minutes for each ward. In Oakland's Oak Knoll Hospital one day, we did six wards. "Ave Maria" was a great favorite with the men. I also played Chopin nocturnes, Gershwin preludes, "Perpetual Motion" by Nováček, "Gypsy Airs" by Sarasate, and other such popular pieces.

At the same time, I began to feel that it was my duty to participate in the war effort overseas. I got in touch with the United Service Organizations—the USO—which arranged entertainment for the troops, told them who I was and what I did professionally, and volunteered to form a group of classical musicians who would be willing to travel and play for the troops. A group of musicians playing classical music for soldiers? The people I spoke to in the USO told me that now and then a solo musician traveled overseas to play for the troops, but there was no such group in the USO. It appeared I had come up with a new idea.

At first, no one seemed to know what to make of it, but I was finally given permission to proceed, and I put together a group consisting of myself, my friend and accompanist Alexander Zakin, and three members of the Metropolitan Opera: the tenor Fred Jagel; a very attractive soprano, Polyna Stoska; and the baritone Robert Weede, who was later to star in the Broadway musical *Most Happy Fella*.

In early spring 1944, I was inducted in San Francisco and issued a green USO uniform. I then proceeded to New York to join the others in the group. Our USO–Camp Show concert group was to be known only as Unit #264. We waited awhile for our travel documents, which, when they arrived, ordered us, with Army logic, back to San Francisco. There we discovered that we were being sent to Hawaii and the South Pacific.

I was in San Francisco the day in April when the news came of the death of President Roosevelt. I remember that I was in the downtown area when I heard the news, and for some reason I entered a building with an elevator. Among those riding up with me were two business-men, and one said to the other, "I'm glad the son of a bitch is dead." I grabbed the guy by his vest and shirt, about to punch him. The others stopped me. I left the elevator in a rage.

Soon afterward, my little group departed San Francisco for Hawaii. We had no official rank—we were entertainers—but if we were ever captured by the Japanese, we had the automatic rank of captain. How they arranged for the enemy to know that I have no idea.

In Hawaii we played in hospitals and at training bases, then flew on to New Caledonia. In a letter postmarked from there, dated May 25, 1944, I wrote that the flight from Hawaii was "smooth and wonderful" and that at times "we became so bored that I would open my fiddle [violin] case and start playing, and Miss Stoska and Mr. Jagel would join me—a concert at 10,000 feet! We crossed the equator playing and singing above the clouds, with a major, a general, and two colonels as our audience."

The letter goes on to say that we played at various bases on New Caledonia and then moved on to other islands, quickly becoming accustomed to

> cold-water showers and shaves and waterless privies. The need for this kind of music is terrific down here—we are the trailblazers in this field and the response has been wonderful and the most wonderful thing for me is the way the idea of music and the value of music in war is so superbly integrated with the total war effort here. . . . We find a complete and smooth-working army music organization, working in full cooperation and with the enthusiastic approval of our Army. We have our own car and driver and a new Steinway upright

war piano and an excellent P.A. system, so that we carry complete ingredients of our show at all times. It's really heart-warming to see some of the responses we've had—we feel swell about the whole thing.

On New Caledonia, we were stationed in a hospital. The island, which was supplied about once a month, was in the third week of its supply cycle and had run out of orange juice and various other important items. Sailors, soldiers, and airmen concocted a drink they called "torpedo juice," which had the same effect as getting the propeller end of a torpedo started, with you as the torpedo. The latrine stood at the end of a very long jetty that extended into the Pacific Ocean; it was what you might call a "natural" latrine system. You sat there and looked out at the South Pacific, and what you saw was a bit of the island and some trees and then the enormous expanse of beautiful blue water.

There were entertainers and performers who toured areas of the South Pacific and Europe that had only recently been combat zones: Bob Hope, Jack Benny, Jascha Heifetz. We were never quite that close, but we played hundreds of concerts—in Hawaii, Guam, New Caledonia, the Canton Islands, Fiji, the New Hebrides, the Florida and Russell Islands, and islands whose names I can't remember. We played anywhere, for whatever troops would be around to hear us, from a group of ten in a hospital unit to 5,000 collected in a field who wanted some entertainment. We also played at some church services. We had the Army Steinway, a small, green-painted upright that had been "tropicalized"—fixed up to take the heat and humidity of the South Pacific. We'd lift it into the back of our truck and go, and we'd set it down wherever there was a place we could play.

The one thing the troops wanted most was to have a good look at blond and beautiful Polyna Stoska. A woman! They'd stamp their feet and whistle and have a great time. She'd play back to them, sing her songs and flirt. Bob Weede would sing some pop songs, and so would Fred Jagel.

I learned a number of important lessons during that South Pacific trip—about myself and about mass audiences. I'd played before large groups before going overseas, and I knew that a musically sophisticated audience is able to gauge instantly the credentials of a performer; pretense is sensed and never forgiven. With mass audiences of the sort I faced in the South Pacific, I discovered very quickly that I needed to connect not only on the level of expertise but also, and more important, with an air of honest familiarity and utter lack of affectation. Therefore, I wouldn't begin with Bach or Mozart but with "The Flight of the Bumblebee," or the theme from the movie *Intermezzo*, or an arrangement of Copland's "Hoedown," or a Stephen Foster song. It was my way of saying hello. Once they sensed your basic honesty, your at-oneness with them, they'd sit back and you could play anything. I'd end up playing solo works by Bach, and they would listen raptly and appreciatively.

One day we had to play for a huge audience of marines, who were on R & R on one of the small islands in the Hebrides. They had been in some severe battles and had suffered heavy losses. Earlier that day, they'd received word that instead of going back into combat, they were all getting home leave. The area in which they had been assembled was about the size of three football fields, and it was packed with those happy marines, who were drinking New Zealand beer, a brew much stronger than ours. And there we were, the five of us, making every effort to perform—until after some good-natured, back-and-forth shouting and bantering, I decided that there was no point in trying to play in an open arena to an audience of marines who were celebrating such good fortune. So I got a couple of beers, sat down near the piano, and just talked and relaxed with the guys. It was wonderful to cut through the performer-audience barrier, to share in the happy release, the exhilaration, that all of them were feeling about going home.

Afterward, we flew to Guadalcanal, where we lived in the tents of the 9th station hospital, just off the beach. The hulls of wrecked landing craft were visible from the shore. We played in the hospital areas and in some of the camps. One or two areas hadn't been cleared of mines, and rumor had it that there were still some Japanese holed up in the caves in the hills. But we never saw any Japanese in the many days we were there, and the story had probably been invented to lend some color to one's presence there at that time.

Over the years, I've carried with me certain vivid memories of that time in the South Pacific. There was no ambient light at night, so the sky was absolutely clear, and the Milky Way was like a woven carpet over your head; you felt you could reach up and touch it. I've never since seen the constellations so close that I almost felt I had to duck down. An extraordinary sight.

On our way back from Guadalcanal to Honolulu, we flew in a B-24: bucket seats and a "head" that was the tail gunner's station, with a window that opened out onto the sky. Early in the morning, I experienced a nature call and made my way to the tail gunner's domain. As I looked out to the left toward the dawn, the first of the Hawaiian Islands was emerging from a blood-red sea. We were high up, at 10,000 feet. Above us, apparently oh-so-close, was a full, searingly silver moon. In all my travels since then I've never seen that again, the silver of the moonlight and the blood of the sun, simultaneously.

Another memory I carry of that time is of something that occurred on the flight from Honolulu to San Francisco, which was then one of the longest overseas hops for propeller-driven planes. We were about halfway across. Everyone was lying on the floor of the plane, covered with blankets and trying to sleep. You're flying, droning on through the night, in an unusual environment, your antennae working differently. The engines had lulled me to sleep. In the middle of the night, I woke with a start. All four engines had stopped. I could hear only the whooshing sound of air. It turned out that the pilot, weary from lack of sleep, had forgotten to flip the switch from one set of fuel tanks to another. The silence lasted only a few seconds, but in the middle of the Pacific Ocean, somewhere between Hawaii and San Francisco, it caused a moment of interesting anxiety.

In all, our group of musicians was away for seven weeks, traveled 20,000 miles by air, and played sixty-one concerts for more than 140,000 servicemen. We returned to the United States in June 1944, shortly after the Allied invasion of Europe.

MY PARENTS and sister had decided to move permanently from San Francisco to New York. They settled into an apartment in Manhattan, at 67 Riverside Drive, and I moved in with them. Between my return from the South Pacific and my next trip for the USO a year later, I played more than fifty concerts in the United States and Canada: at Carnegie Hall, with the New York Philharmonic, Artur Rodzinski conducting; in Philadelphia, with the Philadelphia Orchestra, Pierre Monteux conducting; and recitals, with Zakin, in Cleveland, Fort Worth, Laredo, Columbus, Cedar Falls, Stamford, Akron, New Rochelle, Boston, Joplin, Kansas City, Omaha, Madison, Niagara Falls, Montreal, Quebec City, Perth Amboy, Ottawa, Waco, Houston—to name a few.

The war in Europe ended in May 1945, but the war with Japan continued. Shortly after V-E Day, the USO sent me and my fellow artists to Greenland and Iceland.

To get to Greenland, you had to leave from Bangor, Maine. The plane that was to take us was a C-46, lumbering and loaded with passengers. It had started along the runway when suddenly the pilot slammed down hard on the brakes and we spun around and came to a stop. It seemed that one of the engines had quit; had that happened two or three minutes later, we would have been in real trouble. We were herded into another C-46, and as that one started down the runway, one of its engines caught fire. Back we went. The third C-46 managed to get into the air.

Greenland is an island of 840,000 square miles. Eighty-five percent is ice up to 10,000 feet thick, surrounded by a fringe of mountains rising from the sea. It was a stepping-stone to Europe for the Eighth Air Force and was also used as a weather station for the gathering of vital data necessary in forecasting the weather in Europe. When the war in Europe ended, the Eighth Air Force began ferrying fleets of American bombers, B-17s and B-24s, back to the United States, using Greenland as a refueling station. The base we were in was at Narsarssuak, on the southwest coast, one of the most difficult in the world to approach by air. We had to fly up a fjord sixty miles long below the level of the surrounding mountains in order to be ready to touch down at the beginning of the airstrip, which began right at the water's edge and continued uphill to the glacier.

We played to little groups of fifty, a hundred, sometimes as few as ten lonely boys at weather stations and observation posts. We tried to give them as much music as they wanted, and they wanted a lot.

We were housed in the officers' quarters of the hospital. I remember spending a good part of each night trying to keep officers out of Polyna Stoska's room; they were seeking "private conferences" with her. I appropriated a few bottles of liquor from the officers' mess and distributed them to some of the enlisted men, whom I then enlisted as guards to stand watch at Polyna's door. She was, of course, perfectly capable of taking care of herself, but I thought it couldn't hurt to offer her some help.

One day we flew from the main base to the air force base in the north, and at one point during the flight the pilot let me get into his seat and try my hand at flying an airplane. We were over ice. I used the stick to make a few small right and left turns and some dips and climbs. The next thing I knew, Zakin had burst into the cockpit and was shouting, "I knew it, goddamn it, get your hands off the goddamn wheel!"

The day we were to leave Greenland, the weather turned bad, and we were stranded for a few days. There was no fresh food of any kind except for some onions. The meat was frozen; the vegetables were canned; the milk, potatoes, and eggs were powdered. I did a lot of practicing of the Mendelssohn E Minor Violin Concerto, played a good deal of gin rummy, and even went out seal hunting with one of the officers. We traveled on a dogsled, and I was introduced to the enriching perfume that wafts from the behinds of fourteen or sixteen dogs. We carried rifles but found no seal.

In Iceland, almost exactly one year after having been on Guadalcanal, we were 47 miles inside the Arctic Circle. I remember the baseball game we played at two o'clock in the morning, because there was no night. One night in Reykjavik, we played a full-dress concert at the request of the Icelandic government.

Iceland was an interesting station for Americans in that there were five women—one more beautiful than the next—for every man; acquaintances were quickly made and heartily exploited. The personnel there felt cut off from everything going on elsewhere in the world. One evening in the officers' club, I was made an honorary member of the FBI—Forgotten Bastards of Iceland.

On the flight back to the United States, we were in yet another C-46, occupying bucket seats along the sides of the aircraft. On board with us was a huge German shepherd that belonged to the commander of an army base, who wanted the dog returned to his stateside home. As luck would have it, we hit a bad storm, and the plane, beset by fierce winds, started bucking, dropping, lurching. The dog vomited at my feet. Near where I was seated hung a pair of earphones that enabled one to hear the pilot's cockpit talk. I hooked an arm around a rail so as not to be thrown from my seat, put on the earphones, and heard the pilot saying, "Where the hell is the goddamn field?" and ground control responding, "You're right over us! We can hear you!" and the pilot's reaction, "I can't see a thing!" There was a sudden violent gust of wind, and I looked out the window and saw a break in the clouds, and we were at a forty-five-degree angle, heading straight for the ground. You never felt a nose go up so fast. We landed safely and disembarked, together with a very shaky German shepherd.

In some ways, the war years were heady, freewheeling times. I was involved in a torrid romance with an attractive young woman. There were many parties; sex was rampant. When I returned from Iceland, in the summer of 1945, and while still in uniform, I made a beeline for my girlfriend. I can still remember her opening the door to her apartment, seeing me there, and screaming, "Isaac!" I had walked into a party. All her friends gathered around me. It was a deliciously warm, hugging homecoming. I'd only been away to Greenland and Iceland playing the violin, but to them I was back from the wars.

FIVE

*D*URING THE MONTHS that followed the end of the war, my career began to surge. From early September 1945 to the end of December, I played twenty concerts. And in that same year, I signed my first recording contract, with Columbia Records.

The contract was arranged at a lunch with the then head of Columbia, Goddard Lieberson. Tall, lean, saturnine, an attractive man with a hawk nose and absolutely first-class charm, he was enormously well educated, possessed a beautiful command of English, and was himself something of a composer. He had professional as well as personal contacts with the major classical musicians of his time, and it was also his idea to buy the rights to and make the first cast recordings of the popular Broadway musicals of that era. He backed artists whom others regarded as too young or too untouchable—like Stravinsky, who was his close friend. Lieberson insisted on recording practically all the Stravinsky works then available for recording, and eventually arranged for me to record the Stravinsky Violin Concerto, with the composer himself conducting.

Lieberson had heard me play—I can't recall who made the contact with him; perhaps Hurok—and during that lunch we discussed the fact that Columbia Records was going to offer me a contract. Then we talked about some details and sealed the deal with a handshake. A day or two later, I received a formal contract, which, if memory serves, was one page long. Today it takes about three months of expensive legal advice from both sides to produce a basic contract, which usually consists of seventy or eighty pages of small type, in which is included everything—from the fillings required by the back teeth of the artist to who will get record royalties down to the tenth generation.

The very first recording I made was a violin and piano performance with Alexander Zakin: the Beethoven C Minor Sonata and the Handel D Major Sonata, recorded at the wonderful studio on East 30th Street, a defrocked church with great acoustics. My first orchestral recording, made at about the same time at Carnegie Hall, was with the New York Philharmonic, conducted by Efrem Kurtz, a very amiable and professional musician who always wore a dark blue or black shirt with a tie, always had a smile on his face, and spoke English with a mixed Russian and French accent. His wife, from the noted Rosenwald family, was herself a violinist and owned a beautiful Stradivarius.

The work we recorded was the Wieniawski Violin Concerto in D Minor. In those days, recordings had to be made in small segments, each limited to approximately three minutes and thirty seconds. We had to determine with much care the points at which we would stop; then we would have to back up a little to begin the next segment. Recordings were cut on wax disks, which were later turned into a master that would press out the 78 rpm vinyl records then in use. The concerto was the equivalent of five sides on the wax disks, and it took us only six sides to make the recording. We made no errors, and there were no retakes save one, when someone dropped his bow, creating a noise that couldn't be erased or explained. I might add that there were times when members of the orchestra would deliberately drop a bow or clang their brass instruments against something (by accident, of course) and thereby extend the session and get paid more. But in the instance of my first orchestral recording, the dropped bow was indeed an accident. That recording, which is still available, was literally a live performance, with just one three-and-a-half-minute side played twice. Such was the assurance, the arrogance, and the ignorance of youth!

In the summer of that year, I had played Lalo's *Symphonie Espagnol* at the Hollywood Bowl, with Stokowski conducting. A number of Warner Brothers executives were in the audience, and they decided that my playing had the kind of urgency and style that would suit John Garfield's dramatic performance in the film *Humoresque,* which was then being made. That December, I was handed a script to read and asked to suggest compositions for the movie as well as professional touches that would add to the authenticity of the film.

I proceeded to work closely with Garfield, showing him how to play and pose for still shots with the violin. I gave him tips on what clothes to wear as he performed, coached him on various scenes, discussed music with him, sometimes even advised him on scenes not directly related to music so he could penetrate the character of a musician. At the same time that I was working on the film, I also had concerts to play. In order to satisfy both commitments, I had to cross the continent thirteen times by air.

When you see Garfield playing the violin in *Humoresque,* you are actually seeing three people. Garfield would stand with his hands behind his back, and his chin resting on the violin. Behind him a professional musician would hold the violin and move the left-hand fingers with another person holding the bow, while my music played on speakers. At those moments, the camera filmed from an angle that would show only John Garfield. But when one sees a shot of hands alone, those are mine.

WHEN I WALKED out onto the stage of Carnegie Hall for my March 22, 1946, concert, I tucked under my chin my recently acquired Guarnerius, the Vicomte de Panette, for which I'd paid $65,000. It was a very beautiful violin, in exquisite, perfect condition, and had a lovely reddish-orange varnish and a strong, high tenor sound, rich with clarity and power. In April of that year, I played a concert in Augusta, Georgia, and returned to New York by train. To my surprise, when I got off in New York, my sister was there at the platform to meet me—which already told me that something was very wrong. I looked at her and said, "What's the matter? Is it Papa?" She said, "Yes." I said, "What happened?" She said, "He died." He'd been found by our maid, crumpled on the floor in the bathroom of our apartment, dead of a heart attack.

In the early years, my father had been distanced from me because of my becoming, in his eyes, so American. I loved baseball, tennis, football, movies. He was something of an iconoclast, and remained an émigré to the day he died. My mother and I enjoyed American movies very much; he disliked them, especially Westerns. I remember his saying to me that he saw no point to watching a movie in which nearly everybody was killed. He read the newspapers, was keenly aware of events in the world. He was an American citizen; he voted. But he was deeply connected to Russian culture. The news of the death camps affected him profoundly. He had brought his family to America to escape the persecutions that ended in the Holocaust and to make a new life for us in this land, yet he could never forget his Russian beginnings. He and my mother had married young, in Russia, and from what I could see then and recall now, enjoyed a very good marriage. My mother was always very gentle and affectionate toward him; theirs was a comradeship as well as a warm marriage. A big portion of Mother Russia remained in him his entire life, though he had not the least sympathy for socialism or communism.

We became very close during his last years. When I began to succeed, there was no one more proud of me, though he would never say it, never show it. But he would carefully take my music and put it into marked folders, sew them together, and place them neatly in a drawer so I could easily find whatever I needed. He had been present at my 1944 success in Carnegie Hall, and he knew then that I would make it as a solo performer. I only wish he had lived five or ten years longer; he would have enjoyed my career as no one else could have.

He was buried outside New York City, in a nonsectarian cemetery. That was a natural corollary to our lives at that time—to have had a religious funeral service and to have buried him in a Jewish cemetery would have been contrary to what went on in our house. With the death of my father, the whole early period of my life came to an end.

IN THE NEXT two years, I played 193 concerts, in virtually every corner of the United States—from Redlands, California, to Gloversville, New York; from Nacogdoches, Texas, to Grand Forks, North Dakota. There were occasional trips to Canada. I also played in Havana, Honolulu, and the Town Hall of Auckland, New Zealand. In every one of my recitals, I was accompanied by Alexander Zakin.

About Havana. My memory is that of a happy island, with superb

With my first teacher, Robert Pollack

Naoum Blinder's violin class, March 1935. I'm directly behind Mr. Blinder.

ARKATOV Photo

Naoum Blinder's Violin Class March 1935

No 'Prodigy'
17-Year-Old Isaac Stern
Dislikes 'Sarcasm'

With my mother in a photo from the Seattle Post-Intelligencer, *July 26, 1937*

With Miss Lutie Goldstein

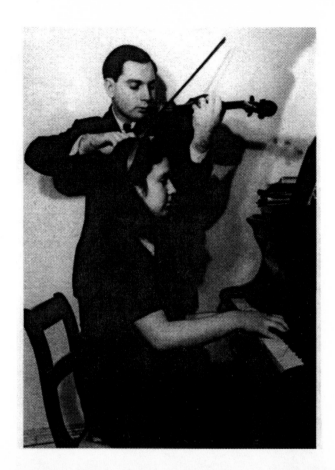

With my sister, Eva

With my father

Reviews as they appeared in the New York Press Jan. 12, 1944

Season's Greetings
from
NORA KAYE
and
ISAAC STERN

Married
NOV. 10, 1948

*Our wedding announce-
ment, cover . . .*

. . . and inside

*Off we go —
Into the wild blue . . .*

*With my mother,
Vera, and Shira*

*Shira, Michael, and
me with violins, and
David in Vera's arms*

On the set of Tonight We Sing, *in the role of Eugène Ysaÿe*

Publicity still for the film Humoresque, *in which I played the musical cues for the character portrayed by John Garfield*

hotel accommodations and very amiable people of all classes. Marvelous cold watermelon juice in little stands on the street, and delicious grilled-cheese sandwiches that you would buy from hawkers along the street. And, most of all, a musical audience that cared deeply about having a civilized life there. It was in Havana that I first heard the great conductor Erich Kleiber, a legendary figure in Germany, which he left in the mid-thirties to travel from one South American country to another, creating and training orchestras; he'd spend a few years in one place building an orchestra and then, satisfied with its quality, leave to do the same in another country. In Havana, he had an orchestra in which there were only two professional musicians. The other players in that Havana symphony orchestra were policemen, firemen, garbage collectors, a couple of doctors—a motley group. Erich Kleiber, who had an international reputation and whose son, Carlos Kleiber, is now a famous conductor in his own right, held at least twenty to thirty rehearsals for each concert. When I told him how astonished I was at the ability of this mixed bag to play so very well, he told me how he would bring each section of the orchestra—first violins, second violins, violas, cellists, bass players, oboe players, clarinets, trumpets, bassoons, horns—in separate groups, to his hotel room, where he would teach them how to play their instruments better and read the music more clearly. He had a demonic passion for training, and was a superb musician. I remember with special pleasure hearing members of his orchestra play the Haydn Sinfonia Concertante, which is written with major solo parts for first violin, principal cello, oboe, and bassoon—a truly fine performance! He was a worker of musical miracles. And always, after building an orchestra, he would say, "I have done my job, and now I must go somewhere else and do the same thing."

I WAS learning during those years that an artist has to walk out on the stage and not apologize for being there; he or she must give every appearance of self-confidence, must seem to be saying, "Be quiet and listen!" I don't mean this in a cheap or egotistical way; it's something about a performer that is immediately evident to the audience and is really impossible to explain. That sort of stage presence can't be falsely created for too long, especially in classical music. You have to go out onstage with your talent and bare face and display your wares. More than anything else, you have to create a bond between you and your listeners; you feel that you're playing for them and that they want to hear you. It's that constant dialogue, that affectionate embrace between performer and audience, that makes them want you to come back and play another time.

There were times during those years when I worked with the same intense effort and concentration I had brought to the preparations for my 1943 Carnegie Hall debut.

I remember the 1947 concert I played in Rochester, New York, with Lenny Bernstein as the conductor. He and I had met socially, but we didn't really know each other as colleagues. He'd had an explosive debut on the musical scene in November 1943, when he'd substituted for the suddenly ill Bruno Walter and conducted the New York Philharmonic in works by Strauss and Schumann with stunning perfection. That evening in Rochester, we were playing my first performance of Prokofiev's Violin Concerto No. 1, in D Major, a very difficult work, which had taken enormous effort to learn. As the two of us performed, we sort of let ourselves go and had a terrific time. We were so successful, we had to repeat the second movement, the scherzo, as an encore.

Starting then, Lenny and I became very close friends. We played together many times, recorded together, spent a lot of time together. He had one of the greatest minds I've ever known, intelligent, curious, involved, almost frightening in its brilliance. It was a mind that absorbed ideas from all sides, like a sponge. He'd received a rigorous education: Talmud from his father, a general education at Boston Latin School, then Harvard. He was virtually Serge Koussevitzky's adopted child. "Lenoushka," Koussevitzky called him. He once gave Lenny a pair of cuff links, and Lenny wore them at every concert. Just before coming onstage, he'd kiss the cuff links and say a brief prayer. He couldn't go out onstage without those cuff links and that prayer.

Early in 1948, I played my first concert with Koussevitzky and the Boston Symphony. Again, it was the Prokofiev First Violin Concerto. I was in my hotel room practicing when the assistant concertmaster,

Alfred Krips, called me and said, "Isaac, remember, this is the first time you are playing with Koussevitzky. Do not, under any circumstances, have any discussion or argument with him in front of the orchestra. Anything you want to say, you say after the rehearsal is over, in private, backstage." I said, "All right, I understand."

That was a very important event in my professional life, my first appearance with the Boston Symphony. I went on practicing in my room until the very last minute and then hurried over to the rehearsal with the orchestra. I had put on some sort of ratty practice sweater. Koussevitzky arrived wearing an impeccable black silk jacket: a gentleman coming to work in an artistic environment. I looked at him and said, "Maître, I'm very sorry, please forgive me. I'm not dressed, really. I just came from practicing." He said, "Hmmph, all right." We went out onstage and started the rehearsal, and after the first four measures we were already apart. I stopped playing, and he said, "What's wrong?" I said, "Maître, may we do it once more?" He said, "Of course." But again we were soon apart, the oboes were not together with me, and I stopped. I went over to him and pointed to the score, and heard behind me a horrified gasp from Alfred Krips. I spoke quietly with Koussevitzky, in Russian—which, as it turned out, meant to him that we were in a private conversation and not in a discussion in front of the orchestra. He said to me, "Remember, this rehearsal is entirely for you. Two hours, whatever you want, you tell me." I said, "Thank you."

It took two hours. We came to the end of the difficult last movement. The solo violin is entirely at the very top of the strings, very uncomfortable. It's all orchestra, it's all color, it's little points of light flashing through, and murmurings, and the fiddle is wandering somewhere above. An ethereal fairyland. We concluded, and Koussevitzky said, "Gentlemen, very nice. But the end must be fantastical." Everyone nodded very gravely. "Yes, maestro, fantastical." Koussevitzky said, "Let us do it once more." Again, we got toward the end, with the orchestra playing exquisitely, and suddenly Koussevitzky screamed, "EET EES NOT FANTASTICAL!!" I didn't know what he meant; no one in the orchestra knew what he meant. But at the performance that evening— with the concentration, the ineffable wonder of playing a concert—it *was* fantastical.

One of the most difficult experiences I had during those years occurred in the early fifties, when I was preparing for my first appearance with William Steinberg and the Pittsburgh Symphony. A young conductor had once asked Steinberg how he memorized a score. Steinberg had looked at him and said, "I don't memorize it. I know it."

That's what I have always tried to do: study a score until I know it.

It so happened that I didn't start studying early enough the score of the work I was to play with Steinberg, a work I had never played before, the Bartók Second Violin Concerto. I began to work measure by measure, page by page, learning, playing. I put aside everything else. I played until I could play no more, until I was exhausted. Then I'd go to sleep for a few hours, get up, and start all over again. I ate at home, didn't leave the apartment, slept in snatches, worked around the clock for three and a half weeks on this piece of music—and when I was done, I knew it. I performed it at Carnegie Hall, ten years and two months after my 1943 debut there.

SIX

*I*N MID-AUGUST of 1948, I took the next major step in my career: I brought my fiddle to Europe.

Traveling through Europe that year, in the aftermath of the war, I played before audiences in Switzerland, Italy, Sweden, Norway, and France. I did not play in Germany. Never in my entire career have I performed in Germany. When I play the violin, I am engaging in a dialogue between myself and my listeners; it's as if I'm making love to the audience. I speak to the people individually and en masse, simultaneously. I know how impossible that sounds, but people have come over to me after a concert and said, "You know, I felt you were playing right to me." My visceral memories of that dreadful, inhuman Nazi period make it impossible for me to talk to and make love to an audience of Germans. That is my own personal burden—nothing is to be gained from its being carried by future generations. I've urged young fiddle players and pianists and cellists to go to Germany and meet members of their generation. Nor have I taught my children to carry that baggage; I'm truly happy that both my sons, musicians, have long-standing relationships with German orchestras and audiences. It's sad enough that I carry that burden.

The manager of my first concerts in Europe was an urbane, educated European named Frederick Horwitz, who had fled Hitler Germany around 1933 and created the Organisation Artistique Internationale—the OAI—in Paris. He arranged my tours in Europe in 1948 and 1949. Then his son, Michael Rainer, who had lived and been educated in the United States, joined him, and upon Mr. Horwitz's death, Michael became head of OAI and my general European manager. He worked with the individual managers in all the European countries where I was to play during the next forty years. He and his wife, Lena, were thoughtful and caring about their artists—Arthur Rubinstein, Rudolf Serkin, Marian Anderson, and many others. His death was a painful loss to the concert world.

One of the basic reasons for visiting Europe was to gain for myself the knowledge of a civilization that had experienced the more-than-four-hundred-year development of music, that had made music essential to its cultural and economic well-being—a very different experience from the rapidly acquired musical culture of the United States. My first impression, however, led me to the conclusion that, generally speaking, there is a good deal of similarity between Europe and America insofar as audiences are concerned: the major cities of both cultures had a core of highly perceptive, sophisticated concert-goers, which then changed to lower levels of musical understanding as one went into the provinces.

But, of course, there were differences as well. The first was the wonderful warmth of a European audience once it had decided to favor the artist. It had no reservations in its expression of friendship and enthusiasm; there was absolutely no inhibition once the artist had been accepted. (At the same time, I was told that rejection of a performer or composer was equally vehement. Luckily, I didn't experience this kind of rejection.) Such a spontaneous positive reaction could be of inestimable value to an artist: it gave a feeling of instant rapport, which made the performance all the more alive for everyone.

A second difference was that, with the probable exception of England, European audiences made up their own minds about a performer even before the reviews appeared. To be sure, there were paper and power shortages in Europe, which often resulted in delays of two days to two weeks before reviews could come out. But in countries like Switzerland and Sweden, where the economies had not been disrupted by the war to any great degree and reviews appeared promptly, there was still the clear impression that those reviews didn't have the overall importance that, say, a New York review had on the minds of the general American music public.

Even before going to Europe, I had had the feeling that the supposed high standards of culture among the concert-going public in Europe was due not so much to a love of culture per se as to the fact that, in Central Europe especially, musical culture was a natural function, not only an artistic one. In countries like Germany and Austria, the great fountainheads of musical training until 1933, the integration of music into the national culture was due in no small measure to the fact that Bach, Haydn, Mozart, Beethoven, Schubert, Brahms, Wagner, Mahler, Hugo Wolf, Strauss, Bruckner, and so on were all local composers and therefore part of the national cultural home and educational background. I discovered that, whereas most Americans would be familiar with *Porgy and Bess* and the songs of Stephen Foster, most Europeans would be familiar with Schubert songs and Beethoven and Brahms symphonies—the result of both cultural and nationalist pride. This pride spread in time to other countries, where new colors were added: in France, the influence of Debussy and Ravel; in Italy, the music of Verdi and Puccini; et cetera.

All of that, I further learned, led to a rather natural case of musical chauvinism as regarded anything that came from the "New World." As an example, one reviewer said that despite my being an American, I had the musical soul of a European. The critics found it difficult to conceive that an American could have any real musical (that is, European) culture. They had no understanding of the extent to which musical standards had developed in America. Indeed, most of the orchestras I heard abroad couldn't begin to compare with the ten leading orchestras in the United States. Of course, there were exceptions: Berlin, Vienna, Amsterdam. But most Europeans were not aware of the amount of new music performed by major groups and small avant-garde associations throughout the United States. America was on the bottom rung of the musical ladder insofar as most of Europe was concerned. In 1948, appearing for the first time on a European stage, I sensed the audience reaction. The people in the concert hall were saying, "Well, go ahead. Show us. We who really know music will judge."

THEY JUDGED. The tour was an enormous success. There was an explosive enthusiasm everywhere that was astonishing and gratifying. I'd never before had so much continuous general approval, and it felt darn nice. There was also a steady demand for definite commitments to return to Europe the following year, but I avoided making promises before I could talk to Sol Hurok.

My first tour of England, in 1948, was arranged by Harold Holt, Ltd. Mr. Holt was a jovial and jolly man, large of frame and full of laughter, and the most respected figure in artist management in Great Britain. When he launched my career, I was put on what was then called the Celebrity Concert Series, a series of concerts in many cities around the country, including Newcastle-on-Tyne, Liverpool, Manchester, and many more whose names I do not remember at this moment. What I do remember is that it was a gray and foggy time of the year and England was just coming out of the post-war difficulties. There was dirt on the train windows and pellets in the various game birds that were offered for dinner in various hotels around the country. Every one of the hosts in every city was as hospitable and thoughtful as could be and made me feel welcome, though I was a completely unknown newcomer. That was never more clear than at the first recital I ever played in Edinburgh. The Usher Hall, later to become the main concert hall of the Edinburgh Festival, held about 1,800 people. And I had a huge audience of about 54 people at this first concert, among them a man named Ian Hunter.

As there were so few in the hall and they were somewhat scattered, I invited everyone to gather together in the first two or three rows and proceeded to play the whole concert for them. Many years later, Ian Hunter became the director of the internationally known Edinburgh Festival, and still later on, some years after the death of Harold Holt, he became the managing director of Harold Holt, Ltd. The name and the prestige of the organization continued, but Ian was the motor running the vehicle.

After that first touring experience with Mr. Holt, I suggested to him that I should no longer play in the provinces but come to England only for one or two concerts with the leading London orchestras and wait for the reputation to build up before going back on the circuit. It was this decision that led to the first concerts in London with Sir Thomas Beecham and the Royal Philharmonic. And the wisdom of that decision was proved by the wonderful and loyal audience that grew over the years.

At the end of the tour, I returned to the United States, where, between November 6 and December 8, I played eighteen concerts. In January, I was in Caracas, Venezuela, giving a recital with Zakin. From there we flew to Barranquilla, Colombia. The area was undergoing a slight revolution, and as we landed, the plane was suddenly surrounded by soldiers with rifles. All the disembarking passengers had to claim their luggage and place it on a cart for inspection. I was, of course, carrying my violin. Under no circumstances would I let some nineteen-year-old conscript with a gun handle my fiddle, so I started to object. The next thing we knew, Zakin and I were being marched at gunpoint into the terminal and from there taken to the city to be jailed. I screamed for a telephone and called the local American consul, who promptly came to extricate us from this "misunderstanding."

I remember the concert I played in Recife, Brazil, during that first South American tour. The hall was, one might say, airy: its warped doors wouldn't close, and its windows were broken. One could hear dogs barking in the distance. It was a battle of wills as to which sounds would dominate—those of the dogs or the fiddler. In the third row of the audience sat a man who kept taking pictures. I motioned to him a few times to put his camera down, but he went on snapping away without pause. Finally, I stopped playing, looked at him, and, raising my arms, shouted, "Out!" The public applauded. I stood there, waiting. He got up and left the auditorium, and only then did I go on playing.

The audiences in South America were generally made up of people with a European background who were involved with the musical scene in their cities. I remember how delighted I was when playing for the first time in Buenos Aires' Teatro Colón, a hall that seats 2,200. It had the classical U shape of the European opera house, with many balconies, and the rows in the parquet were so comfortably distant from each other that one could get to one's seat without having to make anyone move his or her legs. Most astonishing to me was the sheer beauty of the acoustics. We often use the phrase "One could hear a pin drop." In this hall, you could. Its acoustics gave the music a beautiful resonance, warm and rich, and a most remarkable clarity. But because it was an opera house, its stage lights were not too well suited for solo performances. I remember a tasseled floor lamp that looked as though it had come from a lovely home; it stood on the stage near the piano keyboard and added a touch of intimacy to that enormous auditorium. The lamp was still there during my future visits.

I REMEMBER a huge, sudden snowstorm in New York during one of those years, twelve inches of snow falling overnight and blanketing the city. I was due to play a concert with the St. Louis Symphony, with Vladimir Golschmann conducting. But the New York airports were closed. I took my violin and two bags and, knee-deep in snow, carried them two blocks to the subway, and boarded a train at Pennsylvania Station. The train was considerably delayed by the snow, and I arrived in St. Louis about twenty minutes after the concert had begun. I was taken directly to the hall and went onstage in my travel clothes, my trousers wrinkled from the wet snow of the night before, and played, if I recall correctly, Mozart—with no rehearsal. We had a great time.

Once Zakin and I were on a tour in Wisconsin when snow disrupted all travel, and we found ourselves stuck in a snowbank. I left Zakin in the car with our bags and the violin, and trudged to the nearest town, a mile away, for a tow truck to dig us out. We finally got on a train and arrived in Milwaukee half an hour before the concert. The city was paralyzed by the same storm, and fewer than 150 people managed to get to the concert hall. Again, I asked everyone to gather near the stage, and Zakin and I played the entire recital to those who had been brave enough to come.

I have made rehearsals and concerts in Australia from Chicago, in Japan from New York. One of the very few I missed involved a trip to San Diego from Los Angeles—two hours by car, twenty minutes by plane. I chose once to go by plane, fell asleep, woke up an hour later—and we were still flying. Bad weather sent us back to Los Angeles, where I made some frantic phone calls. The Los Angeles Philharmonic, on tour, replaced me with a symphony. I called my friend

Danny Kaye for sympathy and commiseration, and instead got a roaring peal of laughter and an invitation to come over and join him for one of his Chinese dinners, which he loved to cook. He was a great friend, a music enthusiast, and a virtuoso chef.

IN NEW YORK, I was still living with my mother and sister in our sixth-floor apartment in the building on the corner of 79th Street and Riverside Drive. The apartment had a long hallway, with various rooms running off it, including our kitchen. The large dining room and living room looked out onto Riverside Drive and the Hudson River. There was a piano in the living room, and a divan and armchairs and small tables. The bedrooms faced other buildings at the rear of the apartment.

Alexander Zakin and I rehearsed in my apartment four or five times a week when we were preparing programs. If we were just looking over music in general for future programs, we would meet when it was mutually convenient. I felt it so important that Shura (his affectionate diminutive) and I work together on a very steady basis, I entered into an agreement with him for an annual sum comparable to what a pianist of his caliber would earn in any given year, whether we played one concert or forty. In other words, it was not a per-service agreement but a permanent working-and-living arrangement. Where there were performances outside our regular concert schedule—recordings, radio, television—I would always arrange for him to be paid a special fee either by the sponsoring organization or by me. That way, neither of us had to worry about discovering whether the other was free of outside commitments; we were committed to each other. I'm not certain that this kind of working-and-living arrangement was practiced by any other artist. Many pianists were always associated with the major artists with whom they worked—Emmanuel Bay with Heifetz, Franz Rupp with Marian Anderson, and two or three others in both Europe and the United States—but I doubt that those relationships were as close as the partnership that Zakin and I enjoyed all through our more than thirty years together.

We would decide together what repertoire we wanted to play. Our rehearsal sessions were intense and concentrated and took place under the warmest working circumstances imaginable. We had enormous affection for each other and great respect for each other's abilities. Zakin was a superbly trained musician. His playing was immaculate; he possessed extraordinary technical control that never made itself too obvious. He was often of enormous help to me in working out some cadenzas or rearranging certain passages for the piano to make the musical line come through with greater clarity.

Fortunately, the Riverside Drive apartment where we rehearsed was in a very old building with solid walls and floors. We would rehearse day and night without any problems from our neighbors. Probably they heard us to some extent, but they never complained. And we never charged anybody for listening to our rehearsals.

My musical choices for the programs Zakin and I played were based entirely on what I liked. If you play a piece not because you like it yourself but merely because it's the right length, or other people like it, or you need something light or splashy at a certain point in the program, you'll find that you aren't going to make your audience like it. What you are playing at that moment must be your own favorite piece of music. You're playing it because it has meaning for you, and you want to communicate that meaning to your audience. When you're on the concert stage, you can't pretend to like a piece; the audience can hear your conviction, or your lack of it. I'm lucky in that I have always liked many kinds of music, so I've included many kinds of music in my programs: the classics because they're great and beautiful; the contemporary because the composers of my generation say something important to me and to our times; and even the so-called warhorses, those classics that are immensely popular—the Mendelssohn and Tchaikovsky concerti, sonatas by Beethoven and Brahms, Ravel's *Tzigane*, Dvořák's *Slavonic Dances*. I don't tire of them any more than audiences do. They're loved because they have merit. And so Zakin and I would rehearse and play them with pleasure.

I remember we were rehearsing on the day John Glenn first flew into space. I desperately wanted to watch, and arranged for a small television set to be placed on the piano so that we could rehearse until the blastoff. We worked steadily, and when they announced that the rocket was ready for launch, we stopped to watch the last seconds of the countdown. We heard a thunderous noise and saw a billowing cloud. Slowly, reluctantly, the rocket lurched away from the Earth's gravity and began to climb into the sky. As I stood there watching, I began to think about the future. I could see that the people in charge of the space program would eventually be sending rockets to the moon. I turned to Zakin and said, quite seriously, "What would you like to play with me for our first concert on the moon colony, after it's established?" He looked at me, looked at the television screen, looked at me once more, and said, with equal seriousness, "Wouldn't you like to use a local pianist?"

Zakin was a short, light-haired man, a favorite of women until he met Isabelle, the woman who became his wife. He spoke English with the accents of his native Russian as well as Polish and German. He had a somewhat glum view of life. One of his typical remarks, which he would utter now and then at the end of a concert after we'd completed our last encore, was "Well, one more concert nearer the grave." Russian optimism.

My partnership with Zakin was, I think, one of the longest—if not *the* longest—violinist-pianist collaborations in the history of modern music. We traveled all over the world together. He was my companion-in-arms for thirty-three years.

OFTEN MY MOTHER would be somewhere in the apartment, listening to us rehearse. She was short, even shorter than I, and quite stout. Early pictures, taken in the twenties and thirties, show her already heavily built, and she grew even heavier in the ensuing years. Food was one of her great interests—preparing it, serving it, eating it. On all three counts she was enthusiastic. Her eyes were about the same as mine: gray-green. Her voice was feminine, genuinely gentle and with the quintessential sound and accent of a Russian Jew using English quite easily as a second language. Her accent and her syntax had the lilt of another language. When I think of my mother, the words "gentle," "loving," "enormously supportive" come to mind. She was deeply hopeful for a successful career for me, proud as she watched my career growing during the 1940s; but she was never pushy in the way that some stage mothers are. She had only the vaguest interest in politics. I can't remember anything she really disliked.

My sister, Eva, is seven years younger than I—when I was fifteen and already a professional, she was only eight. She was an excellent student and finished Lowell High School in two years. At thirteen, she joined a Zionist group called Hashomer Hatza'ir (The Young Pioneers); it was made up of young people from Los Angeles and San Francisco, who banded together to prepare themselves for a future life in Israel. She was with the group for about a year and then dropped out. She attended the University of California for a year and then decided to continue her education in the East. She went to New York. Through Hy Goldsmith, who was working for the United Nations on atomic power, she got a temporary job at Brookhaven National Laboratories, where she met a physicist, William Hornyak, whom she later married. Wonderfully gifted as a teacher, he became chairman of the physics department at the University of Maryland. The attention given me and my possible future might have made Eva, at times, feel overlooked or that she lacked close family support. But our deep affection for each other never lessened. In our adult years we have become, and remain, very close.

A PERFORMING artist selects and rehearses repertoire with thought for musical variety, with a wish to display abilities and move an audience, and with the realization that the world of music is enormously complicated in that it is without absolutes—except when what you are doing is wrong, abolutely wrong, wrong in tempo, wrong in ideas, wrong in your understanding of the period in musical history when the work was written, what performance practice was then like; all those things. Rehearsing and practicing, you have to learn what the variables are. Most people do not stop to think that the words "piano," "forte," "mezzo-forte," "mezzo-piano"—that is, soft, loud, half-loud, half-soft—mean nothing in themselves. Each of these indications is simply in relation to the sound that preceded it; the kind of piano or the kind of forte that one plays or uses depends almost entirely on where it comes in the body of the work that you're learning or performing. And the relationship between the quality of sound and the amount of sound has to do with the control and understanding by the performer of the composer's total concept. You learn that when you play the first note of a composition, you must already understand where you expect yourself to be when you reach the final note of that movement, if it is a three- or four-movement work; you must know the tonal, harmonic, and tempo relationships among the movements to make a work hold together throughout its entirety, from the first note to the last.

And you remember performances of the same work by many great artists, how differently they sounded—and yet all correct. How can music be so differently performed and yet remain correct? Because as the performer grasps the totality of the composition, he gauges the amount of sound and speed required by the work against his own skills with tonal and volume pressures and technical fleetness, so as to enable him to create feelings and ideas that will make difficult passages seem easy. In every fine performance there is a sense of inexorable logic that forces you to say, "Well, of course, that makes absolute sense. It's clear that's the way it should be." Then you'll hear someone else do it differently, and you'll say the same thing. Beyond the necessary acquired knowledge of the instrument and musical history, every artist also has a very personal and indefinable symbiosis with his instrument, be it violin, piano, cello, or his own vocal cords. As he plays, he hears the composition in his or her own very special personal voice. Every great artist has a distinctive interpretive strength. That is what one searches for through all of one's life: uniqueness and simplicity. The single most difficult responsibility of a performing artist is to know how complicated, how interwoven, how difficult a work is— and how to get it to sound simple and inevitable. That is what Zakin and I strove to achieve with every musical work we selected for our repertoire during those years, with our every rehearsal, our every performance.

SEVEN

*O*NE OF the major political issues of the postwar period had to do with the participation of certain German musicians in the culture of Nazi Germany. Wilhelm Furtwängler was an extraordinary musician—and a pure German. When Hitler came to power in 1933, Furtwängler was the conductor of the Berlin Philharmonic. At first, he did what he could to protect and help some of the Jewish musicians in his orchestra, who were banned from taking part in anything cultural. But when matters became really difficult, he said he couldn't go any further and let events take their course. He believed in Germany; Germany was the very center of his life. That was the difference between him and the brothers Fritz Busch, the conductor, and Adolf Busch, the violinist, and others, who were not Jewish and yet chose to leave Nazi Germany. Furtwängler would have been received anywhere in the world with honor and acclaim, but he elected to remain in Germany. As far as I know, he never became a member of the Nazi Party, but all during the war he conducted music in Nazi Germany.

There was a very well-known conductor named Paul Kletzki, a wonderful musician with whom I've played many times over the years, at La Scala and in Switzerland, America, and elsewhere. He was a Polish Jew of remarkable musical ability, with a lovely Middle European sense of humor, a wry smile, and a pair of huge eyebrows—one went up and the other down, giving a unique expression to his face. He had been a protégé of Furtwängler's, had lived in his house, was virtually a member of his family, a son to him. In 1933, Kletzki fled Germany and ended up in Italy, without work and nearly starving, barely managing to live on three or four bowls of spaghetti a week. He told me that when he read in the papers that Furtwängler was coming to Switzerland to conduct at the Lucerne Festival, he wrote to him there: "Remembering the closeness of our lives together in Berlin for so long, I ask you as a friend to send me some help here to Italy. I would ask you only when you are out of Germany so that you can do this with foreign funds that would not necessarily go through any German authority." Kletzki didn't receive an answer for a long time. Finally, Furtwängler wrote back, "My dear Paul, as your old friend, I would love to help you. As a German, I cannot."

Some years after the war, Furtwängler was invited to the United States to succeed Artur Rodzinski as conductor of the Chicago Symphony Orchestra. A number of artists—Arthur Rubinstein, Vladimir Horowitz, Nathan Milstein, Jascha Heifetz, Gregor Piatigorsky, myself, and others—promptly made it known, in a letter we signed and sent to the management and board, that if Furtwängler was given that position, we would never again play with the Chicago Symphony. The invitation was withdrawn.

During the late forties, when I was on my first European tour, I gave a recital in a small, delicious concert hall, the Salle Gaveau, in Paris, and then was invited for my first major orchestral engagement at the Lucerne Festival, where the conductor was Charles Munch, whom I had known fondly for many years in America. As we relaxed in the dressing room before the concert, a man came in with a group of people. He was in his late fifties or early sixties, tall, cadaverous, with deep eyes, high cheekbones, thinning gray hair. I was introduced to him: Wilhelm Furtwängler. I said, formally and somewhat distantly, "Good afternoon." He greeted me politely, and then he and Munch entered into a conversation. I sat down on a very lumpy leather couch and directed my talk to those around me, but not to Furtwängler. At one point, Munch, who was standing next to Furtwängler, said something very funny. I turned toward him and Furtwängler and burst into laughter—and a flashbulb went off. Someone had taken a photograph, which, as I subsequently discovered, was handed around to a number of people. It showed me and Furtwängler enjoying a good laugh together; everyone else in the photograph, including Munch, had been airbrushed out. The comment that made the rounds, along with the photograph, was "Stern can have pleasure with Furtwängler backstage in Europe, why does he attack him and refuse to play with him in the United States?" I think the photograph was also put into some newspapers by Furtwängler's people. A small example of postwar power politics in a very minor arena.

I have always felt that it was far too easy for those of us living on the American side of the ocean, untouched by the horrors of war, to tell others, "Why aren't you heroes? Why don't you bare your chests to the machine guns?" I can very well understand and sympathize with the position of European musicians like Georg Solti and others who, after the war, found posts in ravaged Germany and helped rebuild its musical infrastructure; they had no alternative; it was impossible for them to leave Europe without some kind of musical reputation, which they did not yet have. But there were men of musical renown who, before the war, could have left Germany and come to America, where they would have earned acclaim and immense financial returns. Wilhelm Furtwängler was one of them.

Unlike Richard Strauss, Furtwängler was never an anti-Semite. He was, I think, quite a nice man, and very broad-minded. But he was also, fatally, a weak man, who preferred to remain blind to what was happening all around him, decided to remain *the* German conductor, and chose to make music for the Nazis.

EIGHT

I CAME to know Sol Hurok very well. I can see him now in my mind's eye. He was about five feet seven, rotund, husky, with an expressive face that was always ready to break out in a smile. There was a lurking humor about him; he would with ease laugh or scoff at others and himself. His voice had a rolling pitch to it and was distinctly colored by his formative years in Russia and his Jewish background. He spoke several languages, all with a Yiddish accent. He used to wear fedoras in a rakish fashion, with one side down, like George Raft in the early movies, and handsome topcoats with fur collars; in later years, he sported a cane with a silver top.

He was more than a manager; he was an impresario, one of the greatest of the century. He discovered, developed, and presented artists and entertainment. That meant he took risks. He would put up his own money, or find money, to back unknown artists. He would take on struggling young artists and try them for a couple of years, see if they caught on; if they didn't, he'd let them go. He made fortunes, he lost fortunes. He was a flamboyant man who believed utterly in himself, the only person I have ever known who would refer to himself in the third person—"Hurok said that"; "Hurok thinks such"; "Hurok did this"—and have it come out simply natural.

He was always thinking about the "people," the common man. And though he loved money and position, he had a conviction about the need for the arts to be available to the greatest number of people. In later years, he had an uncanny sense of what would sell. He was the one who brought European ballet to America. He had an extraordinary sense of box office. When he had a ballet company—Russian, British, French—or any artist appearing in New York, whether for one day or six weeks, he'd be in the theater every night, checking the box office, the audience, the empty seats. His life was his artists, his concerts—to the extent that little else seemed to matter.

Hurok and I became very close, despite the fact that he was my manager. An indication of the kind of relationship we had was the fact that there was never a contract between us, only a handshake. About five years into our relationship, he or his lawyers and accountants decided that there should be a written contract, and one was presented to me. It contained clauses that were completely unacceptable. I rewrote them and brought the contract back to him. He looked at it, put it in a drawer, and that was the last either of us ever saw of anything resembling a contract.

At some point in our relationship I began to feel that my calling him "Mr. Hurok" just didn't suit the closeness I felt toward him. I didn't want to call him "Sol"; it would have been too forward, undignified, I thought, considering the difference in our ages. So I started calling him "Papa" when we were alone together or on the telephone; he had once talked about himself as being Papa Hurok to so many young people.

He taught me many things. For example, when I was on tour in later years and receiving a very good fee, many managers would say to me, "Why don't you get a higher fee? You're worth it, we're making money on you. Why don't you ask for more money?" When I discussed this with Hurok, he said, "Remember one thing. Never ask for more than what you can honestly earn for the local manager. The manager should always earn some money. Ask for a little less, and you can be sure your career will be secure with him." He was so right. In all the years I've been playing concerts, in all the years I've been on tour since 1938, I have never known a bad season, or a season poorer than the one preceding it. I have enjoyed fine and long-standing relationships with managers of all the major orchestras as well as individual impresarios.

Hurok also took a great deal of interest in politics and international affairs, and was a kind of parlor socialist. On Sundays he would listen to radio news broadcasts and, in later years, watch television roundtable discussions. Because he was constantly traveling throughout Europe and bringing artists in from there, he had many influential friends and contacts in the State Department.

He was well known for his wit. There was the time, for example, when Vladimir Horowitz, after twelve years of absence from the concert stage, returned to Carnegie Hall in a recital that was the music event of the decade. It was a sensational performance. Hurok wanted desperately to become Horowitz's manager, but Horowitz would have none of it, because Hurok managed, and was an intimate friend of, Arthur Rubinstein, Horowitz's archrival. After the concert, when Hurok was asked what he thought of Horowitz's performance, he came up with this memorable response: "Huh! What did you expect? Twelve years to practice for only one program." Once a radio interviewer said to him, "You know, you're so extraordinary in picking things that become great box office successes. There's sort of a magic golden touch that you have. What makes it possible?" Hurok said, "I don't know. I don't know what makes box office. One thing I know. If people don't want to come, nothing will stop them."

Sol Hurok's personal assistant was a woman named Mae Frohman. She ran the office, was his most trusted confidante, and served as his contact with his artists. Hurok was deeply involved with ballet: he single-handedly sparked the keen interest of the average American in ballet by bringing European companies to the United States and sending them to cities across the country. As a result, Mae Frohman knew the ballet world very well. She was especially close to Ballet Theater, a company that had been founded by Lucia Chase, a wealthy woman whose family owned a nationally known carpet company. Chase herself was an enthusiastic dancer and an excellent actress and played cameo roles in ballets, often bringing to her dancing a piquant humor and a strong stage presence.

One of the great stars of that company was a ballerina named Nora Kaye. She was a brilliant performer, physically powerful and capable of meeting all the demands of classical ballet. She did not have the ineffable grace, charm, and tenderness that marked such great ballerinas as Margot Fonteyn or Alicia Markova, but she possessed a unique sense of theater and the ability to project whatever mood and character a role demanded of her: drama, tragedy, or humor. Antony Tudor created and revived ballets for her which in time became staples of the Ballet Theater repertoire: *Pillar of Fire, Lilac Garden,* and others.

For reasons that are not important here, Nora experienced a personal and artistic crisis that caused her to leave Ballet Theater and the world of dance. It was during this period that she was introduced to me by Mae Frohman. I knew her by reputation but had never seen her dance. She had a firm, compact body, more rounded than those of most classical ballerinas. Her face was not beautiful: the nose was too large, the eyebrows were too strong. Though the facial structure was striking and immediately attractive, "beautiful" was not the word you would use right away to describe her. Her voice was the most unfortunate part of her physical endowments: it was high-pitched and colored with a Brooklyn accent that clearly revealed her Russian-Jewish ancestry and New York beginnings. The timbre of her voice and her nasal singsong were what kept her from becoming one of our great dramatic actresses on the legitimate stage. To see Nora was immediately to experience a personality, a vivacity, a force able to express easy laughter and an eagerness to enjoy life.

We felt an almost instant attraction for each other, and a passionate affair began. She was thrilled to have a new sense of stability away from what her life had always been: dancing class, rehearsal, performance, dancing class. The life of a ballet star, seemingly glamorous and exciting, is really made up of almost constant work and routine. The body is the instrument; it cannot function unless it is incessantly worked and trained. During our intense courtship—I don't remember that marriage was in our thoughts at the beginning; we were too busy being together—she joined me in Switzerland, in the summer of 1948, when I went to play at the Montreux Festival. I had already arrived at the hotel and was waiting for her to join me in the large suite I had arranged for us. We met and went downstairs to the bar for a drink before dinner. We were so happy to see each other that we started to toast our being together—in the course of which we finished off a bottle of vodka. That's about eighteen drinks each. We went upstairs and passed out cold.

The rest of that night is somewhat dim, but I know that before the weeklong visit was over, we had decided to get married as soon as possible. It was clear to us at that point that we could have a wonderful life together, and that we both wanted it.

As Nora had never met my family, nor I hers, it became a bit of a problem as to where to get married and what sort of ceremony to have. Would it be a formal marriage in a synagogue, with invitations going out to a multitude of people, all done in grand style? As we discussed a variety of possibilities, it became clear that what we both wanted was to get married quickly and quietly, and start our new life together as soon as possible. So, upon returning to New York, we informed our families that we were going to get married, took out a marriage license, and, on November 10, 1948, went down to City Hall and were married by whoever was there at the time with the authority to conduct the civil ceremony. After that, there was a joyous reception— exactly where, I don't remember—and Nora moved into the apartment at Riverside Drive, which was to be our home. My mother had moved to another apartment some weeks before.

After a few months I began to realize that in being with me while I practiced, traveled, played concerts, and met my public, Nora was experiencing a growing sense of doubt about herself. She was becoming restless. I remember saying to her that if she were to tell me that I was never to play the violin again, I would be absolutely crushed, and our marriage would dissolve in complete rancor. I said that I didn't ever want to hear her say that I had kept her from achieving a great career. I urged her to return to ballet, take classes, perform, and then, if she still wanted to be my wife, the marriage would have a true base.

She began to dance again and rejoined Ballet Theater. For the first time, I was able to see her onstage. She was truly extraordinary, filled with charismatic power. She knew everybody in ballet, all the dancers and designers, and I met them: Oliver Smith, Maria Tallchief, Margot Fonteyn, Sono Osato, Lucia Chase. She started touring with the company.

There was an incident that sticks out in my mind. I had been on tour for some time, and Nora was dancing in New York. One of the ballets she was appearing in was *Lilac Garden,* a romantic piece set by Tudor to the *Poème* for violin and orchestra by Chausson. The violin part was usually played by the concertmaster of the orchestra, and the conductor, Max Goberman, was a good friend of mine. I came back to town without telling Nora and phoned Max and asked if I could sneak into the pit just before the ballet was to begin and play. He was delighted with the idea, and we made the necessary arrangements. The curtain rose, and the orchestra began to play. Nora and the other dancers were going through their first routines onstage when suddenly I came in. I could see her stiffen, stop, look down, whisper something, and then go on dancing. Of course, as a performing musician I had always felt that it was outrageous for music to be tampered with, slowed down or speeded up, to suit the needs of the dancers. From my point of view, it was the dancers who had to follow the music, not the other way around. But that's not the right way most ballet companies work (Balanchine's New York City Ballet was an exception), and the conductor always has to watch the solo dancers and make certain that the music fits whatever tempo they've chosen. I would have none of that; I was going to show exactly how the music was to be played, and they were damn well going to dance to it. So I more or less stuck to my guns, giving only a little bit here and there. The performance ended, and Nora took her usual bows in front of the roaring crowd. I went backstage and hugged her, and she said, "You son of a bitch. I knew. I knew." I said, "I saw you stiffen." "Of course," she said. "The minute you started, I turned to my partner and said, 'Damn it, that's Isaac down there.' And I knew we were going to be in trouble as far as the tempo was concerned. But we tried."

That was one of the few moments of artistic collaboration that we enjoyed during our six months of marriage.

It was soon obvious that this was an untenable marriage. Her travels took her in one direction, mine in another. She'd be dancing in South America; I'd be playing in Europe. She'd have to be in Los Angeles; I'd be in Chicago. We discussed our situation in a warm, friendly fashion and decided that it would be best for us to get a Mexican divorce. This was done quickly and quietly, in mid-1950.

Some years later, I met her in Oslo, where, by chance, Ballet Theater was performing on the same day that I was playing a concert. We had a nostalgic dinner together, at the end of which she looked at me and said, "Damn it, I wish we could have known enough to have stayed together." But by then both our lives had taken quite different directions.

She went on with her career, and I with mine. We remained good friends. In 1959, she married Herbert Ross, who was then a notable choreographer and later became a successful film and stage director, and in 1961, she decided to end her ballet career. She and Herb lived on the West Coast, and on occasion, when I was in Hollywood, I would have dinner with them.

Years later, she fell ill with cancer. A long and very difficult period followed. When she died, in 1987, her husband called me in New York and asked if he could come over to my apartment. We talked about Nora and her memorial service, which was to take place in a theater. He broke down in tears. I played at the service, and afterward Jerome Robbins came out onstage and reminisced about Nora and the time when she was married to me. He said, "You know, Nora once told me that all she heard when she was home with Isaac was 'Reppa-reppa-reppa, squeaka-squeaka-squeaka, scrappa-scrappa-scrappa,' Isaac practicing all the time."

His words were true, and they brought down the house.

NINE

I DON'T SUPPOSE there are many people on this planet who, if they recognize my name, aren't at the same time aware that I'm Jewish. Yet, as I've said, my family never observed any kind of traditional Jewish ritual; neither Friday evening nor the Sabbath nor the holidays. We weren't members of any synagogue. Neither my father nor I had a bar mitzvah. And so my attention and education were never focused on anything specifically Jewish. I was busy being a musician.

My generally unfocused attitude on matters connected with my Jewishness changed dramatically in September 1949, when I went to the newly established state of Israel for the first time. That experience proved to be unforgettable, and it affected my life profoundly.

To be in Israel in those years—there was such a sense of ebulliency, such an exhilarating faith in the future. One got drunk with the urge to help create a new democratic society based on humanist ideals. That joy, that willingness to work, that fearlessness in the face of enormous problems!

I went to Israel with an open heart and mind, and was absolutely captivated by the sheer energy, the certainty of hope, the sure conviction that the dreams would be fulfilled. There was a kind of freewheeling, total commitment on the part of everyone to the future of the country. It was the sort of place where Moshe Dayan, who was then chief of staff, would walk down a street and if a soldier didn't salute him, he'd stop him and say, "What's the matter, are you mad at me or something?"

That experience in Israel was among the strongest and most exciting that I'd had in years. It was an excitement that increased as time went on, because my first impression—the city of Tel Aviv—was disheartening. Together with the adjoining former Arab city of Jaffa, which was almost entirely populated by refugee Jews, Tel Aviv was a crowded city built for 100,000 people and containing three to four times that number. Only after leaving Tel Aviv did I get to see a radiant Israel—a healthy, alive, land-loving, proud, and, on the whole, cooperative people. There were many conflicting points of view among them, but the general impression I got was of a people with immense hope and confidence in the future.

Between the concerts I gave, I managed to see almost the entire country. The chief of staff of the army gave me a car, with a driver and military escort, and I went to Haifa, Acre, Nazareth, middle and upper Galilee, up to Lake Tiberias, through Safed, a Jewish city dating back some 2,500 years (and, when I saw it for the first time, smelling like it), and then to within a few miles of the Lebanese border. Later, the army made available a small plane in which I flew down over the Negev. I saw the Red Sea, the Dead Sea, and the Mediterranean, all in five hours. We flew all the way down along the Trans-Jordan border to the Egyptian border and landed at Eilat, the southernmost Israeli city, on the Gulf of Aqaba. The water was the bluest I'd ever seen, the surrounding hills jagged, with gullies and ravines. It was a wasteland both horrible and beautiful at the same time.

Three days after arriving, I went up to Jerusalem and found it to be quite beautiful—so different from Tel Aviv. It had a wonderfully unique character, and a serenity marred only by the fact that it was practically cut in half by barbed wire and mined areas, since the Arabs held the Old City. I was taken up to the Notre Dame mission and the Church of the Dormition on Mount Zion and shown the then newly discovered supposed tomb of King David. Looking across the Arab lines, I could see the Mount of Olives and the garden of Gethsemane. I wasn't able to take pictures because I was in military territory under military escort and in full view of the Arab Legion guards.

I visited several kibbutzim: one was twenty-five years old; another, ten; a third, eight months old; a fourth, two weeks old. I spoke to hundreds of people, to people in and out of the government, to people long settled on the land, and to newcomers, and I was able to get a picture of the country, physically, economically, socially, through all manners of eyes and minds. Living conditions on the whole were very bad; the food was atrocious. Many of the newcomers were from concentration camps; the big problem was how to get them settled and into worthwhile work. An American psychoanalyst, Dr. Paul Friedman, was visiting the country at the time, and in the evenings, after he'd met with people and I'd played a concert, we would get together and compare notes about what we'd seen that day. Invariably, our individual experiences left us filled with optimism, with a sense of the eagerness of the Israelis to look forward, to build for the future.

I found my reception to be simply incredible. People would almost rather go to a concert than eat. At every performance we had at least 250 more people than the capacity of the hall. They crowded in everywhere. I played endlessly: seven concerts in Tel Aviv, one in Haifa, one in Jerusalem, an extra pension-fund concert. Each concert included two and sometimes three concerti. I played Brahms, Lalo, Tchaikovsky, Mendelssohn, Wieniawski, Beethoven, Mozart, Bach. The last three days were frantic. On Monday morning, I rehearsed three concerti; Monday night, we played them. Tuesday afternoon, at 5 p.m., we played two for the pension fund; at 7 we rehearsed another, and at 9 played three more. Wednesday night, three concerti in Jerusalem— and for an encore, a fourth! Some of those performances were among the best I'd ever given, simply because the audiences were so warm and willing to listen that I just relaxed and let the music flow out of me.

The informality of the country was intoxicating. People dressed simply and even came to concerts in shorts and khaki shirts. I'd return to my hotel around midnight after a concert, and the night clerk would say something like "Tell me, why are you only playing the Fifth Sonata of Beethoven, why not the *Kreutzer* or the Tenth? They're much better."

I took no fees for my playing—no visiting solo concert performer did in those days, as far as I know. Certain favors were rendered by way of compensation. One such favor I received was a trip by taxi accompanied by a woman, one of the volunteer workers for the orchestra, to the small house on Keren Kayemet Street in Tel Aviv where David Ben-Gurion, the first prime minister of Israel, lived. I remember the woman paying the taxi driver, who looked at me and said, "Mr. Stern, don't stay too long talking to the old man. Remember, you've got a concert tonight."

Ben-Gurion turned out to be a short man with an enormous personality that radiated from him like waves of electricity. His utter belief in what he was creating shone from him like a beacon. I told him about the excitement I felt playing in a new country and for audiences for whom music was such a vital necessity. He wanted to know why I wasn't emigrating to Israel and plied me with questions about my beginnings, about my family. Years later, when I met him again, he said to me, "You I've given up on already. But how about your children? When are they coming?"

I was also taken to some of the battle areas. A well-known general named Yitzhak Sadeh drove me down in his jeep to his headquarters on the southern front. I remember he had a long beard and was completely bald. He drove like a madman, scattering people, donkeys, chickens—anything that got in his way. I had my heart in my mouth the entire ride. At his headquarters he took out his battle plan and showed me what he had managed to accomplish with very little equipment. During one attack by the Egyptians, he'd had only one battery of six cannons, so he ordered them to fire off a salvo and then move like hell to somewhere else; fire another salvo and then move to a third position and fire again. The Egyptians thought he had eight batteries there, and broke off the attack.

He told me that everybody was in the army, no matter what his profession. He said there was one young man, a gifted painter and poet, about whom he really worried. "I tried my best to make sure the officers knew about him, so he wouldn't be in the advance attack groups. I told them to let him bring the ammunition, let him get the bandages. I didn't want him wounded or killed. He managed to come out alive."

Something else occurred during that first trip to Israel that I've never forgotten. I was supposed to play a concert in Haifa with the Palestine Philharmonic, which later became the Israel Philharmonic. The location for the concert was a horrible movie theater in the downtown section of the city. Earlier that day, I'd been taken to a recently established agricultural settlement headed by Leah Previn, the sister of the pianist-conductor André Previn. A beautiful woman, who later tragically died in childbirth, she showed me around the place. The group that had put up the settlement and was training there for future kibbutz life had originally come from Los Angeles and had been placed near the Lebanese border both to till the earth and to act as an observation post in the event of a military move across the border by the Syrian army. There was nothing but barren soil and boulders in the area. The settlers pulled out the boulders, tilled the soil, and built little houses for themselves and their children. Every house had a magazine or a picture book, and each day they would turn to a new page, which would be their children's reading for the day.

I invited them to the concert in Haifa. I said to bring whoever could come, thinking maybe eight or ten would show up. Forty of them came down in buses and trucks. There was no room for them in the movie theater. I told the people who were in charge of the concert, "They've got to get in." They said, "We don't have seats." I said, "You don't have seats, I don't play." Backstage they found barrels and crates and broken-down chairs and put them all around the stage. About twenty people who came from the settlement had brought with them the scores of the compositions I was scheduled to play, and they sat on those barrels and crates and broken chairs, following me with their scores.

Israel was that kind of place then. It made me feel very proud.

FROM ISRAEL I flew to Rome, in those days a comfortable trip of six hours and fifteen minutes, passing over the island of Crete and the coast of Greece. In Rome I was met by Zakin and his wife, Isabelle, who had been enjoying a delightful and exhausting time seeing Europe and were wonderfully happy and cooing like doves. I stayed only one night in Rome, and the next afternoon arrived by plane in Milan.

On the evening of September 26, I played the Beethoven Violin Concerto at La Scala, with the La Scala Orchestra, conducted by Paul Kletzki. The performance was a great success. Even Zakin was impressed by the Beethoven. La Scala was a wonderful place in which to play, though the orchestra sounded only fair. The next day I boarded a plane to Vienna. The flight was one of the most beautiful I'd ever had. En route, we landed at Venice. On our approach to the landing field, we flew low over the entire city; in the morning sunlight, it sparkled and floated like a child's toy. Our next stop was Trieste, and from there we flew over the southern Alps, some snow-covered, and along the Yugoslavian border into Austria.

Now began a very strange experience: from the moment I arrived in Vienna to the moment I left, I felt peculiarly ill at ease. The instant I saw the German-style uniform on the customs officials, I felt the hairs on the back of my neck rising. Hearing the German language everywhere left me feeling very disturbed.

In the meantime, Zakin and Isabelle were traveling to Austria by train. In those years, immediately after the war, the Russians were still in charge of entry into Vienna. They stopped Zakin because he was an ex-Russian, took him off the train, and made him and Isabelle wait in the station through the night while they checked his papers, delaying his arrival by almost twenty-four hours.

The program I was to play included the Prokofiev Concerto in D Major and the Beethoven concerto. In the car on the way from the airport into the city with the local concert manager, I asked how many times the orchestra had previously played the Prokofiev. His answer was "Oh, we've never played it, we were waiting for you." I was shocked; with the limited rehearsal time we had, it wouldn't be possible to prepare the Prokofiev. I told him so, and requested that we switch to the Mendelssohn concerto instead.

I was scheduled to give a recital with Zakin in the Brahms Saal of the Musikverein—Haydn, Bach, Brahms, Bartók—and then, two nights later, a concert with the orchestra in the Grosse Saal. The Austrians gravely and piously reminded Zakin and me that Brahms had given his very first performances in those auditoriums. We nodded and murmured "Interesting," and went about our work, determinedly unimpressed.

I had, by that time, been invited to dine with a number of Vienna's well-to-do and socially prominent individuals. We discussed some recent history, including the Anschluss (the 1938 annexation of Austria by Germany) and the Nazi period. With some of those elegant individuals I talked about music and literature. At one point, I mentioned that I was eager to travel to Prague and see the city where Kafka had lived and written. Their reaction was "Who? We don't know Kafka."

Among the Americans who were there at the time was a group from HIAS, the Hebrew Immigrant Aid Society. A sister of one of my closest friends, Hy Goldsmith, worked there, and she came to see me and talked about the problems involving the transfer of Jews from Russia to Europe, the United States, and Israel. There were so many Jewish refugees in Austria that a large camp had been set up to care for them until their transfer papers to other countries could be arranged. I remember her telling me something that colored my entire visit to Austria. She said that, a few days before, she had been to a soccer game between an Austrian team and a team of Jewish refugees from the transit camp. At a moment in the game when the refugees were leading the Austrians by more than a few points, she suddenly began to hear from among the spectators chants of "Send them back to the gas chamber." Listening to her, I realized that such moments of horror had been experienced by many Jews during that terrible period, but for me it was the first chilling reminder of how ingrained was their anti-Semitism.

I met several people—members of the Joint Distribution Committee and a number of journalists—from whom I learned that my instinctive feeling of distrust was well-founded: anti-Semitism was widespread and vicious. There was a cynical decadence about Vienna that was inescapable. Badly scarred by the war, with many ruins still in evidence, the city seemed prosperous, its shops filled with food and clothing. Russian troops, much in evidence along the streets and in patrol cars, kept strictly to themselves. But the famous charm of the city was noticeable by its absence.

The recital with Zakin and my concert with the orchestra were a fantastic success, with the audiences in both halls coming to their feet and stamping and yelling with abandon, and with hyperbolic reviews in the press. Yet I still felt very uncomfortable. Those heavy faces, that Teutonic pomposity—it all made me feel especially happy that the concerts had been so successful. I wondered if I was bringing too much imagination and memory of things past to bear on the present; perhaps I had come to Vienna too soon after my experience in Israel, which had had quite an effect on my Jewish consciousness. Maybe I needed a little perspective that only time would bring.

In the end, I decided never to return to Austria, despite the fact that the reviews that appeared in the Austrian press after those two concerts were among the most ecstatic I have ever received in my life.

I haven't an ounce of antagonism, hatred, or disdain toward contemporary Austria and Germany. In fact, I respect, I admire, I envy their need to listen to great music, to live with great music. But there is something about my playing in those countries, about hearing the language—images burnt into my mind are suddenly brought back. Germans and Austrians have lost far less by not hearing me than I have by not appearing before the most musically educated and receptive audiences I could have had anywhere in the world.

THROUGH that fall, Zakin and I played in Holland, France, Denmark, Finland, Sweden, Norway, Switzerland, Italy, and Portugal. My final concert of 1949 was on the 30th of December: the Tchaikovsky Violin Concerto, with the Minneapolis Symphony Orchestra, conducted by Dimitri Mitropoulos. This extraordinary man, with whom I was to have many wonderful musical collaborations, did something that I have never seen before or since. As I was listening to him lead a symphony during the second half of the concert, I suddenly noticed him standing beside me in the wings, while the orchestra went on playing. I looked at him and said, "What's wrong? Are you ill?" He said, "No, I just wanted to show the audience how the orchestra can play just as well at times without a conductor." He continued, "They don't realize that after one rehearses well and gets to a certain point, it is really the orchestra that makes the work come alive, not the man standing in front, waving his arms." Of course, the orchestra went on playing exactly as he had rehearsed them, somewhat in a state of shock, until the end of that movement, and then he walked back to finish the symphony and the concert.

From there I flew home, to celebrate the new year with my family and friends. It was, of course, impossible for me to know what personal and professional astonishments awaited me in the coming decade from two sources that were to become major centers of my life: Pablo Casals and the new state of Israel.

TEN

𝒫ABLO CASALS occupied a very special place in the world of music. He was already a living legend, a man of profound principles and yet extraordinary kindness—truly a unique figure. To that, one must add his enormous musical gifts, which made him the outstanding musician of his time. He was a world all his own, and his influence on those close to him was very strong. When he played, he created music in a manner few had heard before. At times during rehearsals, he would become so emotional that tears would pour down his face and he would have to stop playing.

A Spaniard from Catalonia and an outspoken anti-Fascist, Casals had sworn never to perform publicly in any country that recognized Francisco Franco, who in 1939 had defeated the Republican forces in the Spanish Civil War and now ruled as dictator of Spain. Because the regime was recognized by all countries in the world, Casals could play nowhere without breaking his word to himself, and so for several years he played nowhere.

It was the violinist Alexander (Sasha) Schneider who was solely responsible for the reemergence of Pablo Casals as a major figure in music.

I'd first met Sasha during the summer of 1935, when the Budapest String Quartet was playing a complete cycle of Bartók and Beethoven quartets at Mills College. The quartet had already established an outstanding reputation and was quickly gaining recognition as the premier ensemble in the world, perhaps the greatest quartet of the twentieth century.

I was introduced to the quartet by my teacher, Naoum Blinder; he and Joseph Roisman, who played first violin, had known each other since their student days in Russia. Sasha was the second violin, his brother Mischa was the cellist, and Boris Kroyt was the violist. Boris had a warm and completely individual sound that always fit into the total sound of the quartet as a unit. Mischa Schneider's bass was the Rock of Gibraltar on which everything rested; it was always there, never interfering with the musical line but giving substance to the whole harmonic and melodic structure of the works they were playing.

From his position as second violin, Sasha was a sort of Vesuvian fire that gave a special warmth, spice, and color to the total quartet sound. It was Sasha, as I say, who was primarily responsible for the reemergence of Pablo Casals. In his constant effort to expand his musical knowledge and satisfy his musical curiosity, Sasha traveled to Europe after the war and went to visit Casals, who was then living in the small border town of Prades, in the section of France known as the Pyrénées-Orientales.

The two men began to play chamber music together, particularly Bach sonatas, and Sasha would listen to the solo suites on the cello and to the keyboard inventions with which Casals would begin his days. Very quickly Sasha realized that Casals was, indeed, one of the seminal musicians of our time, a major figure tragically unavailable to the world because of his self-imposed exile.

At first, Sasha tried to prevail upon Casals to break out of his exile and return to public performance, or at least to share his knowledge with others. But Casals refused. After some time, Sasha decided that if Casals wouldn't come out into the world, the world should come to Casals. He spoke to some wealthy friends, among them Mrs. Rosalie Leventritt, whose husband, Edgar, was a well-known financier, and to Mrs. Lionella Pereira. Both were avid concert-goers and highly informed music aficionados. With their sponsorship and the backing of one or two other very wealthy women who knew and supported chamber music, Sasha helped organize the first Casals Festival, which took place in Prades in the spring and summer of 1950.

I had been at home the year before when Sasha called and said, in his heavy Russian accent, "There is a festival next summer, and you must come." I was delighted; nothing could have pleased and honored me more.

In June 1950, I was in Paris. From there I drove down to Prades with a friend from England, Julian Spiro, and Jane Eakin, a painter with whom I was then having a very close relationship. Julian did most of the driving so as to save my hands and keep me from too much body strain, because I was going to have to play well and work hard in the next forty-eight hours. We arrived at the Hotel Moliget-les-Bains up above Prades, at a little widening in the road—not exactly a four-star hotel but adequate—at about two in the morning. I told my two friends that I had to practice, because I had a rehearsal the next morning, the Bach Double, with Sasha Schneider and Casals. In my room I took my violin out and started to play. The window was open, and suddenly the most extraordinary accompaniment came from somewhere outside. My music had apparently awakened a nightingale, which now joined me in sound as I was practicing Bach. It was a special moment.

The next day, feeling the excitement of anticipation and not a little nervous, I was picked up by Schneider and driven to Casals' home, a modest, square stone house. We went in and climbed a staircase to Casals' practice room, where, my pulse racing, I was introduced to a smiling, rotund, genial man who was smoking a pipe. He greeted me with the gentlest affability imaginable. Casals was a legend, and there I was, in his home, about to make music with him.

Sasha and I took out our violins. Casals sat down at the piano to play the accompaniment. He was a splendid pianist and had a lifelong habit of starting his mornings by playing Bach preludes for at least half an hour. We began to play the D Minor Double Concerto, joyfully, excitedly, with everything going better than I could have hoped. It was immediately clear that we all had the same general idea of the music. The piano was a half-tone flat and completely out of tune, but that didn't seem to bother Casals at all, though it was a bit troubling to me, as I have perfect pitch. Every once in a while, Casals would make a comment that would give even more impact or subtlety or surging power to a musical phrase. By the end of the rehearsal, it was obvious that we had found ourselves to be kindred spirits. That was a most important moment of my life, because, though I had confidence in my talent, my instincts, and my vision, I now had my basic musical approach confirmed in a fundamental way by this first encounter with Casals' mind and spirit.

Casals was not an impressive figure physically. He was about my height, five feet six inches, gray-haired, portly, with a twinkling eye that could be either deliciously familial or passionately demanding, depending on circumstances. I've often been asked what was so unique about Casals, and it's difficult to describe in words. The best image I've been able to come up with involves a high brick wall and a garden. Imagine yourself suddenly coming upon such a wall, not knowing that beyond it lay an exquisite garden. What Casals did was open a door into the garden; you entered and suddenly found yourself amid colors and scents you never dreamed existed. He revealed what might be accomplished once you were inside the garden. But how many of the colors and scents you could make your own, giving greater power to your musical imagination—that was your responsibility.

Here is another (impossible) attempt to verbalize Casals' gift. Let us say that you have done all the necessary musical preparation: you've brought yourself as close as possible to the composer's intention through a careful examination of the score; you have a knowledge of the time in which the music was written and of the history of musical performance in that period; you have studied and analyzed the basic musical character of the work you are playing. Having done all that, you then allow yourself a range of, say, two feet, within which you can make your own personal interpretation, based on all the knowledge you've acquired, to give a complete, cogent performance of the composition. You must remember that what ties a movement or an entire work together is its pulse (quite different from tempo), the inexorable continuity that starts with the first note and finishes with the last. Within that continuous pulse, that inevitability that you must have clear inside yourself in any musical performance, lies that margin of two feet, the arena for your personal interpretation.

Casals made those two feet into fifteen feet! He had the enormous conceptual ability to continue that pulse from beginning to end, with the seeming freedom to give the widest of personal interpretations—an intellectual achievement of incredible proportions. He used to describe it as "Freedom, freedom, but with order." I've heard this kind of vaulting musical imagination very rarely in all my years.

Casals had left behind a great estate in Spain, and many things that were close to his heart. In Prades he had this little stone house, with its small yard and a couple of rooms. Spaniards by the hundreds came to him on pilgrimages—some for political reasons, others to ask for money to stay alive. Prades was the last place imaginable for a music festival. Just over the mountains from Spain, in the southwest corner of France, it lay about an hour and a half away from Perpignan. One main street, one big café, one church. A tall mountain in the distance dominated the valley. The hotel where we lived and relaxed that summer of 1950 was on a nearby hilltop, and beyond was another range of mountains. On the other side of those mountains was Franco's Spain.

The orchestra that had been gathered by Sasha Schneider was extraordinary. Musicians came from all over to take part in the festival. The two flutes were John Wummer, of the New York Philharmonic, and Bernie Goldberg, who later became first flutist of the Pittsburgh Symphony. The oboe player was the great French musician Marcel Tabuteau, who not only was the first oboe of the Philadelphia Orchestra but had the most profound influence on the playing of the oboe in America from the mid-forties on. The first viola was Milton Katims, who had been first viola for Toscanini in the NBC Symphony, later a famous soloist, and then, for many years, the conductor of the Seattle Symphony. And so it went, through the various sections of the orchestra: leading musicians who came from everywhere to participate in the festival, not for the money, because no one was paid more than ordinary minimum rates, and none of the soloists received massive fees. All came out of respect for Casals and the desire to be near this great musical mind.

The rehearsals took place in a girls' school, in a room with a ceiling about eleven feet high. The air was very dry. The room could just about seat sixty orchestra members. The acoustics were horrific, but it was the only place in town where we could rehearse. The recordings that were made there became a test of ingenuity for the engineers:

what kind of microphones to use and where to place them in order to get sound in a room that literally had no sound. One day there was a rehearsal of Bach's Fifth Brandenburg Concerto, the one with the famous solo cadenza for a keyboard instrument; originally, it was for the harpsichord, but now it is often played on the piano. Rudolf Serkin was playing. I will never forget hearing him in that rehearsal: all of us in the orchestra just sitting and listening to his cadenza start slowly and begin to build, and then build and build, and suddenly march across the musical landscape with giant boots, and end with a musical volcanic eruption of sheer ecstasy, a climax that leaped out of the piano and roared its way into the coda, at which point we made our orchestral entrance, playing the final few measures, and then finishing the last chord and suddenly jumping to our feet and screaming like crazy, "Bravo! Bravo!" It was one of those astonishing musical moments when everything that could be done with a phrase was done— and a little more.

Many people visited the festival. Janet Flanner came down to write a piece for *The New Yorker*. Gjon Mili, the world-famous *Life* photographer, and a friend of Sasha's, came. Margaret Bourke-White was there, as well as correspondents from major newspapers in Paris, New York, and London. I met a young violin maker and expert violin restorer, Etienne Vatelot, who over the years developed into one of the world's great luthiers. (What a welcoming and happy home he and his wife, Yvette, maintain in France!) It was one of the musical events of the decade, and I don't know of anyone who was there who has ever forgotten it. A glance at the catalogued recordings that were made during those first three festivals will give an idea of how many of the world's great musicians played there. There is no point in listing all the great performers who were honored to accept invitations, but I would like to single out one: Eugene Istomin. He was a friend of Casals' long before the festival was conceived, and would visit and discuss music and play and record sonatas with him.

The festival consisted solely of Bach: chamber music; sonatas for violin, two violins, violin and oboe, piano, two pianos, three pianos; Brandenburg concerti; cantatas; and, of course, the Bach cello suites, performed by Casals. All the concerts were held in the town's only church, in a palpably reverent and awestruck atmosphere. The church authorities were happy to have the concerts there, but because it was holy ground, no applause was permitted. So we played, bowed, and walked off. We played Bach in all its purity and nobility; it was, indeed, God-given music.

By the final few days of the seventeen-day festival, most of us were feeling the need for another kind of music, something with glissandos and vibrant vibratos and lots of rubatos. A few days before the festival was to end, we had an evening free of rehearsal or performance, and we all gathered at the Hotel Moligt-les-Bains and began to play Wieniawski, Chopin, Schumann, Tchaikovsky, anything that was romantic, so we could get away from the classic purity and the prayerful moods we had been involved with for so long. It all ended with a rather raucous party that lasted until the wee hours of the morning, not only in the hotel rooms but in the various houses where the artists were living. The orchestra had many young people, some of them very attractive women, devotees of Casals', and I must say I had a great time. "Conviviality" and "hilarity" are, I think, the mildest words one can use to describe that evening. I remember one incident toward the end of the night when a couple decided, as dawn approached, that it was time to leave. They went out to their little Volkswagen Beetle and climbed in. Burl Ives, who had come to visit and attend concerts, got it into his head for some reason that they shouldn't go, and stood in front of their Beetle and literally picked it up so they couldn't move forward. They stayed a bit longer.

I hadn't the slightest inkling as to what extent all the gadding about I engaged in during the 1950 festival was a reaction to the breakup of my marriage to Nora and the psychic wound it inflicted upon me. For a time after the divorce, I didn't organize myself physically or mentally for playing. The result was that during a recital at Carnegie Hall on November 10, 1950, right in the middle of a very difficult work, two fingers of my left hand froze. I had to work around that complete block. No one seemed to notice what had happened, but that shocking event brought home to me the realization that my preparation for the performance had been inadequate. And then the stress of the performance itself—it had all suddenly leaped out at me. My ability to concentrate, to prepare, to focus on what I had to do in order to be a performer when, at the moment you're performing, the rest of the world doesn't exist, only the music and the audience, and nothing in your life can be allowed to affect you in a way that might hurt the music—all of that had been put into jeopardy those past months. I had gone much too far and had to return to the fiddle. I couldn't go away from the fiddle, otherwise I was not myself. Though the locked fingers quickly returned to full use and I was able to play a concert the next day, that moment of self-recognition was of crucial importance to me.

Let me add some words here about Casals. I remember an interview that I did with him years after the first Prades festival, during which I said, "You won't play in Spain while Franco is alive, and I refuse to go to Spain because of what you stand for." He looked at me and said, "No, you are wrong. You go and play. I have my reason for not playing, but you should go and make music there." And he added, "You know, I will never see Spain again. I will die before Franco does." He was right.

IN 1951, Sasha moved the festival to Perpignan, a lovely French Mediterranean town that was a mixture of three cultures—French, Spanish, and Catalan. The locals had a distinctive, very heavy French accent. We played in an open Roman stadium that was subject to weather and didn't have much to say for itself as far as sound was concerned. We went there because the festival's popularity had grown to such a degree that more and more people wanted to come, and Perpignan was the closest town to Prades where everyone could be accommodated. That year the program contained works by Mozart and Beethoven. But the excitement of Prades could not be repeated in Perpignan, and the festival returned to Prades the following summer. In July 1951, after my stay in Perpignan, I flew to Israel, where I was scheduled to play a series of concerts, starting in Tel Aviv. That trip turned into one of the most fateful journeys of my life.

$\mathcal{T}$HE LADY who had accompanied me and Julian Spiro on the trip to Prades in 1950, Jane Eakin, had also joined me in Perpignan, where we enjoyed a lovely romantic interlude. When I left for Israel, I borrowed a suitcase and an alarm clock from her. We agreed to meet in Paris after I returned from Israel.

In Israel I played a number of recitals with Alexander Zakin. He had a cousin, Tamara Fitelberg, who worked at the United Nations headquarters in New York. Through her he had met a young woman named Vera Lindenblit, who had been living in New York but by chance was in Jerusalem that summer, working as an interpreter.

Before the war, Vera and her parents and older sister, Meri, had lived well-to-do middle-class lives in Berlin, with Lithuanian passports. Around the mid-thirties, they abruptly left Berlin for France and settled in Paris. Then the Germans invaded France. Lithuanian Jews were among the last to be rounded up in Paris, but even so, Vera's father, who was denounced to the Nazis by a Frenchman, was taken to a sports arena, where he found himself with all the other Jews arrested in July 1941.

Vera, trying to obtain permission to see her father, was informed that passes were available only to those who engaged in labor that would be useful to the German army. She got a job in a factory that made gloves for German soldiers, and after a few weeks, she obtained a pass to visit her father, but by the time she arrived, he had been shipped off to Auschwitz, where he perished.

Vera and her mother went into hiding. By then, her sister had met a Polish Jewish refugee, married him, and gone with him to the United States, where she lived during the worst part of the war. Before their departure for France, Vera's mother had sewn gold coins into her dresses. With her father deported, Vera and her mother fled to a hospital on the outskirts of Paris, where they were hidden by non-Jews, whom they paid for food and shelter.

At that time, the Germans issued a regulation stipulating that Jews who could prove they had family in a neutral country would, if they so desired, be issued a laissez-passer to that country. Vera and her mother had relatives in Stockholm, and Vera decided to join them. The journey to Stockholm involved traveling by train through Germany to the North Sea, and then crossing by boat to Stockholm. Vera's mother wanted to remain in France.

On the train, Vera was the only one who spoke German, her native language. During the stop in Berlin, she disembarked and went to the house where her family had lived before fleeing to France. She discovered that the house had not yet been confiscated by the authorities. Everything was intact: rugs, furniture, paintings. Even their old housekeeper was still there. She and the housekeeper spoke together, and wept. She then hurried back to the train and journeyed on to Stockholm, where she moved in with the family of her father's brother and took a job working with children.

When the war ended, she returned to France, found her mother, and went to work at the Swedish consulate. She had an astonishing facility with languages, and in Stockholm had quickly learned Swedish. In later life, she possessed an impeccable command of English, French, German, and Swedish, and knew some Spanish and Hebrew as well.

By 1947, Vera's sister, Meri, had moved to New York. Vera and her mother decided to follow her. Vera found a job as a translator at the United Nations, and in the translators' pool was Tamara Fitelberg, wife of Jerzy Fitelberg, a professional composer and Zakin's cousin. Mrs. Fitelberg and Vera became good friends. Though Vera lived only a few blocks away from me in New York, we had never met there.

During the following three and a half years, she became an ardent Zionist, and in late 1950 she obtained a visa to the new state of Israel. She sold her belongings, took with her on the boat only a few important items (including a refrigerator), and, leaving her mother and sister behind in New York, arrived in Israel in May 1951, two months before I got there from Perpignan. In Israel, she attended classes to learn Hebrew and began to look around for work. As it turned out, the World Jewish Congress was to meet that summer in Jerusalem, and she obtained a job as an interpreter.

Zakin and I were scheduled for a recital at the Edison Theater, a miserable little hall in Jerusalem. The city, at that time, had no concert hall. The World Jewish Congress was meeting at the Binyanei Ha-Oomah, a newly built convention center. Vera had bought a ticket to the concert but had given it to her boyfriend, who was in the army and returning for the concert. She tried to obtain a ticket for herself, only to discover that the concert was sold out. She called Zakin and asked for a ticket, and he told her to meet us and he would try to arrange to get her in. Zakin and I arrived backstage, which I remember as an alley with leaking garbage cans near the rear door of the theater, and there was this beautiful girl standing there. I took one look at her, ushered her inside, found a seat for her, and asked her what she was doing after the concert. She said, "Well, I have some friends here." I said, "Could you tell them that you've been invited to a party?" I was being given a post-concert party by the head of the Jewish Agency for Palestine. She said yes, she would join me.

At the party we started talking, and I discovered that we had very similar backgrounds. Her family had come from Russia, as had mine. She told me about their life in Berlin, their flight to France, her father's arrest in Paris and death in Auschwitz, the months she and her sister and mother lived hidden from the Germans, her years in Sweden and New York. We stayed up very late that night. She tried to talk me into moving to Israel. I explained to her that my profession was not exactly one that could flower in this tiny new land. We saw each other the following night, and then the night after that. I persuaded her to come along with me to some of the concerts I played in various parts of the country. Whenever I was free during the day, I traveled to Jerusalem to see her. One week before my tour in Israel was to end, I proposed to her, and she said yes.

I was thirty-one; Vera was twenty-four.

FALLING in love quickly in Israel was one thing; getting married quickly was another matter entirely.

Israel's marriage laws required that the intent to marry be published in advance of the ceremony. But I had to leave for Belgium in a few days, my first stop on a concert tour of Europe. Furthermore, Vera was technically stateless: she had left the United States, did not yet have an Israeli passport, and might encounter a great deal of difficulty returning to America. In addition, as far as Israel's rabbinate was concerned, I might have a wife somewhere; could I prove otherwise? Finally, I was told that the Air France flight I was scheduled to fly out on the morning after the wedding was fully booked, and there was no seat available for her.

The marriage was made possible through the efforts of diplomatic officials of Israel, the United States, France, and Belgium. The first person I saw was Moshe Sharett, Israel's foreign minister, who agreed to arrange for the papers that would enable us to leave Israel. I then went to Monnett B. Davis, the American ambassador, who agreed to send an official witness to the ceremony to expedite Vera's reentry into the United States. The French and Belgian consuls agreed to open their consulates on Sunday to issue visas for her. The Israel rabbinate waived the requirement for the posting of banns. And Air France miraculously found seats. *L'amour, toujours l'amour.*

On the 17th day of August, exactly seventeen days after we'd met, Vera and I were married by the Chief Rabbi of Ramat Gan, a suburb of Tel Aviv. I remember the rabbi: a man with a long, straggly beard, broken teeth, and twinkling eyes. It was a sunny day. The ceremony took place under a chupah, the traditional wedding canopy. In those days, nearly everything was rationed in Israel; new clothes were out of the question. Vera wore the best clothes she had—a blue suit. The laws of Orthodox Jewish marriage require that the bride wear a veil, so one of Vera's cousins cut down her own veil, and Vera wore that. The reception that followed the ceremony took place in her aunt's home on

Rothschild Boulevard, a lovely place with a garden. There were people present from the Israel Philharmonic and from Vera's family; friends I had made during my previous trips to Israel came as well.

The very next morning, we boarded the Air France flight to Paris.

I PLAYED a concert in the casino at the Belgian resort of Le Zoute, and afterward the local manager took Vera and me to supper. The roulette tables were right behind the dining room, and I excused myself and went over to play. I loved to gamble, and I especially loved roulette. I lost and came back and asked my manager for some money; I hadn't yet received my fee. I went on losing. The manager kept looking at Vera and saying over and over again, "Ah, pauvre Madame Stern." He saw a very bad future for her with this gambling maniac of a new husband. I lost most of my fee, but in the end we had some money left, and I got some additional money from my local manager, and the tour continued.

I had promised Jane Eakin that I would phone her when I arrived in Paris. I called and stunned her with the news that I'd met a woman in Israel and married her there. We arranged to meet on the corner of a street near the hotel where Vera and I were staying. I explained to Jane what had happened, and fortunately she was as gallant and thoughtful as anyone I've ever met. She had brought with her a lovely French cookbook: a gift for Vera. She also gave me a very beautiful drawing of a mournful lady standing against a wall with an arrow through her heart. I have that picture to this day. We embraced and said goodbye.

Sasha Schneider was in Prades. I called and said that I wanted him to meet Vera. The two of us drove down to Prades. Sasha wanted to drink a toast to our marriage, and we went to the café and he ordered champagne. At first, Vera wouldn't drink—she simply wasn't a drinker—but finally she did sip some of the champagne.

We continued on the tour. That was a difficult time for Vera—traveling with a new husband who had friends everywhere, professional and personal, people who'd been part of his life for years.

She had to catch up on all that. But she was in possession of unique strengths: her command of languages, her vivacity and unpretentiousness, and her having experienced and overcome so many hardships during the war. There was about her a toughness of character that assisted her tremendously during those months. And helping both of us was the similarity of our cultural backgrounds: the Russian-Jewish world from which our two families had come, and our respect and affection for Israel.

I mentioned earlier the gambling spree I went on during the early days of our marriage. Some years later, in Biarritz, where we were on vacation, I started to play at a roulette table, and I lost so heavily that I had to wire my manager in Paris for more money. At one point, I was down to my last thousand francs. I said to myself, "What the hell," and bet double or nothing, and won. I then hit a winning streak, won back all the money I had previously lost, plus enough to pay for the entire Biarritz vacation and some pretty clothes for Vera. Maybe that's one of the reasons gambling can become so addictive: you never know when you may hit the right streak.

But then, in a way, so many artists are gamblers. We gamble every time we go out onstage. Early in our careers, we place our bets on our fingers, on our knowledge, on our abilities. At the moment when we begin to play, we make our bet, we put our total assets on the table. If we're lucky, the result is a career. If not, we have to settle for whatever we can get.

But there is a difference between the gamble of the artist and that of the roulette player. To this day, I believe that talent more or less makes its own luck. It's true that it can be enormously helpful if a friend gets you an audition for a conductor, but the outcome depends entirely on how you play, on your talent. If the audition for a conductor or a fellow musician goes badly, or you falter at a poorly attended concert where an important critic is present—if none of those opportunities succeeds, there is nothing that can make up for the lack of your abilities to take advantage of the door that has been opened for you. I know that there are many who will point to careers that have been arranged and paid for; but in the final analysis, the careers that truly last, that go on longer than a few engagements for a couple of years, the careers that are lifetime involvements, come from the talent and commitment of the individual artist who gambles on his career every time he steps out on a stage to play music.

The European tour came to an end. In the second week of November, we arrived in the United States and took up residence in the apartment at Riverside Drive and 79th Street.

TWELVE

*D*URING THE EARLY YEARS of our marriage, Vera would travel with me on my tours to major cities in the United States and whenever I went abroad. We were together at the Casals Festival in the summer of 1952, when it was moved back to Prades.

I have a particularly vivid memory of that festival. We were in the midst of a rehearsal of the Brahms G Major Quintet—Sasha Schneider and I the violins, Milton Thomas and Milton Katims the violas, and Casals the cello—when, in the very middle of it, with all our joyous playing, Casals abruptly stopped. It turned out he had suffered a mild heart attack.

Though we did not perform, we continued to rehearse. Paul Tortelier, a superb French cellist who led the orchestra's cello section and played much chamber music, filled in for Casals. We spent many days rehearsing and waiting for Casals to recuperate.

After dinner one evening at the Grand Café, the only café in town, we all looked at each other and, suddenly, one of us, I don't remember who, said, "Why don't we go up to the school and record the Brahms? We've been rehearsing it, and we know it really well."

Everybody was enthusiastic about the idea. Our wives immediately set out to prepare a snack for the middle of the night. They loaded up with fresh baguettes, cheese, sausage, and wine and water. We went to collect our instruments and, in the light of a full moon, walked over to the little schoolhouse, woke up our recording engineers, got everything set up, and very near midnight, began to record.

It was one of the happiest sessions that I remember in all the fifty-odd years that I've been making records. We played easily; we laughed a lot; we listened to each other. At about two in the morning, we stopped. The women brought out the bread, sausage, cheese, water, and wine they had so thoughtfully prepared. We ate, and we went on. That recording turned out to be one of the best in which I've ever participated. There is a quality of sheer abandonment in it. We had been rehearsing a great deal; we were all thinking of Casals. In the joy and surge and ebb and flow of the music, we found a measure of peace and optimism. We all knew the music was there, and we felt that both the music and Casals would continue forever.

There is one particularly interesting point about that recording. The opening measures of the quintet call for the two violins and the two violas to play forte, in unison, a series of quick repeated notes representing the basic harmony, while the cello trumpets the great solo theme that is really like a fanfare and has to be heard above the din created by the other four players. In most instances, no cellist can overcome four of the upper-string instruments sawing away like mad without the others dropping the sound a great deal so that the cello can come through. If one does that, however, one loses the urgency, the forward thrust of those first measures, which is what Brahms intended. We were determined to play it full out, and yet to have the cello heard. In rehearsing it and checking with the engineers and listening to a test tape of the balance, we decided to have an extra microphone placed directly in front of the cello. That microphone could be controlled by the engineers to add more power than we could get from the ones that were covering the violins and violas. So we played full power—and you can hear the cello coming through as if it were a trombone. That sound resulted simply from the use of microphones, and we made the musical intent of the composer audible in a way that it rarely could have been in a concert hall.

Casals recovered and was able to finish out the festival that summer. He played in the Brahms Sextet, op. 18, and in the Schubert Two Cello Quintet, op. 163. It was a very special joy to have him back in our midst.

I remember that when I first met Casals, his companion was Madame Capdevila. A stately woman with a rather hawkish, gray look, she'd been running his household for many years and was always seen with him. In the early 1950s, a lovely young woman from Puerto Rico named Marta Montañez came to study with him. She had huge black eyes and a wonderfully beautiful face, and was well educated and a gifted cellist. After the death of Madame Capdevila, Casals' roaming and appreciative eye fell on this cellist, and on August 3, 1957, they were married. For the next sixteen years she was his devoted wife. Some years after his death, she married Eugene Istomin, my friend and playing partner. Today, twenty-four years later, she is as beautiful as ever, and a most effective and intelligent arts administrator, who still lights up a room when she enters it.

JAPAN, where Zakin and I, along with our wives, went on tour in September 1953, was a new world for me: new sights, sounds, tastes, habits, attitudes—everything. We traveled with open eyes to as many places as we could. The first concert in Tokyo took place in Hibiya Hall, which had about 150 steps leading up to the front entrance; I remember those steps more clearly than I do anything else about that concert.

Zakin and I gave many recitals throughout Japan—in Tokyo, Shizuoka, Osaka, Okayama, Hiroshima, Fukuoka, Nagoya, Sapporo, Sendai—to capacity houses. The first four concerts in Tokyo were announced four months in advance and were sold out in two hours; the concert in Sendai, in thirty minutes. There had been very few Western artists in Japan since the war.

The day after we arrived in Tokyo, we attended a large reception in our honor. Present were most of the diplomatic corps, cabinet members, and foreign-press representatives. One of the most prominent musicians in Japan was there: Professor Michio Miyagi. He played the *koto*, an ancient Japanese instrument with thirteen strings on a long, hollow soundboard with movable ivory bridges on every string to vary the pitch. I was intrigued by the sounds that came from the instrument and by Miyagi's facility with it. At my invitation he joined me in one of my last recitals, and we played a work originally composed by him for the koto and the native flute, the *shakuhachi*. The audience was charmed and delighted, and the whole affair did nothing to hurt Japanese-American relations. That was the first time any major foreign visiting artist had done something like that.

In certain ways our trip to Japan might almost have been called a diplomatic tour, as we were always regarded as semiofficial ambassadors of American culture. We tried to behave accordingly, by displaying our sincere interest in the Japanese and their traditions and cultural development, and at the same time emphasizing that Americans, too, possess dignity and cultural maturity—something that others were not always willing to grant us. Press conferences took place in every city, and in addition to the usual questions, there were many pointed and searching enough to allow me the chance to talk and promote American standards and beliefs.

I wanted very much to play in Hiroshima. The concert hall there had a capacity of one thousand, but when Zakin and I played, they managed somehow to find room for an audience of 1,600. The recital was followed by various speeches, and I learned that there was a group in Hiroshima seeking to link the horror of the nuclear bombing to what had happened to the Jews in the Holocaust.

Later, traveling through the city, we saw the epicenter of the bombing and the efforts under way to rebuild the city. There was a bustling, a sense of buoyancy, about the people. But I learned later that all the money raised to connect the Hiroshima Memorial to the Holocaust had been placed in escrow because a considerable political campaign had been directed against that linkage. In the end, the effort did not go through, and the money was distributed to various charitable institutions throughout Japan.

A few days before we left, the American Cultural Center director arranged a roundtable discussion with a few of the best musicians in Tokyo and reporters from the three leading music magazines in the country. The entire two-hour discussion was taken down verbatim, to be published in the news and music magazines. As the final major effort in our private foreign-policy program, Zakin and I decided to set aside a portion of the earnings from our last three concerts in Tokyo to establish a fund for young Japanese musicians to go abroad for studies.

I should add that we also played several times in American armed-forces hospitals around Japan, twice making special trips by airplane and once by helicopter. The night before we left Japan for India, General Christenberry, chief of staff to General Hall, gave us a dinner party, where he presented us with gold medallions for playing in the hospitals.

During the six weeks we were in Japan, we were broadcast five times and on television twice, and we hardly had a waking hour when we weren't traveling, playing, or being officially entertained. In forty days, we played twenty-three public concerts and at seven armed-forces hospitals, and we traveled the length and breadth of the three major islands.

The remarkable Japanese affection for Western music—I have my own interpretation of that phenomenon. My first indication of the direction of Japanese musical listening habits came on visits to local bars in some of the smaller cities outside Tokyo. For example, in Sapporo, I went out to a small bar for a nightcap with our Japanese guides and companions, and coming out of the loudspeaker was not jazz or traditional Japanese music or light music, but—to my astonishment—Beethoven quartets, Bach Brandenburg concerti, and Chopin piano music. Upon returning to Tokyo later in the tour, I was invited to one of the early performances of *Fiddler on the Roof*, which was being premiered in Tokyo by a completely Japanese cast. I went as a guest of the actor who was playing the leading role of Tevye. Everyone on the stage was dressed in absolutely correct costumes. The play, of course, was presented in Japanese, with simultaneous translation into English. It lasted a little longer than the performances I had seen before—I was at the opening night in New York, when Zero Mostel played the lead, as well as at two other performances with Mostel onstage. Each time I saw it, I wept. And there I was, seeing it in Tokyo, in Japanese, and I looked around at the audience and saw half the women in the traditional kimono and half in Western dress, and practically everyone there was crying, too, including not a few men.

Somewhat mystified by that reaction, I went backstage afterward to meet the actor who had been my host. I entered his dressing room, and the first thing he said to me was "How could Americans write so

Japanese a play?" That took me by surprise. Then I began to think about the central theme of *Fiddler:* the idea of tradition. There is the moment when an anguished Tevye is confronted by his daughter, who is leaving with a young man of whom he disapproves. Tevye refuses to recognize them. His daughter puts her hand out to him and urges, "Papa, say goodbye." He reaches for her, but just before their hands touch, he abruptly turns away and starts singing, "Tradition." Well, that was precisely what was happening in Japan at that time: the breaking of age-old traditions by General MacArthur and the American occupation forces. The play was a kind of release mechanism, a catharsis, for what the country was still experiencing eight years after the war: the diminution of traditional Japanese culture.

There is yet another way of understanding the Japanese relation to Western music—especially classical music. As far as I know, Japan has no pure music as such, in the sense that a quartet or a symphony is pure music. The identical rules of address that applied to class interaction in Japan—superior, equal, inferior—applied to traditional Japanese music, as well as to poetry. Except for temple music, all other musical expression was accompaniment to either dance, song, or the spoken word. It was all program music of one kind or another. When Western music began to penetrate their culture—to some small extent before the war, and in a major way afterward—for the first time, anyone, regardless of class, station, or economic position, could relate to a mood or a feeling and experience it personally. Western music gave each Japanese the possibility of being a person, a self; of being able to feel as a separate individual despite what the corporation one worked for required, despite what the rules of etiquette dictated. You could laugh, cry, sing, sit quietly, read, think—while you listened to the music. Western music seemed to offer the Japanese people a release that perhaps they could not find in their own traditional forms of music.

That may account for the fact that in Tokyo today there are ten symphony orchestras and, I think, more than seventeen concert halls. It may also explain why so many young Japanese attend concerts.

· · ·

FROM JAPAN we flew on to India, arriving in Calcutta at the end of October.

The Indian authorities had made it clear to us that they could not afford our usual fee, and we had agreed to play if they took care of our travel expenses and gave whatever money the concerts earned to a recognized charity. As it turned out, the charity they chose was the Prime Minister's Fund. And one of the rewards for the concert in New Delhi was the opportunity to meet and spend time with Prime Minister Jawaharlal Nehru.

I'll never forget that first week of November 1953. When we arrived at the prime minister's residence, we were met at the door by his daughter, Indira Gandhi, who informed us that her father would be delayed because the Congress was still in session. She was an attractive young woman, dressed in the traditional sari and very gracious. As I entered the house, she handed me a letter from Kashmir that was addressed to me. It turned out to be a fan letter from someone who had discovered that I would be in the home of the prime minister. The writer requested an autograph. In Nehru's residence!

We were all sitting there politely having tea when Nehru entered, dead tired. He was very much like the pictures we had seen of him, not as tall as one might have expected, but with that handsome, if ascetic, face. Nothing could have interested him less at that moment than the presence of four itinerant people in his home. There ensued a rather uncomfortable half hour. Nehru looked weary, bored, and we were somewhat intimidated by his presence. The air was filled with lengthy silences broken by moments of forced conversation, which was going nowhere until I suddenly said to him, "Mr. Prime Minister, I've traveled a great deal in the world, but I've never seen conditions as terrible and as dreadfully difficult as those we saw in Bombay."

He suddenly came to life, his eyes opened wide, and he began to lecture us about what it meant to have the refugees from the war with Pakistan flooding into India. "Do you know how many refugees we have from Pakistan in one month?" he asked. I said no. He said, "Ten million. That's right. Ten million." The figure was unfathomable to me. That number of refugees would destroy the infrastructure of any city; in the instance of a city with so marginal an infrastructure as

Bombay, those refugees clearly were a major disaster. We had seen people lying about wherever we'd gone, defecating in the steets, dying; children begging; flies everywhere, on food, on faces—impossible scenes of the most sordid poverty imaginable. Nehru said, "Do you realize what it means to bring the country out of this? We are trying to do something. While you are here, you must go and see what we are doing in Agra. It will become clear to you where we have been and what we are trying to do." Agra was the location of the Taj Mahal; I said we were planning to go there. He said, "Good! I will tell my secretary to let the people there know that you are coming. They will take you to a model farm I wish you to see. That is the future of India. That is the only way we can turn this problem of poverty around—give the people land, a cow, a mule; let them till the land for themselves and rebuild the country from the ground up."

We visited Agra and saw a world of difference between the model farm there and life in the cities. I haven't been back to India, but I've been told by recent visitors that the problems that were endemic when I was there in 1953 haven't changed much.

During that visit, we were introduced to a woman called the Raj Kumari Amrit Kaur, who was the minister of health. She said to us, "Do you know how many hospital beds the British left us? Six thousand. We have one and a half million cases of active tuberculosis and two million incipient cases. And that is only in one disease. The problems we face are very nearly inconceivable."

She invited us to her home for tea, and to hear Indian music played by some of India's best musicians. She accepted and liked Western classical music to some degree, but she was determined that I should learn how far superior Indian music was.

That was my first experience with Indian music. I heard the sitar and other local instruments and listened to ragas for the first time. She explained the intricacies of the melodies, how they became increasingly complex and convoluted and wilder, always in a certain numerical order. She went on about the sophistication of the music, insisting that it was superior, emotionally and intellectually, to Western music. I didn't agree with her then, nor do I now. But I don't believe that we in the Western world should go about with the attitude that there is little if anything of value musically in other cultures. I may not deeply appreciate the music of India, but that gives me no license to be disrespectful toward it.

I remember that the weather in India was so bad—hot, steamy; the hotels without air-conditioning—that my fiddle became slightly unglued and opened up. I inquired if there was anyone who could repair it, and was told of a man who took care of musical instruments. I went to his place and found a man there, naked to the waist. He worked up a batch of glue, applied it to the fiddle, and reset the top.

The fiddle was my precious Guarneri. When I returned to New York, I needed to have it thoroughly examined and cleaned and so brought it to one of the world's great violin repair experts, a luthier, Fernando Sacconi. I stood by as he started to open it, and I heard him say, "Who put that glue in there, for God's sake? It's almost impossible to open!" He worked at it very carefully. There was a slight ping with each release, and suddenly the violin cracked. It was like seeing my child eviscerated. But it was the glue that had cracked, not the violin itself. He cleaned off everything, put the top back on correctly, and redid the bass bar. My relief was overwhelming.

I REMEMBER the 1953 tour of Japan with special warmth: the careful way it was organized; the meticulous attention paid to details and the respectful regard for our needs; and the audiences, the press, the critics—even those who were unaware of modern tendencies in Western music and were more than skeptical of the way I played—and, always, always, the parties, the food, sushi and sashimi and yakitori, shabu-shabu, all the different kinds of Japanese food I adore. And Zakin would have a drink from time to time; once he actually got roaring drunk—to the enormous embarrassment of his wife and to the amusement, I must say, of Vera and me.

From India we went on to the Philippines. In Manila, Zakin and I gave a recital—and learned of the tragic death, in an air accident, of the wondrously gifted young pianist William Kapell.

I'd heard him play often; we had also played together privately. Short, with wild black hair, a pimpled face, and a wiry body, he seemed to walk electrically; it was as if he needed only to touch the piano and it opened up to him. He was a brilliant, explosive virtuoso, a Promethean pianist. During the past two years, his perceptions had matured; his palette of colors and ideas, the inner substance of his music, had grown larger, and he was able to give ever greater scope to his performances and develop more and more music of various kinds—classical, contemporary, romantic, impressionistic. There was literally no limit to his talent. He was headed for a major career, not only because of his intrinsic ability as a musician but also because he possessed what I call the "X" factor, the most important attribute for any person on the stage: the mysterious quality of personality, describable but unexplainable, that enables the performer to extend across the footlights and mesmerize the audience. William Kapell had it; there was a tension in his playing that attracted audiences to him. And now he was gone. A terrible loss!

By the end of 1953, after thirteen years of our musical partnership, Zakin and I had traveled hundreds of thousands of miles together, nearly all of it by air. All my adult life I have lived with a fatalistic sense about travel. If something were to happen—well, there was nothing I could do about it. I certainly would never let that possibility rule my life.

THIRTEEN

*I*N VENICE, in the fall of 1954, I played for the first time Lenny Bernstein's composition *Serenade.*

Lenny had originally intended the *Serenade* for someone else, who, for several reasons, was unable to accept it. He then asked me if I would want it, and I said I'd be happy to do it, and he started to complete the work.

Every once in a while, he'd ask, "Is this doable?" or "How does this seem?" or "Which way would it be better?" He'd ask me only about matters having to do with feasibility. I've worked this way with Lenny and with Dutilleux, Rochberg, and Penderecki, with every composer with whom I've collaborated. If I were asked about the viability of a musical passage, I would do my best to help; then, when the piece was done, I would proceed to learn it. If I saw that there was a contradiction in the direction the composer had taken, I wouldn't hesitate to point it out. I had some questions once about a composer's final movement, and when he said he'd written it five times, I responded, "Wouldn't you like to try for six?" In another instance, I sensed a great difference between a composer's closing passages and the music that had preceded it, and I asked him whom he'd had in mind when he was finishing the piece. He said he'd written the final part shortly after the death of one of his children. I have never told a composer what to write—my job was to play what they wrote, to play it as well as possible. In the final analysis, I have to be the composer's vessel.

Lenny would send me parts of the *Serenade.* I had a slight problem with him, because at times he composed in key signatures that were completely correct musically but difficult for string players, who tend to think *enharmonically* in fingering quick passages. In the last movement, the music suddenly turned jazzy. It was pure Lenny. He had this synthesis of great music, from Mahler to Brubeck. It came instinctively from his gut.

Lenny was an inveterate night owl, an insomniac. He'd be awake through the night and then sleep from about four a.m. to noon. A couple of nights before the first performance, at La Fenice in Venice, we went to dinner together in the Hotel Bauer Grünwald, where we were staying, and we started talking. After dinner we came upstairs to his suite and talked some more. We talked and talked and talked, two friends opening their hearts and talking—about music, about their families, about people they knew, about their most intimate dreams; random thoughts, one idea flowing into another—and suddenly it was six o'clock in the morning! That was one of the very special moments of my life.

Before the concert, Lenny sent me a note, which he wrote on the hotel stationery.

> Isaac, my Isaac:
> Whatever happens tonight, fair or foul or flop, I want you to know how much I will always cherish your work on our *Serenade.* Nobody can play like you, and nobody can play the piece as you can. I have an eternal debt to you, and besides, I love you anyway. Thank you with all my heart.
> Lenny
> 12 Sept. 1954

With Lenny conducting and me on the fiddle, the *Serenade* was premiered by the Israel Philharmonic Orchestra, then on a world tour. It was well received, though in all candor it did not stop musical history in its tracks. After I returned to the States, we played it again, with the Symphony of the Air Orchestra, and then we recorded it. Today, happily, it is part of every violinist's repertoire.

IN LATE December of that year, Zakin and I traveled to Iceland. Ten years before, we had played in Iceland on the USO tour. Though we were again on board an army plane, this time we wore no uniforms, and we were to give concerts mostly for civilians, residents of Iceland.

That tour in Iceland was an important milestone in a succession of travel experiences—in Europe, Israel, Japan, India, and elsewhere—that were leading me to an awareness of the role the arts could play in international diplomacy. In India, for example, I had pointedly been told of the powerful cultural delegations that the Soviet Union had sent there—their finest dancers and best musicians.

Since Iceland was not on most concert itineraries, it was one of the few countries where Sol Hurok, our manager, hadn't yet arranged an appearance for us. In early December he had called me to say that, at the request of the State Department, the American National Theatre and Academy (ANTA) had recently set up the International Exchange Program to send artists and groups abroad. Some of the members of the Music Society in Reykjavik had remembered us from our last visit ten years ago and were now inviting us to come back. How about it?

We had just returned from a round-the-world trip. Getting back on a plane and spending Christmas week in Iceland was the last thing in the world we wanted to do. So we said yes.

I wondered why the State Department had become involved in a cultural-exchange program. Perhaps its people, together with members of ANTA, had become aware of the implications of a recent visit to Iceland by a Russian delegation of musicians and dancers. This troupe not only had given formal concerts but had gone out of its way to make friends. The pianist and cellist had traveled from village to village and invited local chamber music enthusiasts to join them in performances. They had made quite a hit.

The night of our arrival, we played at the civilian club of the Keflavik Air Base. Service in the adjoining dining room stopped at 8:15, and the jukeboxes were turned off for a few hours as we played for an audience of American soldiers and their wives stationed near the top of the world.

Our concert in Reykjavik was held in the city's largest movie house. As in so many American cities at that time with a population of about 50,000, the movie house was the concert hall. The theater, a simple, clean, modern building, seated 350. Zakin and I had to perform our program twice, since the number of subscribers was double the theater's capacity.

Recitals were only one facet of Reykjavik's musical life. There were also local string quartets, several chamber music societies, and a national symphony orchestra, which recently had strengthened its ranks with several brass and woodwind players from Germany and Austria. The orchestra also played for opera performances in the National Opera House, which was new and modern and seated about 650.

We were not the only American musicians who had appeared in Iceland. Blanche Thebom had given a concert there; so had the Philadelphia Woodwind Quintet; and on our plane was Ervin Laszlo, who stopped off, en route to Europe, to give a piano recital.

It turned out that Zakin and I had a free day between our last recital and my performance of the Mendelssohn concerto with the orchestra, so we asked if we could play for and speak to the students at the University of Reykjavik. An announcement was made over the state radio, and the next day the room in which we spoke, which seated 350, was jammed.

At first, the students were shy. But soon they were asking questions that were much like those we had heard from students in schools all over America. What is the value of music? How do we choose our programs? Do audiences differ around the world? Why do we play modern music? And so on.

In the decade since our previous visit to Iceland, Zakin and I had given concerts around the world. To our dismay, we had seen potential friends of the United States alienated by the nation's material wealth. The arts, which could create better understanding, were being largely ignored by our country in areas of the world where music, painting, and literature were regarded more highly than refrigerators and automobiles as evidence of civilization.

Our experience in Iceland was, of course, only a small segment of the important work being done by the International Exchange Program. The *Porgy and Bess* troupe sponsored by the program had just scored a huge success abroad. And the Philadelphia Orchestra, under Eugene Ormandy, would soon be setting out on another tour of Europe. It was made clear to us in Iceland that the language of music could bring people together.

I wrote a piece about our tour of Iceland and sent it to the *New York Times,* which published it on January 23, 1955, and appended to it, without my prior knowledge, the following:

> Mr. Stern's gesture as a cultural ambassador to Iceland was supplemented by his action in contributing the proceeds of his concerts to the university for the establishment of a music library and music room.—*Ed.*

My friend Lionel Rudko went to Iceland to help them install the audio and earphone equipment. (Lionel is one of my oldest friends. We first met about fifty years ago, when he was the owner of one of the most select classical record shops in New York City. In later years, after he sold his business, he was for a time the general manager of Carnegie Hall.)

Late in the following year, 1955, I was invited to play in the Soviet Union. And in April 1956, I flew with Zakin to Moscow, two years before the cultural-exchange program between the United States and the Soviet Union was formally initiated.

My TOUR of the Soviet Union, the first by an American artist after the Second World War, had its origin in Antwerp, in 1951. I had played a concert and was backstage when into my dressing room walked the Russian violinist David Oistrakh, one of the greatest fiddle players of our century. He was a solid figure, with a stocky build similar to my own, except that he stood five inches taller than my five feet six inches. Accompanying him were two men from the Russian embassy. He greeted me warmly and said, "Why don't you come to Brussels for the concert?" Brussels was the location of the Queen Elizabeth International Music Contest. I said I would love to, but I didn't want to be on the jury, I would come only to listen. When I said that I'd be arriving in Brussels a few days later, he suggested that we meet at the Russian embassy. I was hesitant, and proposed that we meet in my hotel. We compromised and agreed on a café near the Palais des Beaux Arts, where the competition was being held. I remember Zakin saying, after Oistrakh had left, "What do you want him to do for us? He's going to come with two security people. You won't be able to say anything; there won't be a conversation." I said, "Let's see what happens. I'm going to meet him."

I went to the café as arranged. Oistrakh arrived alone, carrying a camera. We were supposed to meet for half an hour. About an hour and a half later, he got up, went over to the telephone, and dialed. I heard him say, "This is Oistrakh. I won't be back for lunch."

That half-hour meeting lasted five hours. We spoke in Russian; he had no English, and I couldn't fathom his heavily Yiddishized German. We talked about everything: life in our countries, politics, a life in music, various soloists. His interests were broad, and he possessed an absolutely natural humanity.

By the time that meeting was over, we had formed a close friendship that was to last for twenty years. Our lives from then on seemed to be inextricably linked. We always made it a point to meet whenever we played in the same city, but by mutual agreement we never wrote to each other, because life could grow complicated for a Soviet citizen who received mail from a foreigner.

The last time we were together was in London, about three months before he died. He was sixty-six, had put on a lot of weight, and looked awful. I said to him, "Why don't you come out? You'll be honored everywhere. Within a year you'll be a wealthy man." He said, "I can't. They don't let my family travel with me. I can't do that to my wife and children." I asked him why he was working so much in Russia, playing, conducting, teaching from morning to night, performing local concerts in the provinces. "You don't stop," I said. His response was one of the most chilling things I've ever heard, something I won't forget to my dying day. He said, "If I stop even for a little while, I'll start to think. If I think, I'll die."

He was an astonishing, adorable human being. And the first Soviet violinist Sol Hurok was able to bring to the United States.

By the mid-1950s, Hurok had managed to get close to the Soviet minister of culture. Hurok really wanted the Bolshoi Ballet, and was happy to start with Oistrakh and the pianist Emil Gilels. I went to Oistrakh's first appearance at Carnegie Hall, in November 1955. He played Beethoven's Sonata No. 1, Prokofiev's Sonata No. 1, Tartini's Sonata in G Minor, Tchaikovsky's Waltz Scherzo, and other pieces. It was an incredible concert, utterly magnificent. Soon afterward came the call from Hurok's office. The Russians were talking about reciprocating: we had invited their leading fiddler to tour America; they were inviting our leading fiddler to tour the Soviet Union.

The actual invitation arrived in January 1956. Details were discussed by letter and cable in the ensuing weeks. I remember remarking to someone at the time, "The Russians sent us their Jews from Odessa, and now we're sending them our Jews from Odessa." The remark ended up in *Time* magazine and was not taken kindly by either our State Department or the Soviet authorities.

In early April, Sol Hurok traveled to the Soviet Union and finalized the details. He informed the necessary people at the State Department and received their tacit, informal blessing. They were eager that we go, even though there was as yet no department policy officially backing exchange programs with the Soviet Union.

Which is how it came about that in late April 1956, Zakin and I were flying to Moscow.

We were scheduled to play the first concert on May 3, but we left the States on April 28 because I wanted to be in Moscow in time to see the May Day parade. The flight was a difficult one for me, filled with sorrow and foreboding. A few days before, I had played my last concert in Cuba. I knew I would never play there again; the Castro regime was poised to take over the country. I had then flown with Zakin to Miami, where, because of phone calls and shopping, I missed my flight to New York. Zakin was frantic, but they wouldn't hold the plane for me, and he went on alone. I took a plane to Philadelphia and a train to New York—in time to learn that Mae Frohman, Sol Hurok's trusted assistant and lady Friday, had suddenly died. It was Mae who had run the office; it was she who had introduced me to Nora Kaye.

I rushed to Hurok's office, and we talked and cried for hours. He was bereft. We sat there reminiscing, hugging, weeping. Then what was left of me went back home and repacked for the trip to Russia.

At the airport, Zakin and I boarded a Pan American Stratocruiser and were soon airborne. I was a wreck, a complete wreck. Zakin was feeling very nervous about the flight. I slept out of sheer exhaustion, like a dead man.

The next morning, in London, we were met by my English manager, with whom we had breakfast, and then boarded a flight to Copenhagen, where we had lunch with my manager there. Then we took another plane to Helsinki, where we had dinner with some friends and stayed overnight. The next day we boarded a Russian plane that took us to Leningrad, and from there another plane brought us to Moscow on the last day of April.

It was dark when we landed. We were met by delegations from the Soviet Ministry of Culture and from the various musical organizations that would be our hosts. Also present was a man from the American embassy and Daniel Schorr, the correspondent for the *New York Times*, whom I had met sometime before in Amsterdam. Flowers were handed to me and Zakin, and welcoming speeches were made, to which Zakin responded in his excellent Russian and I in my incredibly poor Russian. I was determined to speak Russian as long as I could be understood, no matter how cruelly my bad grammar grated on Zakin's ears. The man from the American embassy then asked me and Zakin to accompany him to the embassy to meet with Ambassador Charles (Chip) Bohlen before checking into our hotel.

The airport was forty kilometers from the city. The first view I had of Moscow that night was of the university, which was brilliantly lit by floodlights, with red stars pinpointing the spire of the central structure and the four corners of the basic buildings around this center. The streets were crowded with people and traffic, and there were signs everywhere of the coming May Day celebration: pictures of the political leaders, loudspeakers playing music, shops still open though it was 11 o'clock at night.

Ambassador Bohlen was a good-looking man, six feet tall, with a square face and a warm, confident manner. He was new at his post, respected by the Russians, admired by seasoned diplomats and cynical journalists alike. Ably assisted by his charming and cultured wife, he was doing his job well. His Russian was excellent. We met in the one room in the embassy that they were sure couldn't be bugged; it was insulated with lead and checked frequently. We talked for an hour, and he understood that I knew enough not to be persuaded by what I would be shown and told officially by the Soviet authorities.

Zakin and I returned to our car, which took us past the walls of the Kremlin to the Hotel Moskva, just one short block from Red Square. And there, to my joyous astonishment, were David Oistrakh and his son Igor, with a bottle of Russian champagne and a little jar of caviar. They'd been sitting in the lobby for more than three hours, waiting to greet us! That was the nature of the relationship Oistrakh and I had established. The four of us went to the hotel restaurant for a late supper and some warm and friendly talk.

The room assigned to me was a small suite facing an inner courtyard, "so that," as the desk clerk politely explained, "it will be quiet for you if you wish to rest or work." Zakin had a suite with a small upright piano. We learned later that these were among the smaller suites in the hotel. By arriving two days earlier than expected—the Ministry of Culture had known of our arrival time, but the information somehow had not been conveyed to the hotel—we had thrown the hotel, jammed with delegations from abroad, into a frantic search for space. But we were the guests of the ministry; all our hotel and food expenses would be paid by the ministry. And so space was found and every effort was made to see to our comfort.

The next day, I showed the special pass I had been given and was ushered into the VIP section on Red Square. The square was impressive, with masses of people and colorful banners. The military part of the parade was brief and not particularly impressive: tanks and guns and rocket launchers. Of greater interest were the groups of athletes who followed, with their formations and acrobatics. Then came marching farm groups, factory workers, women's organizations, and the like, all of them bearing banners, each group pausing to shout a greeting to Khrushchev and other members of the Supreme Soviet who were standing on the dais constructed over the tombs of Lenin and Stalin. It seemed to me that hundreds of thousands of people were going by.

After about four hours of that, I began to grow weary and decided to leave. I saw the police and realized that no one was supposed to depart until the parade was over, but I pulled out my American passport and showed it to the guards, and they waved me through.

In my suite at the hotel there was a three-inch television set. I turned it on and saw May Day parades taking place all over Russia. May Day parades—everywhere! I suddenly realized that in two days I would be playing in Russia for the first time. I took up the fiddle and started to unlimber a few muscles. I walked back and forth, thinking about parades, thinking about Russia, about Sol Hurok and Mae Frohman, and about Vera in New York, nine months pregnant and due to give birth any day now. As I went on walking back and forth in the suite, playing, I tried to think only about the music. The night was quiet, peaceful. I played on, my fingers finding their own course. At one point I looked out the window, and then at my watch. It was four in the morning. There was a faint dawn in the sky.

I remember saying to myself, "My God, I've been playing all night! I must've kept people awake." I opened my door to see if the *dzizhurnaya*—the woman found on every floor of a Russian hotel, who traditionally guards the room keys and watches and reports the comings and goings of the guests—was anywhere nearby. She was right there, standing quietly against the wall near the door. I stepped into the corridor and said, "I'm very sorry if I was waking anybody with my practicing." She said, "Oh, no, not at all, you play very well, it's been such a joy standing here and listening." Then she looked at me closely and said, "Mr. Stern, you have a concert tomorrow and you're soaking wet." I was drenched in sweat. "Get out of your clothes and take a hot bath." She hurried into the bathroom, returned with a towel, and started to dry me off. Then she ran down to the end of the corridor and returned in a short while with a pot of hot tea. She didn't leave me until she was sure I had gotten into the tub, taken a bath, and was asleep.

Thus my first contact with the natural warmth and humanity of the true Russian soul.

Zakin and I spent the early part of the following day resting from the rigors of our long trip. Later, we stood on the street for some hours, watching the people going by. That evening, we visited the Bolshoi

Theatre, to see an opera by Glinka. The theater was large and quite beautiful, and the audience seemed to be made up of a cross section of Russians, with many people from the provinces. Foreign delegations were there as well. The Russians were by and large dressed in their everyday clothes, most of which looked awkwardly cut. Some of the men wore boots, and many women had kerchiefs around their heads. Others wore shirts with gaily striped ties. There were many men in army and navy uniforms; the military seemed quite prevalent in Moscow. The performance onstage was beautifully mounted, and the orchestra played well, though the sound didn't have the rich, pulsating quality to which Zakin and I were accustomed from the better American orchestras. The singing was quite good but not outstanding. The staging was first-rate; the sets, magnificent. Fatigue overcame both of us, and we couldn't remain for the entire opera.

The next day, we gave our debut performance in the Great Hall of the Conservatory, the Russian equivalent of Carnegie Hall. It was a lovely space, done in white and gold, with many windows and huge portraits permanently mounted on the walls: Tchaikovsky, Glière, Glinka, Rimsky-Korsakoff, Bach, Mozart, Beethoven, Brahms, Schubert, Mendelssohn, Chopin. The acoustics were clean and alive, with just enough reverberation to give the kind of ping and lift so important to the performer. The hall's seating capacity was about 1,700, but people were crowded into the aisles, boxes, entranceways—everywhere except on the stage, where they were not permitted—and that night the audience numbered 2,000. I was informed that every violinist within 500 miles of Moscow was in the audience. The performance was an enormous strain on me; yet it was also a great joy, that first concert of mine in the Soviet Union. As Zakin and I went onstage to begin the program, I had no idea what to expect. I looked out at the audience and saw all kinds of faces: old and young, a few I recognized, musicians I had already met, staff members of the American embassy, foreign-embassy representatives, officials from various Russian ministries. And professional musicians of all kinds: composers, conductors, members of symphony orchestras—all watching and waiting, in what I sensed to be a most friendly attitude.

We began with a Handel sonata. It was very well received, though the applause was hardly thunderous. I had noticed that in the slow movements the professional musicians had turned to one another with smiles of approval as I'd expressed various nuances and brought certain phrases to an end. The Handel was followed by the Bach Adagio and Fugue in G Minor. The applause was stronger that time, more excited. Then, to close the first half of the program, we played the Brahms D Minor Sonata. The house burst forth into its first really tumultuous applause. It was gratifying to hear that reaction, but Zakin and I had been under such stress during the opening half of the concert that we had no way of judging the real nature of the audience response.

During the intermission, which in Russia can be anywhere from twenty to forty minutes, Oistrakh came backstage to tell me what an enormous success the concert was proving to be. I looked at him and said, "Is that really so? Are you really pleased?" He put his arm around me and said, "I couldn't be more pleased." I cannot begin to express what that touching personal encouragement meant to me.

After the intermission, we opened the second part of the program with Aaron Copland's Sonata for Violin and Piano, which didn't prove to be a rewarding work for the people in the audience. Its musical language puzzled them; their cool, polite applause clearly reflected their difficulty in accepting the contemporary sound of this composition.

We then played a Mozart rondo, and at its conclusion, the house erupted. Both Zakin and I were completely taken aback. The reaction of the audience was astonishing; it was almost as though a physical force had assaulted us, so concrete was the expression of sheer pleasure we heard and felt.

We followed the Mozart with the *Nigun* by Ernest Bloch. That sad and dramatic composition must have brought to the audience many memories of other times and places, of people they had known and been close to. The reaction was remarkable: in the few rows just in front of me I saw some people weeping openly, and others with restrained and pensive looks, sober thoughts clearly written on their faces.

The program ended with a bravura work by Wieniawski, to which the audience reacted with acclaim—insistent, excited, yet friendly. It was a kind of warmth I had rarely felt, and it seemed to me to signal a willingness on the part of the Russians to listen to another style of interpretation, to be moved not only by the virtuosic, the dramatic, the technically brilliant, but also by the slightest nuances, by a phrase spinning out of a long phrase in a Brahms slow movement, by the fleeting swiftness of Mozart in a rondo, the impressionism of Szymanowski, the elegance, gaiety, and quicksilver brilliance of the *Rondo capriccioso* of Saint-Saëns.

After that first concert I began to relax. My realization of the Russian love of music made it easier for me to play long phrases in a quiet manner and to have them completely, instantly understood. I could underplay, be gentle, make love to the audience, laugh and cry with the violin, and be assured that even the least idea and feeling would be appreciated. I was now certain that the main purpose of our visit—to play good music—would be accomplished, and I felt entirely justified and at ease about having come to Russia.

We played another concert the following evening, also in the Great Hall, and on May 8 we played in the Tchaikovsky Auditorium, a hall with a circular stage, a latticed ceiling with recessed lights, seats for an audience of 2,000, and acoustics that were not very good. Even the Russians told us they didn't like the acoustics in that hall. Moscow also had the Hall of Columns, a place with excellent acoustics, where we didn't play. The American ambassador told me he was just as glad we didn't—it was in the Hall of Columns that the 1937 purge trials were held.

I was not the first American violinist to play in Russia since the end of the war; Yehudi Menuhin had been there before me. I was told that he had played only in Moscow. It seems I may have been the first American violinist to do a tour of the major Soviet cities.

Our first stop after Moscow was Leningrad. By then I was very anxious about Vera. I had discovered that in the Soviet Union it took quite awhile to place an overseas call and that to receive an overseas call, you might have to wait up to twelve hours. Telephoning home from Moscow had been a problem, but I had finally managed to get through to say that I'd arrived safely. The day we were to play in Leningrad, I was backstage, rehearsing, when suddenly someone came in and said that there was a telephone call for me. I said, "For me? Here?" "Yes."

The call was from Vera. She had given birth just thirty minutes before. To a girl. We would name her Shira, the Hebrew word for "song." As far as we knew, no one in either of our families had ever had that name. I hung up the telephone, overjoyed, exhilarated. People were congratulating me. I remember wondering, in the midst of all the happiness, how that call had managed to get through to me so quickly, and later I learned that she had called the American embassy in Moscow, where my itinerary was known down to every detail, and the Russian operators, informed that a mother was calling about the birth of a child, had pushed the call through in only a few minutes. What an anomaly that country was!

The Philharmonic Hall in Leningrad, where we played, had been the ballroom of the Club of Nobles when Leningrad was St. Petersburg, the czarist capital of Russia and the center of its imported Western culture. It was all done in white, with great marble columns and enormous crystal chandeliers that blazed with light throughout the concert. Its acoustics were brilliant, perhaps not as rich as those in the Great Hall in Moscow, but marvelous nevertheless. I played three concerts in Leningrad, and then we continued our tour, which next took us to the city of Kiev.

On May 17, Zakin and I gave a recital in the Shevchenko theater in Kiev. Every seat was taken. An enormous crowd of people who couldn't get in refused to leave, and soon they were banging on the doors to the theater, demanding to be admitted. The doors were opened; the crowd poured in; somehow room was found for everyone.

While in Kiev, I came down with a cold and a fever. I wanted to be certain the cold wasn't spreading to the lungs, and asked that a doctor be called. At midnight, after a concert, there abruptly marched into my hotel room a lady doctor, followed by a platoon of assistants carrying medicines and instruments. I said, "For heaven's sake, all I have is a cold." The response from the doctor was a smile and a firm command: "Strip!" This I unhesitatingly and unblushingly did. I was thoroughly examined and informed that I would live, though there would be some discomfort for a while from the cold. I was handed medication, my hand was shaken by everyone in the delegation, and they all departed. The medical service, incidentally, was entirely free of charge, available to all visitors and most citizens in an emergency.

Almost everywhere Zakin and I traveled in the Soviet Union—we went on to Baku, Tiflis, and Yerevan—we played in splendid halls. The only exception was in Tiflis, the capital city of Georgia, where they had a summer hall behind the philharmonic building, a closed pavilion in the garden, with stage lights and seats for about 1,000 people. The warm spring weather had already set in, and we played two recitals in that pavilion and one in the opera house.

That pavilion, I ought to add, was especially convenient inasmuch as it was but a few steps from a splendid restaurant run by the philharmonic, in that same garden. There we were royally wined and dined. Georgian wines are famous, very pure, delicious—and very potent, as Zakin and I soon found out. After my first encounter with them, I couldn't tell whose chin held the fiddle. From then on, we would drink that wine only after a performance—a necessary prudence.

All the audiences during the tour were, it seemed to us, a cross section of the population, as had been the case in Moscow. Large numbers of professional musicians attended. We encountered music lovers of all ages: carefully attentive children who shared their seats with their parents, older people who had obviously been concert-goers from before the Bolshevik Revolution. At times I could see the interest of the older ones become increasingly aroused as the concert progressed; they'd sit on the edge of their chairs, visibly trying to absorb every musical sound, physically drawing from us every shade of musical emotion we could impart. When you have that kind of an audience, you can't help giving the very best that is in you to try to meet this open thirst for musical satisfaction.

The audiences seemed never to be satiated; they always asked for more. After each concert, hundreds of people—not only professionals, composers and local musicians, but also people from the streets, from all walks of life—would wait near the backstage door to applaud us and say thank you. Many asked us about American concert artists who had performed in Russia before the war, and about the current work of

Heifetz, Milstein, Piatigorsky, Horowitz, Francescatti, Szigeti. They asked about Menuhin and about my teacher, Naoum Blinder, whom some fondly remembered, and about the nature of musical life in America. And they would wish us Godspeed and good luck, and ask us to return soon, and offer their greetings to music lovers and musicians in America. They seemed so very eager to be in contact with people in the rest of the world.

One evening, in the capital of Armenia, Zakin and I had dinner with the composer Khachaturian, and I took the occasion to ask him about his background and musical influences. He told us that he was born in Tiflis, Georgia, the son of a shoemaker, and that for many years, as a boy and a young man, his only musical contact was with Armenian folksinging. His earliest experiences with classical music occurred when he entered the local conservatory, where he heard, for the first time, the great traditions of Western music and began to study musical history. As a result, he said, whatever he now thought and wrote in the way of music was bound to be influenced by the folk-music background of his beginnings. "It is in my heart, my blood, my flesh," he said. "How else can my music sound?"

He and many of his colleagues felt that this was the most solid ground for creativity. I pointed out to him that while this folk basis was undeniably healthy and had its historic validity, it must be used as a basis only, as a beginning from which must come a new language and experimental ideas. I cited Bartók, who, employing folk music as the foundation of much of his composing, enlarged upon that music through the use of the most contemporary of harmonic language, and in orchestration and form vastly expanded the knowledge and effective ideas of music. Khachaturian remained dubious, unconvinced.

The general reaction of Russian audiences to the new music that Zakin and I played—the Copland, the Bartók—was a mixture of awe and puzzlement. Their comments tended to be cautious: they would have to hear more before they could arrive at a real opinion concerning such music. Among the older composers I felt a definite reluctance to accept the necessity of the contemporary musical language. The younger composers were at least eager to learn more about it. When I played the Bartók and Copland pieces before the members of the composers' unions in Moscow and Georgia, I told them that they didn't have to agree with what was happening in the world of music outside Russia, but they owed it to themselves at least to know what that music was all about.

Zakin and I returned to Moscow for our final concert there, scheduled for the 30th of May. David Oistrakh asked me to come to the Moscow Conservatory to hear several of his pupils. A number of the more advanced students were chosen to play for me, and the works they selected were intended to show to the full their technical abilities. Oistrakh then asked me to comment on their performances, and I pointed out some musical values that I felt they had overlooked. It was amusing and touching to hear Oistrakh utter the all-too-familiar remark: "You see, I've told you these things several times. Now you must believe me."

It was difficult to get the students to talk and ask direct questions; they were shy, intimidated by my presence. At the same time, they were terribly eager to understand and try everything suggested to them. While discussing a musical phrase with one of the students, I picked up his violin and demonstrated what I'd been talking about, at which point Oistrakh asked me to play something for them, which I did, accompanied by the staff pianist. I then invited Oistrakh to join me in the Bach Double Violin Concerto, and a student was sent to find the music. Together, we played an impromptu performance for the students. As word raced around the conservatory that we were playing, the door to the room kept opening quietly and other students and professors stole in until the place was jammed. The only sound in the densely crowded room was the music—and the whir and click of movie and still cameras.

On May 29, after rehearsing Bach, Mendelssohn, and Beethoven for four hours, until 1:30 in the afternoon, I returned to the hall at 4 to give a special free concert to the students of the conservatory, as well as to student delegations from various music schools. More than 2,100 young people packed the hall. Just before the concert was to begin, a representative of the students, a young violinist, came backstage to ask me if I would remain onstage for a while after the concert and answer questions from the audience. I instantly agreed.

The directors of the conservatory were concerned that, with 2,100 students in the hall, any organized question-and-answer period would be impossible, and they asked to have it transferred to a small room in the building, with twenty or thirty selected students. But I insisted on keeping to the original arrangement, and we agreed that the questions would be written down, collected, and read off from the stage.

The concert was a success. When the time came for the discussion, I asked the interpreter to be with me on the stage and, speaking in Russian, I explained to the students that I feared my control of the language wasn't adequate to give them the accurate answers I would prefer. But a shout came up at once from the students: mistakes and all, they would prefer I spoke in Russian. Which I did, for forty-five minutes.

The questions they asked were general and very similar to those put to me by student groups in Rochester, Kansas City, Montreal, St. Louis, and elsewhere: my educational background, my methods of practicing, American violinists I knew, and so on. At the conclusion of the questions, three young women came onstage with a bouquet of flowers, which they handed me. I subsequently learned that they were the wives of three of the best-known young violinists.

Later, in my dressing room, students presented me with a large package containing recordings of performances by David and Igor Oistrakh, Gilels, Richter, Rostropovich; of Russian operas; of Shostakovich symphonies. More than fifty recordings. A treasure, all on Russian long-playing records.

Toward the end of our stay, Zakin and I discovered some unusual facts about Russian music criticism, which made the writing of music reviews somewhat different from the way it was done in the United States. It was interesting to learn, for example, that there were no regular music critics on the staffs of the newspapers. The review in *Pravda*, a lengthy piece that appeared ten days after our first concert in Moscow, was written by the composer Shaporin. It reviewed two recitals and two orchestral performances. Shaporin had told me of the review and apologized that it had not appeared sooner, but important announcements concerning new pension plans for all workers took up all the space in the paper for several days; *Pravda* published only six to eight pages. The newspaper *Sovietskaya Kultura* published two reviews by different people, the second by a leading young violinist named Bezrodny. It seemed common practice to invite professional musicians to review their colleagues. Bezrodny, too, apologized to me; it appeared that his review, an excellent and quite lengthy one, had been cut almost in half. He told me that he had almost come to blows with the editor over the cuts. To my surprise, another review focused on one of my latter performances, when I had played Mozart and Brahms concerti a second time. The reviewer compared the two performances, praised them both, but commented on what he perceived had been the lesser intensity of the second performance of the Brahms—a natural occurrence on the part of many performers, who, thinking that the critics have heard the first concert, often relax and play the second for their personal enjoyment. In retrospect, I found the idea of reviewing both concerts to be rather a good one. It serves to keep performers on their toes at all times!

Images of Russia I have never forgotten: the wonderful folk dancing and singing, sometimes in an opera, in a new ballet, or in a performance proudly, touchingly, and magnificently put on especially for us, or just in a restaurant, with wine and vodka as catalysts; the sight of women doing manual labor, digging ditches, operating steam shovels, working on high scaffoldings as plasterers and carpenters; the miles and miles of farmland tilled by wooden plow and horse, and other farms with tractors and the most modern farm equipment; and the garden party at the British embassy, where I was introduced to Khrushchev, Bulganin, Molotov, Malenkov, and other of the better-known local citizens, Bulganin lifting a glass of champagne to congratulate me on the tour, toasting "better cultural relations between the U.S.S.R. and the U.S.A.," and Khrushchev interjecting that he would like to amend that to say that "perhaps artists, through their efforts in cultural exchanges, can show others, even diplomats, the road to understanding each other better."

Khrushchev was no doubt making reference to a major stumbling block that lay in the path of a final cultural agreement between the Soviet Union and the United States. Congress had enacted legislation requiring all foreign artists visiting the United States to be fingerprinted. The Russians found this to be abhorrent: to them, it smacked of a police weapon for use against criminals. Before leaving for the Soviet Union, I had been asked to smooth over that issue at every opportunity, to try to persuade the Russians to send us their artists despite that legislation. Now here I was at a British garden party, and in front of me was Mr. Khrushchev. Speaking English carefully through the official interpreter (this was not a moment for my at-times-unpolished Russian), I asked his help in bringing to fruition a true cultural exchange between the United States and the Soviet Union. He looked at me and said, "Well, then, this fingerprinting is impossible. It is totally unacceptable." I said, "That was passed by a group in Congress with a political agenda other than that of the majority of the people." He said, "Well, tell the president to change it." I said, "Mr. Khrushchev, the president cannot change the laws. Congress makes the laws; he can only sign them or veto them." He said, "That reminds me of a story. A man was driving across the snow on his horse-drawn cart. The cart hit a stone, the man was thrown out, his head hit another stone and split open. His brain spilled out and was lying beside him on the ground. A peasant came along and said, 'Oh my, let me give you back your brain.' The injured man replied, 'I don't need it, I'm only going to a meeting of our Parliament.' " That some-what cutting reference to Congress made the front pages in the United States. Hurok was on the phone immediately, screaming at me: What had I done? How could I have allowed this to happen? I replied, "I didn't say anything. I was just trying to do what you and everyone else had told me to." That innocuous conversation set the signing of the cultural-exchange program back about two years. Dangers can lurk in casual remarks made by well-meaning artists to political figures. For me, the idea that the efforts of artists can have good effects on political policies, except in areas directly related to the arts, is still dubious.

At 6:30 on a clear June morning, we left Moscow. All the tumult, the happy shouting, the myriad impressions, the differences in living habits and comforts, were soon to be behind us. Three sleepy people—the faithful translator, the director of the Great Hall of the conserva-tory, and Daniel Schorr—accompanied us to the airport. A delegation was due to meet us there with flowers, speeches, and gifts, but because of a mix-up, it arrived an hour and a half after we had left. So it was a quiet and pensive departure. Too much had happened too fast. We talked of inconsequential things. Just before we boarded, two boys hurried up to us. They were from the conservatory. Learning the evening before that we were to leave in the morning, they had spent the entire night at the airport just to say goodbye and talk a bit.

That night we had dinner in Paris, and the next day we were home. How wonderful it was to see Vera and our new daughter, even for a brief homecoming. Zakin and I were to depart for a two-month tour of South America only a few days later.

WHEN ZAKIN and I left the Soviet Union, I was convinced that as artists and as Americans we had in our country one of the most powerful and as yet unexploited means of speaking to people everywhere—especially in countries where the written word was not always trusted and outside information was often distorted. I felt that it was most important to make every effort to get the Russians to know us, and us to know them, through the medium of cultural and artistic exchange—and we had to try to accomplish that to the best of our abilities.

In Russia, I had discovered one of the most musically perceptive audiences anywhere in the world, a people to whom music was as natural as breathing. How better to communicate with the Russian people than through a language they could immediately understand, a language that didn't employ words that could be twisted or taken out of context—the language of music.

I was even more convinced of that nine years later, when, in a profile of me that appeared in *The New Yorker*, I remarked that "other people, especially the French and the Russians, have long considered their traveling artists ambassadors of their national culture. . . . All practitioners of the arts—creators and re-creators alike—are accepted everywhere. An artist can argue openly where statesmen and diplomats often cannot speak."

FOURTEEN

VERA, in New York with our newborn child, had known about the South America tour. It hadn't even been discussed by us; it raised no problems. Tours were arranged a year or more in advance, and I never canceled them; that was a given in our lives.

At the end of that tour, Zakin and I flew directly to Europe, to play in France and Switzerland. Vera met me in Geneva that summer and brought Shira, who was now two months old. The sensation of holding my daughter—our first child, a gently moving, exquisite bit of humanity—while she nibbled at my ear is completely indescribable. I had to learn about building a relationship with a new human being.

I remember that summer in Geneva, holding Shira, walking with her in her carriage, looking at her, just being with her. I had rented a house: tiled floors and lots of space. People kept dropping in. There were evenings of chamber music with many friends, among them the great violinist Nathan Milstein. I had brought with me from Russia two boxes—five pounds!—of fresh beluga caviar, and we ate it by the spoonful. Weeks later we were still scraping little grains of caviar off the tiled floor. Eventually, we all wearied of it. Never had I felt so tired of caviar.

We stayed in Geneva, in a world of clean streets, smooth highways, bountiful greenery, and beautiful mountains, for six weeks, resting, eating, playing music, enjoying friends. Then Vera and the baby flew home, and Zakin and I started on a European tour, which lasted into early October.

Immediately upon returning to the United States, we began to prepare the repertoire we had chosen for our next tour. I was often asked, during those years, how I prepared myself to play, what my practice habits were. In my student days, they had been no different from those of any other student. By the mid-1950s, however, the work I put into learning a new composition and into the constant refining of often-played compositions was greater than before. With experience and knowledge, the goals grow higher, and one becomes aware of how much more can be done. By and large, my practice habits were governed by the amount of work I had to put into any given composition. When on tour, I didn't have a steady practice schedule, but I worked at all possible hours. During periods without travel, I would average about four to five hours a day.

Zakin's remarks cited in *The New Yorker* profile on me fill out another part of the picture: "Isaac practices logically. He has the great gift of selective absorption. He absorbs the good things and ignores the bad ones. He doesn't practice just because 'you have to,' as so many fiddlers do, but concentrates on special difficulties of intonation, speed, dynamics, bowing, and fingering. By using different strings, he achieves different tone colors. He accepts no fingering—not even from famous teachers or editors—but always devises his own. He learns fast; in fact, he needs less time to master a piece than any other musician I know." Zakin was perhaps a little too generous in his comments.

Whenever I studied a work, I would first look at the score to see it in its totality. With Zakin's help at the piano, I would play it through, to acquaint myself with its structure; then play it again, to hear its melodic line. Once I had a clear conception of the work, I would begin to study it technically. When necessary, I would work ten to twelve hours at a stretch, until I felt saturated with the composition.

In November of 1956, we began a five-month tour of the United States. I was then playing more than one hundred concerts a year, which averaged out to almost one performance every three days. To me, the stage was home. I loved to play. I loved people, and I loved speaking to them with my violin, watching them turn exultant or sad or reflective, as the case might be. Playing music for people was the reason for my existence.

Why did I play so many concerts? First of all, I hugely enjoyed traveling—meeting people and making friends in so many cities all over the world. For me, the concerts were never an end in themselves, but a means to an end, the most severe testing laboratory, in which the constant development of ideas, the different challenges, the struggle with mistakes, was going on all the time. It wasn't the concert itself that was the final destination but my relationship to music and the clarity necessary in performance. How closely interwoven with it was I? How completely did I control my medium, the violin I held and played? I could only find that out in battle, on the concert stage.

OF THE MANY violins I've owned, my favorites are my two Guarneris del Gesù. Only about 160 of his violins are known, made in Cremona, Italy, between 1726 and 1744. In addition to their intrinsic qualities as fine instruments, violins have unique personalities. Sometimes there is a deep psychological affinity between an instrument and its player. I have certainly felt that way about my Guarnerius del Gesù called the "Panette," which was 208 years old when I bought it from the collection of Ralph Norton in Chicago in 1945. Before that, it had been in the New York Wanamaker collection. Around 1835, it was in the possession of the French violin maker Vuillaume, whose son-in-law was the famed French violinist Delphin Alard. Often violins are named after a former owner, and according to the Guarneri book by Hill and Sons of London, it was known as the Vicomte de Panette, named for a pupil of Alard.

My most beloved violin, though, is my "Ysaÿe" Guarnerius. It was made in Cremona in 1740, and I purchased it in 1965. It has strength, excitement, songfulness, masculinity—a thrust that resonates in my inner ear. How I've treasured it over the years! Even among the very greatest instruments, it is one of the finest. It had once been owned by the preeminent Belgian violinist Eugène Ysaÿe, for whom I have always had unbounded admiration. If I were given the opportunity to hear any two violinists in the entire history of the instrument, I would choose without hesitation Paganini and Ysaÿe. My Guarnerius still carries the message on the small label that Ysaÿe, the year he died, placed above the maker's label. He wrote, in red ink, "Ce del Gesù fut le fidèle compagnon de ma carrière. [This del Gesù has been the faithful companion of my career.] EUGENE YSAYE 1928." I shall add an additional little label: "*La mienne aussi.*" (Mine too.)

IN JUNE of 1957, I took off for a trip to Israel with Frederic Mann, whose philanthropic gift was making possible the construction of a new concert hall in Tel Aviv. Freddie was an astute businessman who had earned a great deal of money and who loved music and musicians throughout his life. He and his wife, Silvia, had a welcoming house in Philadelphia, where their affectionate embrace included many of the best musicians of that period. They had befriended me in my early days, and it was in their apartment that they had arranged for me to play for Eugene Ormandy for the first time.

During the four days I spent in Israel, I heard several youngsters play the violin. They were between the ages of nine and fifteen, and among them were several who were really gifted, two in particular—a boy named Itzhak Perlman, who was a polio victim and had to play seated in a chair, and another to whom I listened with great admiration—Pinchas Zukerman. They were so talented and eager to learn. I've been asked many times what I listen for in a new young person playing for me. Some years later, I realized what it was in the playing of Perlman and Zukerman that so enchanted me. They looked at me, put their fiddles up under their chins, and dared me not to listen. They didn't ask whether they could play; they demanded my ears. It is that innate certainty that one has something to say, even in the very earliest years—a kind of reveling in one's own talent—that distinguishes the really uniquely gifted ones from so many others. My heart broke at the thought that these young Israeli violinists might not get what I thought proper direction. I was finding it more and more necessary to relate some of my ideas about violin playing to the teaching and helping of others. How I wanted to personally take them in hand!

The tenuousness of one's life as a fiddler was brought home to me shortly after my performance at the Casals Festival in Puerto Rico in 1957. I was playing tennis, a passion of mine since my teen years in San Francisco. That may seem a strange attraction for a violinist, who should be more cautious than most people when it comes to hands, but I had never paid much attention to my hands and had discovered early in life that if I didn't worry about them, they'd take care of themselves. I'm aware of them in a natural sort of way. For example, once I boarded a cable car in San Francisco, in 1938, and stood leaning against the rear gate, reading a newspaper account of Hank Greenberg hitting his fifty-eighth home run. The car started suddenly and I tumbled backwards out onto the street. Instinctively, I folded my arms across my chest and took the impact of the fall with my shoulder rather than my hands. Fortunately, there were no automobiles coming down the hill.

That day in Puerto Rico was bright with sun and very hot, and I was playing well. I went up in the air to hit an overhead smash, but I was sweating a lot and my grip on the racket slipped, and I turned my wrist. The pain was immediate and awful. I immobilized the wrist and flew to New York, where a friend of mine, Dr. Leo Mayer, an orthopedic surgeon who was also an enthusiastic if execrable amateur fiddle player, attended to me.

He said, "Look, you've sprained your wrist quite badly."

I said, "I have to play in three weeks." I was scheduled for the Lewisohn Stadium in New York City, where the New York Philharmonic Orchestra used to perform during the summer; it stood near the campus of Columbia University and has since been torn down and replaced by yet another university building. More than seven thousand people would come with their picnic baskets and wine, sit outdoors, listen to the concerts, and have a good time.

Dr. Mayer was not at all certain I would be able to play. He said, "I'm going to isolate the wrist so you won't be able to use it or flex it in any way until you've let it rest. Then we'll take another look at it."

He put the wrist into a cast. I went back to him a few times during the next two weeks, and he'd break the cast and look at the wrist and say, "Not yet," and put another cast on.

The enforced layoff became rather pleasant in that I began to really enjoy the new apartment on Central Park West that we had moved into the year before. We were using the terrace to great advantage: we had turned it into a child's playground. Shira had a sandbox, a little plastic wading pool, and toys all over the place. I would sit there listening to her happy gurgling and watching her play. It was during that enforced, wrist-healing vacation that I traveled with Fred Mann to Israel and listened to the young Itzhak Perlman and Pinchas Zukerman play the violin.

Four or five days before the concert, I returned to the doctor. "Let's take the cast off and see how the hand is working," he said. It wasn't working. The hand was completely stiff. I couldn't flex it and had no free motion for the necessary control of the bow. Nothing.

I said, "What am I supposed to do now?"

He said, "Go home and pick up the violin and play it for ten minutes. An hour later, play it again for ten minutes, and an hour later you'll also play for ten minutes. Do that five, six times. Tomorrow, the same thing, but you'll play for fifteen minutes. The next day, for twenty minutes. And then you'll have the rehearsal and the concert." I went home and followed his orders, but after three days the wrist didn't feel any better—and now I was facing the day of the concert.

The conductor was Alexander Smallens, a favorite at the summer seasons at Lewisohn Stadium. I called him and said, "Look, I have this problem. I don't know if I can play. I'm going to try, but I think you'd better have a symphony or something prepared in case I can't do it."

He said, "Well, all right. We'll see what you can do."

I went over to play the rehearsal. It was the Brahms concerto, which demands power in the right hand, great control through the fingers and the wrist as the bow moves over the chords and octaves. A lot of very brilliant work. I hobbled along, sweating bullets. The orchestra tried to help me. We got through it, but it wasn't a decent performance.

Smallens said, "What shall we do?"

I said, "Look, I'll get dressed tonight and I'll try it. If I find I can't play, I won't. I'll stop, and you'll have to take over."

The white jacket I wore that evening—appropriate garb for the summertime concert stage—was matched by my face. I walked out on the stage. In the wings stood Dr. Mayer with a hypodermic syringe to anaesthetize the wrist in case I tore something again. I tuned the fiddle, nodded to Smallens, and closed my eyes—and forty minutes later, I opened them. I'd played the entire concerto. No pain. I flexed my wrist, and it was as though nothing had happened to it. It seemed to have forced itself back into shape because I needed it. That's one of the things the body (or brain?) can do sometimes, in moments of great need.

I didn't start worrying about my hands, and I didn't stop playing tennis. Artistic control of one's medium should never be achieved at the cost of draining the joy from life.

SOON AFTER I returned from the festival, an exchange of letters took place between me and Jack Benny.

During the mid-1950s, offers had come my way from TV shows, but I hadn't really been inclined to go on any of the late-night talk shows, where I knew I would be asked to put in an appearance with the fiddle as though in some circus act, chat briefly with the host about something or other, and then be gone. I had the sense that such shows used the classicist—whether in the realms of music, the theater, ideas, or writing—as a kind of comic object, as someone "different" from our nice, friendly, normal fellow man. This was a persistent problem in the acceptance of music and its allied arts in the daily life of an American.

When an offer came from Jack Benny, however, I instantly agreed. I admired the gentleness of his comedy, especially as it related to classical music. He never denigrated or mocked either the music or the makers of music, but only himself, and his inabilities and pretentions. He willingly and openly made himself the target, and he never evidenced less than the most profound respect for those who were musically accomplished.

My admiration for him grew when we met. As it turned out, he was hardly the greedy and enthusiastic miser of his public persona; on the contrary, he was a very gracious person, gentle, generous, and utterly incapable of saying a bad word about anyone. And he really did love to play the violin. He was very lucky that he was never good enough to do it professionally, and thus became one of the most beloved comedians in history. We grew to be very good friends—and the following correspondence is about that friendship and about violins.

Dear Jack:

I had planned to write this some time ago when I first heard the good news that you had acquired a fine Stradivarius violin. But, as usual, the pressure of events here kept me from attending to this pleasant idea until now.

I was very happy to hear that you had finally chosen a good instrument, and I hope you will have as much pleasure using it as I have from mine. I know what fun at least *you* get out of the violin when you play, and anyone who has been as faithful to his first love as you have been to violin and music deserves a fine instrument. . . .

> Cordially, as always,
> Isaac

Dear Isaac:

I received your letter and was very happy to hear from you as I always am.

Yes—I finally bought a Stradivarius and I think it is a real good one. I used it for my concert at the Philharmonic here which I am happy to say was a very big success. The laughs seemed to be bigger than ever, and believe it or not—I even played better. Of course, you could have shut your eyes, and still have known that I wasn't Stern or Heifetz, but it was a little smoother than usual. This is either because I have been practicing, or the Strad that I have—played a little easier than most of them. Am very anxious for you to see it.

My next two concerts will be in Chicago and Toronto sometime in the fall, and if you and Vera can possibly make it—I want you both to be my guests from the time you leave your house in a taxicab until you get back home. Naturally I'll appreciate it if you will use the bus. . . .

Thanks again Isaac for your letter, and I would like to add, I am very proud of our friendship. Mary joins me in love to you and Vera and all good wishes—always.

> Jack

WITH THE WRIST healed, I entered the summer circuit: the Robin Hood Dell in Philadelphia; Ravinia Park, near Chicago; Tanglewood; San Diego; the Hollywood Bowl; and the S.S. *Flandre*, on the Atlantic Ocean, my first steamship voyage to Europe.

Zakin joined me in Milan, where we gave a recital. I then flew on to Israel, and, with the Israel Philharmonic Orchestra under Lenny Bernstein, I played the Mendelssohn Violin Concerto in the newly built Frederic Mann Auditorium in Tel Aviv and Prokofiev's Second Violin Concerto in Jerusalem. A few days later, we gave a recital in Florence, and then returned to the United States for the fall and winter tour.

On January 26, 1958, I played Bartók's Second Violin Concerto with the New York Philharmonic Orchestra under Lenny Bernstein at Carnegie Hall. I appeared again at Carnegie Hall with Lenny Bernstein and the New York Philharmonic in April of 1959; we played the Beethoven Violin Concerto. And that December 3, 4, 5, and 6, we were together once again on that great stage.

The December 6, 1959, concert was the fifty-second time I'd appeared at Carnegie Hall since my debut there in January 1943, and everything pointed to the likelihood of its being the last time. Carnegie Hall, America's promissory note for the future of music, was soon to be demolished.

FIFTEEN

I HAD ALWAYS thought of Carnegie Hall as our country's affirmation of the human spirit. The great artists who had played in it since its opening in May 1891! The music that had resonated within its walls! When I played there that December, I knew that the edifice was to be torn down within the next few months. On the site would rise an office skyscraper with an exterior colored Chinese red.

For nearly seventy years, it had been one of the truly great concert halls in the world. Though it was named after Andrew Carnegie—in its early days, it was known as "the Music Hall founded by Andrew Carnegie"—in truth, he had subsidized the dream of about half a dozen people, among them Walter Damrosch, the conductor and musical director of the New York Symphony Society and the Oratorio Society. Actually, it was Damrosch's father, Leopold, founder of both societies, who had first conceived the idea of a grand concert hall for New York. The Symphony Society had a difficult time finding space for itself: the only hall large enough for its audiences was the Metropolitan Opera House, which placed it last in line for bookings, after the resident opera company, the New York Philharmonic Orchestra, and visiting European orchestras and opera companies. Often the Oratorio Society was forced to give its concerts in the showrooms of the Knabe, Chickering, and Steinway piano companies.

Then, as luck would have it, in 1887, Damrosch boarded a ship for Scotland, together with his close friend Louise Whitfield and her new husband, Andrew Carnegie, who were on their honeymoon cruise. By the time the ship docked, Carnegie had agreed to bring Damrosch's dream of a new hall to life.

A stock company was formed in 1889. The architect William Burnet Tuthill drew up the plans, and construction was begun. The opening festival took place from May 5 to 9, 1891, attracting the finest of New York's music lovers. The Symphony and Oratorio societies performed, under Damrosch and the composer Pyotr Ilich Tchaikovsky. The acoustics were superb; the concert auditorium was graceful, luxurious. One reviewer called it "the most beautiful Music Hall in the world." Carnegie Hall was hailed as a triumph.

Over the decades, the physical appearance of the building underwent some changes: two studio towers were built, as well as street stores, marquees, and a fire escape across the Seventh Avenue façade. The artists who performed there were among the greatest: pianists Godowsky, Josef Hofmann, Paderewski, Rachmaninoff, Schnabel, Myra Hess, Rudolf Serkin, Horowitz, Rubinstein; violinists Kreisler, Ysaÿe, Heifetz, Elman, Menuhin, Milstein; cellists Pablo Casals, Gregor Piatigorsky, Emanuel Feuermann; guitarist Andrés Segovia. And singers: Enrico Caruso, Lily Pons, Marian Anderson, John McCormack, Maria Callas, Paul Robeson, Renata Tebaldi, Leontyne Price; as in our day, Luciano Pavarotti, Beverly Sills, Joan Sutherland, and Placido Domingo. And all the great orchestras and conductors. Jazz debuted there in 1912, with a concert of ragtime. Rock artists played there. Knowing all that, what an astonishment it was for me, in the mid-fifties, to learn that the hall had been sold to developers who intended to tear it down and erect a tall red office building in its place. That deal eventually fell through—but not before a full-page picture of the proposed new building, which I dubbed the "Red Menace," appeared in the September 9, 1957 issue of *Life* magazine. The new Lincoln Center was being built in midtown; into it the New York Philharmonic Orchestra, Carnegie Hall's main tenant, would soon move. The board of the Philharmonic had decided not to purchase Carnegie Hall, thereby rendering the building's continuing existence pointless, according to Mr. Simon, the then owner. But he had no wish to see it torn down and was willing to sell it for $3 million. There were no buyers, however—too many believed that New York would not be able to support two major concert halls. Mr. Simon had spent years trying to save it; now, as far as he was concerned, Carnegie Hall was a dead issue.

Various groups had formed, some made up of tenants and employ-ees, attempting to halt the wrecker's ball. Committees of earnest citizens held protest meetings and rallies, some in the hall itself, where they tried to raise the money needed to purchase the building, plus an additional $1 million for renovations. Every effort had failed.

FOR ME, Carnegie Hall was the Holy Grail, the be-all and end-all of musical life in this country for all performing artists. No other place we played in had its unique history. The whole measure of American musical performance was created at Carnegie Hall. We were all its children. I could not see the one building that represented the American tradition of music internationally be torn down—I just could not bear the thought of it. Any artist who came to the United States to play music, no matter from where, invariably came to Carnegie Hall. It was the source of the amalgam that had created what we called the American standard; all our musical benchmarks had been set by the triumphs and the tears of the artists who had played there. Further, I did not believe for a moment that a city the size of New York had room for only one major concert hall. There were New Yorkers, I was certain, who wanted to hear good music at prices they could afford; and they had the right to hear such music in proper surroundings, with superb acoustics, and with the sense, if they so wished, of linking themselves to the history of the city's culture. How could so remarkable a structure be destroyed?

I hadn't the least idea, at that point, how to proceed. I started to talk to people, conveying to them my feelings about the hall, and got nowhere. Everyone was sympathetic; no one knew what to do. But the more people I talked to, the more I came to understand that the usual route of protest meetings and save-Carnegie-Hall committees was the way *not* to go. A way to arrive at a route that would lead not just to protests but to a practical plan that was a solution—*that* was what we needed. As I went on talking to people, it slowly became clear to me that what was really necessary was some kind of road map that would enable us to resolve the issue politically. We had to convince the city and its politicians that Carnegie Hall was necessary, viable, central to the cultural life of New York.

I want to say, at this point, that many people were of enormous help to me in what then occurred. I was, perhaps, instrumental in gathering certain individuals together and infecting them with my enthusiasm, but no one person could possibly have accomplished the task alone.

I remember the bitter cold night that early December, some days after my Carnegie Hall concert, when I went to the home of Jacob Kaplan, one of the most civic-minded wealthy men in the city. Jack Kaplan had made his fortune in Welch's Grape Juice. He was a short, trim man, with bright eyes and a ready smile, who favored bow ties; an individual of great warmth. I talked with him at length about Carnegie Hall, and after listening attentively, he told me that he, too, would like to see the building saved and would give serious thought to what might be done. A few days later, I went off with Zakin to play in Durham, and by the time I returned, Vera and I had our second child, Michael.

The birth of our son filled me with enormous joy—and with an even greater determination to save Carnegie Hall, for future generations of music. I called a number of friends and persuaded them to meet with me. We assembled on January 10, 1960, in my apartment on Central Park West, a small group—Jacob Kaplan, Jack de Simone, Raymond S. Rubinow—which soon became the Citizens' Committee for Carnegie Hall. Added later to the committee were Colonel Harold Riegelman, head of the Citizens' Committee of New York and once Republican candidate for mayor of New York; Frederick Richmond, a business partner of Mr. Kaplan's; Bob Dowling, a New York financier and banker; and John Barry Ryan, a young man in the New York investment community and a member of one of the city's leading families. An immediate outcome of the meeting was the telegram I sent that same day to John D. Rockefeller III, who was president of Lincoln Center, requesting that he consider supporting a movement to save Carnegie Hall. The appeal failed. His commitments and responsibilities in regard to Lincoln Center forced him to the reluctant conclusion that he would be unable to cooperate with us.

The response was a disappointment. At a second meeting with Jack Kaplan, plans began to be set in motion for a serious lobbying effort. The investment banker Frederick W. Richmond agreed to join our effort, and he and Jack in turn brought in their associates, Raymond S. Rubinow, the executive director of the J. M. Kaplan Fund, and Jack de Simone. Mrs. Claire Feit was engaged on a temporary basis as a secretary, her expenses underwritten by the Kaplan Fund and de Simone. While Zakin and I were again on tour, Rubinow got in touch with Sol Hurok, in a letter dated January 26:

> As Isaac Stern no doubt explained to you, the purpose of the meeting at his home on January 10th was to assess the situation and constitute a center of continuing interest in his absence, without which the possibility of doing anything would be completely lost. . . .
>
> Mr. de Simone and I have been in continuous touch with each other and I have kept Mr. Stern abreast of developments. We are still in the stage of gathering all the information we can so that we can formulate a case for saving Carnegie Hall *for* something as well as against destruction. There are four priorities: 1) ascertaining what the time factor may be; 2) finding out what are the requirements of the music managers; 3) stockpiling ideas for new and additional uses of Carnegie Hall; 4) exploring any possible city, state, or federal interest. . . .
>
> Of course, in thinking about this problem we are much interested in the opinions you offered on the need and use of additional halls in New York, and your own leading role in bringing ballet and musical events to this city. . . . [W]e are eager to have your own views on what would be required if ballet-theatre enterprises were to be brought to Carnegie Hall.

One day later, at a special meeting of the Board of Directors of Carnegie Hall, Mr. Simon noted, according to the minutes of the meeting, that "Isaac Stern had started to assemble a group, amongst whom were Frederick Richmond and Claire Feit, to try to 'save' Carnegie Hall." He added that "this was the first time that people of ability had associated with a Save Carnegie Hall movement," and concluded the meeting with a report on the agreement for the "production of a final concert or two to memorialize the closing of Carnegie Hall" and with a request for "advice as to the disposal of the Carnegie Hall organ."

I returned from the tour in time for a meeting of the full Citizens' Committee for Carnegie Hall, held in the Kaplans' home on February 7. We had enlarged the group, adding to it Republicans who could lobby the mostly Republican state legislature and Democrats with influence in the largely Democratic city government. After much debate, we agreed to a strategy, a key element of which was to obtain the support of Robert F. Wagner, Jr., the mayor of New York City. I took it upon myself to write to the mayor.

The letter, however, was delayed by the demands of yet another tour and by a family illness. In the meantime, on March 2, there took place a further meeting of the Board of Directors of Carnegie Hall, at which time, according to the minutes, Mr. Simon noted that "due to the provisions of the cancellation of the Nedick's lease he would like authorization to enter into a contract for the demolition of the Main Building in the event that the Helmsley-Wien deal [to net-lease the Carnegie Corporation's property] did not go forward." The minutes record that "authorization was granted."

On March 11, I sent a telegram to Mayor Wagner:

> . . . In our society of expanding interest in music a great city such as the one you head should have more than one great musical center to meet growing demand. Having played in concert halls all over the world I know that destruction of Carnegie Hall would remove from the musical scene one of few acoustically perfect concert halls. Run as a tax-free institution, Carnegie Hall will make it possible to offer a platform for vast talent of young people in this country who need opportunity to develop through repeated performances. . . . The possibility of early creation of a future American youth orchestra based at Carnegie Hall and serving as ambassador of good will throughout the world has tremendous implications and is enthusiastically supported

by the greatest of our musical leaders. . . . I am hopeful that I will have early opportunity to explain to you in person why it is so important that New York City act to preserve the great institution of Carnegie Hall.

I was asked to serve as chairman of the Artists' Committee, a spearhead group of the Committee for Carnegie Hall, and in that capacity I wrote to twenty of my colleagues, asking them to endorse a letter I had drafted in which I detailed the importance of the hall:

I affirm my belief in the importance of keeping Carnegie Hall as a permanent cultural monument.

It is of historical significance in the musical development of the United States, the embodiment of our musical heritage. This is a consecrated house. It holds memories of all the great performances of all the world's great artists shared by many generations of music lovers.

Leaving aside all sentimental reasons, Carnegie Hall, for the world outside the United States, has become the symbol of the greatest achievements in music. In the minds of civilized men everywhere it is the gateway to musical America. To destroy it now for "practical reasons" is an act of irresponsibility damaging to the United States and our prestige in the entire civilized world.

Every great city in other countries has several concert halls and opera houses. For this reason we welcome the creation of Lincoln Center as an addition to our musical life. But Carnegie Hall must remain to serve the needs of an ever increasing musical public and as an inspiration and home for the development of the musicians of tomorrow.

Every musician I wrote to signed the letter: Pablo Casals, Vladimir Horowitz, Jascha Heifetz, Myra Hess, Fritz Kreisler, Charles Munch, Gregor Piatigorsky, Arthur Rubinstein, Leopold Stokowski, Leonard Bernstein, Van Cliburn, Dimitri Mitropoulos, George Szell, Bruno Walter, Mischa Elman, Mieczyslaw Horszowski, Eugene Istomin, Erica

Morini, Nathan Milstein, and Eugene Ormandy. Not a single one refused.

In the meantime, a number of vital legal matters had to be addressed, and to that end Republican and Democratic members of the committee were in touch with state and city representatives. Legislative action was needed to permit the city to acquire by condemnation any property with special historical or aesthetic interest or value. Senator MacNeil Mitchell, in whose district Carnegie Hall was located, introduced bills to that effect in the state legislature in late March.

But that still left us with the problem of where the money would come from that would enable the City Council to vote in favor of acquiring the building and then leasing the property to the private nonprofit corporation our committee was in the process of legally becoming; we didn't think the City Council would be inclined to spend $4.5 million or more of the taxpayer's money on such an acquisition. It would take us nearly a year to raise that sum through a public subscription campaign. We didn't even have the time to secure the down-payment and fund-raising "nut" of $225,000. The city might offer a self-liquidating bond issue to acquire the hall, with repayment guaranteed in thirty years, but even that could not be done until the bills introduced by Senator Mitchell, sponsored by Mayor Wagner, and supported by a strong letter of endorsement from Governor Rockefeller were passed and signed into law.

The hall was scheduled for demolition in May.

ENTERING CITY HALL on March 30 for a meeting with the mayor, I had with me the letters signed by my fellow artists. Together with the other members of our committee who were there to present our case for saving Carnegie Hall, I hoped that the letters might make a difference to the city's own deliberations on this issue. We found the mayor and his staff warmly receptive to our presentation, but the fact remained that, without the necessary state legislation, the city was unable to appropriate the funds to purchase Carnegie Hall. With only three days remaining until the end of the current session of the state

With Pierre Monteux . . .

. . . Fritz Reiner . . .

. . . Charles Munch . . .

. . . Sir Thomas Beecham

With Arthur Rubinstein . . .

. . . Leonard Bernstein . . .

. . . *Igor Stravinsky*

With Alexander Zakin in Paris

With Eugene Istomin and Leonard Rose

With Zubin Mehta

With Pablo Casals (left) and Sasha Schneider (right)

With Jean-Pierre Rampal

With Nathan Milstein, David Oistrakh, Eugene Ormandy, and Sol Hurok

legislature, there seemed little chance that the bills would be brought to a vote.

But—astonishingly—they were voted on the very next day. And passed. Now all that remained was for the governor to sign them into law. And for the city to decide whether or not—and, if the decision was positive, then precisely how—to acquire the property.

On the evening of April 11, my wife and I attended Passover seder at the home of Rabbi Israel Goldstein on Central Park West, about four blocks from where we lived. The seder was an annual affair, to which Rabbi Goldstein invited about twenty people: Jews, Catholics, Protestants. To my absolute surprise and pleasure, I found I'd been seated, by sheer chance, next to Mayor Wagner and his wife.

We all sat around a large table. I remember it was a very warm evening. The seder went on and on—while not the first seder I'd attended, it was certainly one of the longest. When it came to an end, my wife and I and the Wagners left together and began walking along Central Park West. As we came near the apartment house where we lived, I said to the mayor, "Bob, how would you like a cold beer?"

His response was "That's the best thing I've heard tonight."

When we were seated comfortably in the apartment with our cold beers, I said to the mayor, "By the way, I have something I'd like to tell you." And I began to talk to him once again about Carnegie Hall.

He listened and said, "I used to go there as a child to Walter Damrosch's children's concerts. I'm an honorary member of Local 802." That was the musicians' union.

I said, "Then you understand the reasons that Carnegie Hall is so central to all of us. It's not just a piece of real estate. For the musicians of the entire world, New York and Carnegie Hall and the United States—it's all one thing."

He understood so very well. We talked for a long time, and Bob Wagner became my first really important and powerful ally in the city government, for which I will always be grateful to him. But both of us were aware that the city could do nothing unless the two bills passed by the state legislature were signed into law.

Five days went by. I was due to leave on a tour of the Soviet Union,

Czechoslovakia, Poland, and Western Europe. On April 16, Governor Rockefeller signed the bills. That same day, on the eve of my departure, I issued a statement about the long struggle to save Carnegie Hall:

> We are delighted not only with the fact that the Governor signed both bills, but also with the accompanying message, which parallels so closely our basic philosophy. . . . I would like to express publicly my appreciation for the support given our committee by Frederick W. Richmond and Jacob M. Kaplan and Harold Riegelman, without whose dedicated and knowledgeable efforts we would not have achieved our present success. We are very hopeful that the Mayor and the Board of Estimate will complete action so that we can within a very short time accept contracts for all orchestras in Carnegie Hall for next season. We have assured the city that not only will this be a self-liquidating investment, but that Carnegie Hall will most assuredly never be a burden on our city's taxpayers. Within the next few months we hope to announce plans outlining expanded activities for Carnegie Hall, and it is our belief that together with our friends at Lincoln Center we will see the establishment in New York City of musical activity of major importance in the world.

At the very height of the Carnegie Hall campaign, Zakin and I left New York for our second tour of the Soviet Union. I remember so vividly the thunderstorm of applause that broke over Zakin and me in Odessa on the opening night of the tour as we stepped out onto the stage. Militiamen had to be called to restrain hundreds of people left outside who were trying to break down the doors of the concert hall, which was packed with ticket holders. Yehudi Menuhin had been in Moscow not long before we went to the Soviet Union the first time, but, if I'm not mistaken, ours was the most extensive tour undertaken by an American performer in many decades. The tour included Odessa, Moscow, Leningrad, and Minsk; then Vilna, Riga, and Tallinn, the capitals, respectively, of Lithuania, Latvia, and Estonia.

While the tour was being organized, I had been asked if I would play in Tashkent. I think all of us have certain magic places we dream of visiting someday. Samarkand was such a place for me. The name evoked images of flying carpets, magicians, exotic foods. I told the Soviet authorities who were arranging the tour that Zakin and I would be willing to play in Tashkent if they would agree to arrange for the two of us to spend a day or two in Samarkand. They agreed.

When Zakin and I arrived at the airport in Tashkent, we were greeted by members of the organizing group; in every city in Russia, the organizing group is called the Philharmonic. We were taken to our hotel and then to dinner. In the restaurant, strolling fiddlers entertained the guests. We were sitting and talking, and I grinned at the fiddlers, who had recognized me as the visiting American violinist. As we went on eating, I noticed that one of the fiddlers was coming closer and closer to our table. He began to play directly to me, and I smiled at him; he came up to me and placed his violin between my face and the rest of the group at the table and whispered in Yiddish, "Be careful of that bastard who's the head of the concert committee, he's the local Communist leader." That happened fairly often during my travels in the Soviet Union: recognition by a fellow Jew; a cautious gesture, a word, a warning, a fraternal greeting.

The next day, before the concert in Tashkent, I asked one of the organizers when we were leaving for Samarkand, and he said, "Oh, we're sorry, but they're rebuilding everything down there and the roads are very bad and there's no way to get there and back." I said, "Thank you," and went to the head of the concert committee, who I now knew was the local Communist leader, and said, "I've just been told I can't go to Samarkand," and he said, "Yes, we're sorry." I said, "Fine, let's cancel the concert here in Tashkent. You get us on the next plane to Moscow. If you can't find us a plane, I'll call the American ambassador and have him send the embassy plane to pick us up. I will hold a press conference telling them how you went back on your word." In twenty minutes, I had two tickets for a flight to Samarkand.

When we arrived there, I understood what they meant. To call the hotel filthy would be an understatement, a compliment. It was indeed under *remont,* the Russian word for rebuilding. In the evening, we went to the local market and sat there eating the wonderful flat bread of Azerbaijan, with hard-boiled eggs and raw green onions and shash-lik, and drinking vodka and beer, and watching the camel caravans come in. Zakin and I spoke in Russian with the camel drivers about what they were carrying to the market and how conditions were. Back at the hotel, neither of us took off our clothes. We slept in chairs, because there was no way we would go near the beds. The next morn-ing, we were told there was no plane back until very late in the day. I said we would rent a car and drive—it was only about seventy miles back to Tashkent. They said, "No, no. We will provide you with a car and driver." We left in the early morning on a road that ran through the steppes of Central Asia; it was one long series of awful potholes. People were tilling fields with a horse and a wooden plow. Suddenly, in the distance, we saw skyscrapers and a city, but as we got closer we could see that the streets were sand and mud and the skyscrapers were showing cracks. About two hours later, we stopped for breakfast at a major town about halfway between Samarkand and Tashkent. Our driver suggested we go to a local teahouse in the center of town. There we encountered men wearing full, flowing silk shirts, loose trousers, and embroidered skull caps, sitting on the ground with elbow rests, sipping their morning tea and having a breakfast of hard-boiled eggs and green onions. We joined them on the ground, ordered tea and eggs and onions, and had some of the wonderful flat bread we had brought with us from Samarkand. The locals, seeing that we were probably Americans, began hesitantly to ask us questions. When they found out that we could speak Russian, the questions poured out: How do people live in America? What does a worker earn? Can a worker have a car, a refrigerator? Their friendliness was overwhelming. That was a memo-rable breakfast. We returned to our car, and it took us four hours to get back to Tashkent.

It was a rather tense period politically. President Eisenhower was due on a state visit to the Soviet Union, but an American spy plane had just been shot down over Soviet skies and its pilot, Gary Powers, captured. Khrushchev was now raging at President Eisenhower. After all, the Soviet government had spent enormous amounts of money cleaning the streets, paving the roads from the airport, repairing and repainting many of the buildings for the visit. The Russian people themselves were so looking forward to it that one had the impression they would have all gladly laid down on the road from the airport and let Eisenhower walk on their backs into the city. Of course the Russians gloated over the capture of the pilot. In this unpleasant atmosphere, Zakin and I went on with our tour, undeterred. At the same time, the musical *My Fair Lady,* with an American cast, was playing successfully to enormous crowds in Moscow. We were all in the Soviet Union as part of a new season in the Soviet–United States cultural-exchange program.

Meanwhile, another sort of cultural exchange was taking place in New York: the city's Board of Estimate, with the encouragement of Mayor Wagner, authorized the Department of Real Estate to begin negotiating with Mr. Simon for the purchase of the hall. The city was offering $3.5 million; Mr. Simon had been offered a good deal more by developers. It was understood that if a price could not be agreed on by the city and Mr. Simon, the city would condemn the property and ask a court to set a price.

In mid-May, the city offered to purchase the hall for $5 million, a price agreeable to Mr. Simon, and then to lease it to the Carnegie Hall Corporation, the nonprofit entity established in place of the Citizens' Committee for Carnegie Hall. The city would sell thirty-year bonds worth up to $3.5 million to acquire the property, and the corporation would reimburse the city through admission fees and other revenues. Once the thirty-year bonds were paid, the corporation would be given ownership of the hall; in the meantime, it would lease the building from the city.

Mayor Wagner named Frederick W. Richmond chairman of the new corporation, and on May 18 he sent me a telegram: "I have the pleasure of confirming your appointment as a trustee and member of Carnegie Hall Corporation, the purpose of which is to perpetuate Carnegie Hall as a great music and cultural center." There was another message from the newly formed corporation, informing me that I had been voted president of the Carnegie Hall Corporation.

The concerts that were intended to mark the demise of Carnegie

Hall never took place. On June 22, I wrote to Lenny Bernstein from the Grand Hotel in Florence: "Though I felt certain it would be successfully concluded, I didn't really quite believe it until it was all over."

In the last week of September, I flew to New York after playing a concert in Geneva, and on the evening of September 25, I stepped through a door onto the stage of Carnegie Hall to play the Beethoven Violin Concerto with Leonard Bernstein and the New York Philharmonic. They had just returned from a triumphant, record-breaking 20,000-mile tour; I was between engagements on a European tour that had been planned more than a year before. I'd come in to play at the concert, which was both a benefit for the orchestra's pension fund and the opening event in the life of the reborn hall. At the conclusion of the evening, I was due to fly out of New York to play a concert the next day in London.

Lenny and I had played the Beethoven a little over a year before on that same stage, with the hall then in the shadows of the wrecker's ball. Now the interior of the auditorium was redecorated: fresh white paint concealed the previous reddish hue on the walls, which were also adorned with gold trim; and the seats were covered in new red velvet. The side of the building that faced 57th Street had been steam-cleaned, with the result that a lovely buff color came to light from beneath the grime. To add to the festive air, orchids had been flown in from Hawaii. The entire auditorium was jammed with politicians, diplomats, New York society people, artists, and a huge crowd of well-wishers—a multitude overjoyed that Carnegie Hall was standing with a new face to the world.

As I made my way out onto the stage, I actually felt my knees shaking. Stage fright was hardly unfamiliar to me, but I had never before felt it to that degree. The atmosphere was charged with emotion. Also, it was an uncomfortably warm night; the hall was not yet air-conditioned. I had taken barely a half-dozen steps from the stage door when the audience rose and burst into a clamorous ovation. When the applause subsided, the orchestra and I began to play. As luck would have it, during the first movement a string broke on my violin; I instantly exchanged violins with the concertmaster, John Corigliano, and continued to play. Swiftly and with great skill, Corigliano replaced the string and returned the violin to me. Despite the wearying flight from Geneva, the heat in the hall, the broken violin string, and the emotion I could feel in the audience—despite all that, the Beethoven was a success. I remember that in the midst of the tumultuous applause that greeted Lenny and the orchestra and me at the end of the performance, Lenny leaned over to me and said into my ear, "Isn't it wonderful to be young and famous!"

I was forty years old.

TWO YEARS later, Carnegie Hall was confronted by a new competitor, Philharmonic Hall, which had emerged in September 1962. But that seemed to have little effect on the venerable hall, which was enjoying a lively season. In December, the *New York Times* critic Milton Esterow wrote that "Carnegie Hall is still flourishing."

It was obvious that New York was indeed able to support more than one major concert hall. Since the opening of Lincoln Center and Philharmonic Hall, and the saving of Carnegie Hall, the city was enjoying an expansion of musical activity. More concerts were booked than ever before in the city's history, and almost all were succeeding at the box office. Of great importance was the fact that the additional halls were proving to be of benefit to young artists. The mezzo-soprano Grace Bumbry, who had made a highly successful first appearance at Carnegie Hall in November 1962, was rebooked for December. In previous years, it would have been difficult to get another date so soon because of the paucity of concert halls in the city.

The Carnegie Hall Corporation was concentrating on the building: completing the redecoration of the auditorium, renovating the boiler plant and the electrical system, installing air-conditioning. We were in desperate need of funds. Through Sir Isaac Wolfson, a generous Englishman, and Raphael Recanati, head of the Israel Discount Bank, I was able to obtain a $250,000 line of credit—a fortune to us and the life-saving blood we needed at that moment.

At the same time, we were attempting some rather venturesome musical programming. Julius Bloom, then executive director of the hall, believed that the whole experience of listening to music was undergoing a basic shift. The *New York Times* quoted him as saying, "We're going from an era in which a program for orchestra or soloist was a pretty well formulated affair. We need another dimension to the musical experience for the artist and the audience, one that relates music more directly to the great jumble of ideas of our time." As an example, he explained, Carnegie Hall had, in a previous month, presented Stravinsky, Schoenberg, Webern, Milhaud, and Messiaen—five directions of modern music, each illustrating the widening of contemporary musical creativity—and combined them with works that were already very familiar to us.

There was no doubt in my mind that programs were becoming more inventive, presenting the accepted great compositions and at the same time including lesser-known but equally valid works of art.

The bustling new life at Carnegie Hall in December 1962—indeed, the enhanced musical life of New York—certainly vindicated the effort that had gone into preventing the death of the hall only two and a half years before.

NOTHING in my life had prepared me for the fight to save Carnegie Hall. I was a musician. Music was my whole being. I had no idea where my sudden ability to deal with politicians, lobbyists, and financiers had come from. Perhaps it had something to do with having grown up during the years of the Great Depression, watching what it took for my father barely to earn a living. And then the Nazis and the war. Maybe without knowing it, I had learned during those years that you really can't sit back and say that politics don't involve you. Everything that happens politically has an effect on your life, on the way you think, on the kind of civilized society you want this country to be. By early 1960, I had two children. How could I look at the world and say that I didn't want to get involved?

The conductor George Szell once told me that if I hadn't spent so much time doing other things and had just practiced more, I could have been the greatest violinist in the world. But I think I had already begun to feel, even before the issue of Carnegie Hall arose, that if my whole life were to consist only of music and performances, of the next work, the next concert, the next tour, if my life were to be forever limited to that—I would sooner or later climb the walls.

As I think of the last thirty-nine years of Carnegie Hall the name Judith Arron immediately comes to mind. In 1986 we were on a countrywide search for a new executive director. I had met Judy on concert visits with the Cincinnati Symphony, whose artist director she then was. She had been a cellist growing up in Seattle, knew and loved music, and seemed to be a wonderful executive. I facilitated a unanimous board invitation to Judy to be interviewed and the board immediately engaged her as the new executive director. During the next two or three years, she learned all about New York, and how it operated socially and financially. Most of all, she learned how to administer a huge staff, engage talented executives, and really understand a balance sheet. Her last ten years saw an explosion of imagination and organization unlike that in any other house of music in the world. A broad statement—but from my own experience and knowledge I believe it to be absolutely true. And it was so recognized by performers, composers, and fellow arts administrators worldwide. She will be lovingly remembered.

The struggle to save Carnegie Hall was a watershed event in my life. It taught me things about myself I hadn't known before: I could sway influential people through speech; I had the ability to stir crowds not only with music but also with words; I possessed an instinctive ability to navigate with some skill the tricky waters of politics and power. Nothing was ever the same for me after Carnegie Hall.

SIXTEEN

*T*HE GOALS of anybody who thinks about what he's doing change constantly. The more you learn, the more you recognize the absolute inability of any one person to achieve omniscience and perfection with regard to his art. The most you can hope to do is learn what the possibilities are, and then employ your own proficiencies to achieve at least some of those possibilities. And you come to realize that you can never really plumb the entire truth of ideas in music. That in essence is the power of music—the fact that the art form is larger, deeper, and far more varied than any single person can divine in one lifetime—and realizing it should give pause to any artist who starts to consider himself all-knowing. We are all simply steps in a continuing age-old tradition. When we do something that enhances that tradition, that makes it richer, purer, clearer—then we have done what we were put here for.

After Carnegie, those "steps" for me began to involve more than my own music-making. Music, of course, was still at the very heart of everything I did, but there was no doubt in my mind that its possibilities had been broadened. I had used politics and diplomacy with success, for the sake of preserving and enlarging the domain of music in New York. Why not continue to use that same judicious persuasiveness beyond the borders of my city?

During the following years, making music, being an advocate for music, and teaching music were the core of my life. I'd had a tough, hardening apprenticeship that taught me the value of values. The truth was, I didn't make power; I was granted power. My fiddle was my power. I couldn't just keep saying "Look at me!" I felt I had to give something back. I couldn't just *take* all the time—it was as simple as that.

Of course, the tours and the making of music continued. During the first few months of 1961, Zakin and I were in, to name only a few places, Minneapolis, Boston, Buffalo, Detroit, Montreal, Denver, Philadelphia, Albuquerque, San Francisco, Toronto, and Chicago. In April, we crossed the Pacific and played in Tokyo and Osaka. And in early May, we flew to Australia.

Eugene Ormandy, conductor of the Philadelphia Orchestra and a dear friend, was following my itinerary, and on May 10, 1961, he wrote to me in care of the Australian Broadcasting Commission in Sydney. In the letter, he chided me about the "jumps you are making." He wondered if I had listened to him at all when he'd told me that I had to slow down. "Even though you are only 40, you are over-doing it and I don't want you to pay for it later. So listen to the fatherly advice of a loving friend and slow down. You don't need world fame—you already have it. . . . I hope you will have an opportunity to rest and relax when you leave Australia."

Zakin and I were in Australia for eight weeks. Twenty-seven concerts: recitals with Zakin, solo appearances with local symphony orchestras, a memorial concert for William Kapell in the Sydney Town Hall. In recent years, the media and the film *Shine* have made much of a meeting I had in Perth with a young pianist named David Helfgott. I have met and spoken with many talented musicians during my more than fifty years of concertizing throughout the world, and the encounter in Perth, as reported, did indeed occur. But I don't have any clear memory of the meeting or his performance at that time.

During a radio interview I gave in Melbourne, I urged that music be made an active part in the education of all children, in order to develop the natural music that was in them. That would bring an end, I argued, to the current situation in which music was an acquired social habit for only part of the people. Australia could do well by establishing a ministry of culture, I added, such as existed in the Soviet Union and in various European countries, and to a degree in Great Britain through the Arts Council. Music and other arts, I pointed out, were rapidly becoming vehicles for breaking down international barriers and promoting understanding and good will. And I urged that a plan be set up to ensure a steady income for professional artists. "Young people in the arts should be able to earn enough to enable them to live in comfort. They spend fifteen to twenty years studying and too often get very little in return."

Invariably, news stories about the tour would remind readers that I was "the man who had recently saved New York's famous Carnegie Hall from the wreckers."

One day during lunch, I found myself in a discussion concerning the design for a new cultural center and National Gallery: Should the design include a concert hall? I urged that every effort be made to have a concert hall that could seat at least 2,500 people as part of the projected Culture Centre. That would be "an appropriate place where artists of international standard could give their best performances," I said. Yes, the concert hall was an excellent idea, said Eric Westbrook, director of the National Gallery. They would build it if they could raise the finances. Georges Tzipine, conductor of the Victorian Symphony Orchestra, readily agreed.

We returned home from Australia in mid-June, and about ten days later I was in Puerto Rico for the Casals Festival, where I played Haydn and Mozart, with Casals conducting, and the Brahms Trio in C Major, with Casals on the cello and Claudio Arrau at the piano. Casals was eighty-three years old that summer and still in possession of wondrous instrumental control.

EARLIER that June, I'd received a letter from Eugene Cook, editor of *Bravo!*, a quarterly music magazine about to be launched, with a projected circulation of 750,000 readers, mostly subscribers to organized concerts. Mr. Cook wanted to know if I would be interested in writing an article for a forthcoming issue.

A number of tape-recorded conversations with the editor and members of his staff followed, and a transcript of the interviews was to be sent to me for review before publication. As it turned out, I received the transcript after the article had already appeared, in the magazine's fall 1961 edition.

In the article I expressed my commitment not only to making music but also to being one of its most forceful advocates. I stated that we were living through "a very important and dramatic and perhaps dangerous moment in our musical history." Western musical civilization as we knew it, I said, was going to be thoroughly tested and tried in the next ten to fifteen years. Unless we were very alert to this and the dangers involved, we might be facing the end of the kind of culture we had known. I thought that remedial actions had to be started immediately.

> Since 1935–40, the center of standards has moved slowly westward from Europe to the United States with the great conductors, the great performers, and teachers who came to the United States to live. We have inherited the best of traditions very much in the same way that we have inherited our mores and our ethics from older civilizations. . . .
>
> We are, then, to make a very big phrase, the standard-bearers of the best of Western civilization. Within the next five decades great, young and powerful forces will come into being: Asian and African standard-bearers. . . . China particularly will make a powerful advance. Within two or three years, it will probably develop its own atomic bomb. This will lead it directly into the world stage power area. . . .
>
> I think that the world in which we live will not resort to war, but that cultural and economic penetration will be the first, and perhaps, in the long run, the most powerful weapons. . . . [I]f we have any kind of faith in the traditions that nourished us, then it's up to us to take the responsibility to see that those traditions are not only nurtured, but expanded, and encouraged to become a potent force in our cultural and geo-political lives. . . .
>
> In the United States, this means certain things. In the first place we must, very quickly, accept the idea that we will be

responsible for setting standards. The shoddy elements in our musical life must be removed.

Musically, we have been fortunate in our development in the last fifteen or twenty years particularly in one area—our universities. The growth of university music schools has probably been the most encouraging sign of a musical coming-of-age in the United States. . . .

What we lack lamentably is a standard of teachers and teaching in primary education. Here, we are dangerously ignorant. . . .

The fault lies in two things: first, the lack of recognition of the kind of life that a cultured society needs to truly be a civilized country. The second fault lies in our economic setup: why should parents encourage their youngsters to spend ten or fifteen years of very hard work to learn an instrument and enter a field where they *might* be able to earn three or four thousand dollars a year [*sic!* this was 1961], when a plumber or an electrician or a stagehand can earn a great deal more and with some security?

If this sounds like a plea for Federal subsidy, it is not—at the present time. I believe the study of the arts will be a necessity. But I don't believe it is either psychologically or politically possible now on a Federal basis, because we are not trained for it, we are not geared for it, we haven't been educated that way.

We do have one of the most substantial governmental subsidies operating anywhere but in a peculiarly American form—it's called tax exemptions and foundations.

That is direct government subsidy via the tax route. But it is not enough. The point is, what can one say constructively, what can one do now?

First . . . acceptance by professional musicians of their responsibility to the public—even more important—to young people, both as listeners and as future performers. The public taste must be guided and excited and the young would-be professional given an understanding of the rich traditions that he and she inherit, and must, in the natural course of events, enhance in their own way.

The most important group in this country is made up of the young people of college age. . . . Within five to ten years they become an influential group. . . . How articulate they will be as voters depends largely on the level of their cultural environment and experience.

They become parents, therefore they can begin, via their own experience, to demand a beneficial educational pattern for *their* children.

This means, then, that the first attack must be made on the wall that has been built up around music and its process of work and development between the professionals on one side and listeners on the other. The listeners must be brought into the mainstream of American cultural development. They must feel that they have a part in it, that they have a goal to reach, that they have a voice in it, that they belong to it. There must be outlets created and subsidized by local money—that is, state, municipal foundation and labor union funds to develop a musical life to which youngsters can aspire, and in which they can begin to earn a living. Our youth can thus become a pool from which the major professional organizations can draw. . . . Through such subsidies, many more people can attend performances at popular prices. . . .

If this is done at a local, municipal and state level, it is only a question of time until this habit becomes so ingrained that a national form of subsidy can be thought about. . . .

I don't say that anyone should stop lobbying for Federal subsidy—it should be continued—but I don't think it will be immediately successful, at least not in time to save a glorious musical culture that I fear may die out if it isn't helped rapidly.

This brings us to the question of teaching standards. . . . [We need] an institute or series of institutes to set our standards. . . . There is no reason why, with all the talents that we now have in the United States, both foreign and American-born, we cannot have the same kind of standard-setting institution in the arts (ballet, architecture, painting, music) that we have in the sciences or in medicine. We can just as well have music schools that are the equivalent of the Massachusetts Institute of Technology and the Harvard and Yale Law Schools, and such great medical centers as Johns Hopkins. It's simply a question of having those qualified to transmit these ideas brought together in one area; then, realizing what can be done both politically and artistically, organizing this into one driving force. . . .

Speedy action can help create, not only young performers, but far more important, an alert, efficient and dedicated group of young teachers to do what performers cannot do: take the time and trouble to develop a base upon which can be built what might be called a Golden Era in the Arts. I firmly believe that this can be done by the enthusiastic cooperation of America's best minds and talents.

ONE OF the young performers whose career I was fortunate to have helped a little was Pinchas Zukerman. After listening to him in 1957 in Israel, when he was nine, I made a mental note to hear him again at some future time. When I returned to Israel in October 1961, to play Viotti and Bartók with the Israel Philharmonic Orchestra in Jerusalem, I made it a point to listen to the then thirteen-year-old Zukerman. He was prodigiously talented.

One year later, an organization I helped to establish, the America-Israel Cultural Foundation, brought him to New York to continue his musical studies. We arranged for him to live with the parents of the pianist Eugene Istomin. Pinchas—Pinky, we called him—was a restless young man; he'd get himself into all sorts of trouble by playing hooky and doing other somewhat silly things. But the talent was incredible!

One day he came over to my studio to play the Beethoven Violin Concerto for me. Two hours later, we had managed to get through only the first twenty measures of the violin entrance—because I wouldn't let him play a note unless he answered my question "Why are you doing it that way?" Again and again I gnawed at him, "Convince me that you're right." He left in tears. But over the years I've found that the greater the talent, the more pressure it can take. Zukerman had the innate ability then, as he has now, to play a musical line and make it sing. He has a natural articulation in his left and right hands that I find astonishing.

Nor was I likely to forget the other young performer I had listened to in Israel in 1957: Itzhak Perlman. Credit has been given to Ed Sullivan for finding him, bringing him over, and having him come out on his crutches and play. But it was more complicated than that. When I heard him again in October 1961, he played the violin with an ability that was breathtaking. I flew out of Israel to continue my European tour, and from France I called Sol Hurok, who was then in London, and started to tell him about Perlman. He said, "Well, we have to talk. Why don't you come over here?" I said I couldn't, I was in the middle of a tour. "Papa," I said, "come over to Paris. I'll treat you to caviar at Fouquet's and we'll talk." He said, "I haven't got the time." I said, "I haven't got the time either. I need to rehearse. I need to play." We compromised. I would fly to London, he would meet me at the airport for an hour, and I would fly back to Paris.

I arrived in London on time. We sat in the airport and talked. I said, "I have another great talent for you." I'd already told him about Zukerman, in whom he'd become immediately interested. But Perlman, I knew, was a special case. "There's this boy, Itzhak Perlman," I said. "I think he's the most fantastic talent I've heard. What he does now is incredible. But there's one problem. He's on crutches." Hurok said, "Crutches! No! Don't start. It's not possible!" I said, "Papa, listen to me. This is a real talent. One of the great talents of our time. Perhaps one of the very few really great talents. You take him. His father is a worker, they don't have money. Bring him to New York, pay him $500 a month. When he starts to tour, pay all the expenses, the publicity, the pianist, whatever it costs, $25,000 or $50,000. Do it for two years, and then make a contract with him. Trust me." Hurok looked at me and said, "You're really that serious?" I said, "Yes." We shook hands. The one-hour meeting had lasted four hours. That's how Perlman came to Hurok, and how his musical growth was assured.

When Perlman arrived in New York, I arranged for him to be seen by my doctor friend Leo Mayer, who loved the fiddle and who devised special arm crutches for him. Both Perlman and Zukerman received scholarships from the America-Israel Cultural Foundation. Many years later, when Itzhak married Toby, the wedding and reception took place at the home of the Foundation, in New York.

Zukerman and Perlman have gone on to major worldwide careers in music. Perlman is perhaps the most successful violinist since Heifetz—he is a hugely dominant figure in the violin world. His appreciation of music and his ability to play all kinds of music in all kinds of styles with equal ease have made him into a very special figure. And Zukerman has not only developed into a very good teacher and a world-class artist and conductor, but he is also involved in promoting the quality of teaching everywhere and in getting good teaching established as widely as possible. I always think of these two superb musicians with affection and respect. I regard them as friends. And they have remained faithful friends.

I came upon another young performer in a most unusual way. It happened in 1962, during my European tour. I was in Paris, at the workshop of Étienne Vatelot, *the* luthier of Europe. I'd become very friendly with him early in my European career; to this day, we're like brothers. He had written to me earlier about a Chinese family, and now he said, "They have this young boy, about six, seven years old. You should hear him. He's unbelievable." So it was arranged that I would listen to him. The boy had been born in Paris, and his name was Yo-Yo Ma. The cello he played looked larger than he was. I was astonished, truly astonished. Some years later, Yo-Yo and his father, mother, and sister emigrated to the United States. I called on the director of the École Française, which our children attended, and arranged for Yo-Yo's father to be the conductor of the student orchestra.

Yo-Yo was at the time studying with a well-known cellist in New York, but I felt that the best teacher for him would be my friend the great American cellist Leonard Rose. I called Lennie and asked him to listen to Yo-Yo play, and Lennie took him on immediately as a student.

Yo-Yo learned so much from Lennie—about bow-arm technique, about playing in general, about practice habits. After he'd been with Lennie for a while, I listened to him, and I was excited as I've rarely been in my life. I talked to Sol Hurok about him, and Hurok signed him up. Together with Shlomo Mintz on the violin and Yefim Bronfman on the piano, Yo-Yo played the Beethoven Triple at Carnegie Hall around the beginning of 1977, with Sasha Schneider conducting the New York Youth Orchestra. It was one of the best performances I had ever heard. Yo-Yo had a turn of phrase and a mastery of his instrument that were unsurpassed then or now, and an instantaneous and infectious communicativeness with his audience. Musicians would turn around and smile with delight at one another as they heard the phrases flow forth with beauty and ease from his cello. I'd rarely witnessed that. And he himself was not only a superb performer but also a delightful and thoughtful person.

Then I did something that someone had once done for me when I was young. On April 7, 1937, Pierre Monteux, then conductor of the San Francisco Symphony Orchestra, had written to Vladimir Golschmann, conductor of the St. Louis Symphony Orchestra:

In writing you this letter I am doing a thing which I do not often make a practice of, which you know very well, but I have been so filled with a really intense and profound emotion this last week, that I feel it is my duty as a musician, to do what I am about to do.

A San Francisco boy, seventeen years of age, named Isaac Stern, just played the Brahms Concerto for the violin, with me in my last pair of concerts, and I have no hesitation in declaring that he is one of the first truly great violinists of today. In fact, he reminds me greatly of Kreisler young.

You would be doing me a great favor, and yourself an immense pleasure, by having this boy play with you next season. He is not a prodigy, but his whole musical training has been so intelligent, that he has become a violinist, we might almost say, of the old European school. I feel very sure that he will be a sensation wherever he plays, and already from the National Broadcasting of his concert, we have received hundreds of telegrams and letters.

I wrote to five major conductors—Lorin Maazel of the Cleveland Symphony Orchestra, Seiji Ozawa of the Boston Symphony Orchestra, Stanislaw Skrowaczewski of the Minneapolis Orchestra, André Previn of the Pittsburgh Symphony Orchestra, and Georg Solti of the Chicago Symphony Orchestra—asking that they consider inviting Yo-Yo to play as a soloist. They all did so, and at the end of each first rehearsal, he was reengaged. There are many ways to gauge objectively a performer's success over the years: the number of conductors who ask the performer to return, the rank of the cities in which he or she is asked to perform, a steady increase in the number of performances, an incremental rise in fees. But to be asked back after a first *rehearsal*! That is astonishing indeed.

There is no way I can describe the thoughts and feelings I've had when performing at Carnegie Hall with fellow artists whom I came upon when they were still quite young. They are now walking the stages of the world. What an extraordinary, ecstatic emotion that is for me!

THAT FIRST post-Carnegie year, 1961, I was involved not only with young performers but also with professional artists in possession of young ideas. Let me move back from 1961 for a brief while and address the matter of innovation in music: how certain new ideas have affected me throughout my years as a performer.

When I first started my career, back in the thirties, solo violinists regularly played concerti for violin and orchestra at their recitals— works like the Mendelssohn, the Wieniawski, the Beethoven—with a piano reduction. Kreisler, Heifetz, Menuhin, and the others would play the fiddle, and the piano would take the part of the orchestra. In the forties, after my Carnegie Hall debut, I decided that at my solo recitals I would play only works originally written for piano and violin and would eliminate concerti. Hurok once said to me, "What's the matter? You want to make the second half of a recital as boring as the first half?" I told him I thought there was plenty of good piano and violin literature around, I could make up exciting programs. And over the years I did just that, successfully. In the late fifties and early sixties, I began to notice that others had also stopped putting concerti on their programs and were playing only pieces originally written for the piano and the violin.

Something similar occurred with another innovation in which I participated. Again, we have to go back, this time to the summer of 1950 and the Casals Festival in Prades. Eugene Istomin and I were the two youngest soloists there. Deep and long-lasting musical connections and friendships were formed that summer, not least those between Eugene and myself. Eugene believes that the partnership came about as a result of the remarkable generative spirit of Casals, who acted as a catalyst at a time when Eugene and I were still young enough to respond to his creative force. It meant a great deal to us that we were regarded as major artists by a musician of Casals' near-mythic stature.

Two years later, at the same festival in Prades, Eugene and I performed together for the first time, and it was then that we started to talk about forming a trio. We needed a cellist, and we chose Leonard Rose, who had begun his solo career in 1951, after playing as first cellist in the Cleveland and New York Philharmonic orchestras. He and I had played a number of recitals together and had performed the Brahms Double Concerto in concert and then recorded it with Bruno Walter and the New York Philharmonic.

Originally, the three of us played as a group for the sheer pleasure of it; we simply loved making music together. Then, at some point, we decided to do some concerts. We wondered what to call ourselves. There were then only two very famous trios that played more or less regularly. One was the Cortot-Thibaud-Casals Trio; the other was the Rubinstein-Heifetz-Piatigorsky Trio, the so-called million-dollar trio, which played only four or five concerts a year and made some recordings. We decided to call ourselves the Istomin-Stern-Rose $683,926.50 Trio.

Most people were aghast when we announced our existence and our eagerness to play together publicly. Each of us was an accomplished soloist. Many wondered how we could possibly fuse together to form an ensemble. In fact, we played together marvelously well. All of us were such good musicians that the differences among us were minor. Most often we found ourselves instinctively in agreement, and where we differed, we would try to reach a consensus, because we all had the same goal: a musical result that would be as clear and as right as we could make it. We were driven by the same sense of purpose: to arrive at the composer's intentions as best we could. Each of us brought to the ensemble years of personal knowledge and experience, the reservoir of information we had about given moments in the music. One of us would say, "Well, it reminds me of this . . ." Another might remark, "You can hear it in that work . . ." Still another would recall, "There was this performer who played it . . ." Discussions were often quite animated. We were three men in a room, trying to work in unison, while acknowledging the primacy of a higher authority, the composer. Professionally each of us possessed a unique and personal voice. We listened together to the fourth voice; we listened to him tell us what to do. We were good enough friends to be able to cuss each other if we had to, but the basic concepts were clear to us from the beginning; it was the fine-tuning that we sparred about, the nuances, the way to reach as deeply as possible into the soul of the composer and to arrive at the joyous culmination, the explosion of finality, *that* is marvelous in music—to do something precisely the right way at the right moment and have it all come out gloriously.

The three of us respected one another, and when we finally worked through a piece, we were convinced that we felt the same way about it. Sometimes we were so close together in our understanding of a composition that we didn't even talk, we just played. Lennie and I would look at each other; I would glance at Eugene's hands, Eugene would watch my gestures. At times, one of us would suddenly come up with a new idea. On occasion we did things without thinking about them, and they'd work, and we'd smile, with the music still going. Lennie and I matched as few people have in ensembles. We instinctively listened to each other. Both of us had wonderful bow arms, and we knew how to use them. And Eugene Istomin had the most uncanny ability to make the piano sound as if he, too, had a bow, and a brilliant sense of the harmonic basis of any phrase, and a flexibility in phrasing that was as natural as using the bow was to Lennie and me. If one of us needed to play a phrase in a certain way, the other would watch and do the same thing. Each of us still had an individual sound, but we tried to put the musical impetus together in the same way. And Lennie and I managed to achieve the single most important—and rare—technical cohesion: the fusion of vibratos. Our vibratos were virtually identical in speed and width. Eugene said that Lennie and I fit together like hands in gloves. We felt the trio was ready to go public.

But the critics thought otherwise. We appeared in public for the first time in Chicago, an outdoor concert at the Ravinia Festival, in the summer of 1955, and the critical response was rather chilly. So we decided to go our separate ways and to let the idea of the trio rest for a while. We played together whenever we could and waited for another opportunity to make a serious public appearance.

That came in September 1961, at the first Israel Music Festival. Casals had agreed to attend, together with Sasha Schneider and Rudolf Serkin. The performances were to be held at the ancient Roman outdoor theater in Caesarea, near the sea. The trio would inaugurate the festival; ours was to be the first musical performance heard in that theater since antiquity.

That tour of Israel—and the trip to play in Teheran that interrupted it—was one of the most fulfilling and exhausting periods of my life. I'd spent virtually the entire summer before the Israel Festival on my usual summer tour: the Casals Festival in Puerto Rico; the Robin Hood Dell in Philadelphia; Tanglewood; the Hollywood Bowl; Vancouver; and Ravinia Park, where the trio had played six years before to negative reactions by the Chicago critics. I had no idea how time-consuming my commitment to playing with the trio in Israel was going to be. Both Eugene and Lennie knew the literature far better than I, and I had to work very hard to catch up on the pieces before we could begin to make musical sense. We ended up playing nine concerts in Israel: in kibbutzim, the Galilee, the Negev. A lot of tiring travel. When not traveling, we would rehearse three to four hours a day. During our first concert in Jerusalem, Lennie suddenly felt terrible pain in his left hand and almost completely lost his sense of touch in the first finger of that hand. He made it through the concert but had to have traction in the hospital. He was given a neck brace to wear several hours a day, to relieve pressure on the nerve that was causing the pain. He'd been through the same trouble eleven years before, and was treated and cured, but the healing needed time and, above all, rest. Under any other circumstances, he would have canceled the concerts, but he most gallantly played them all, and played gorgeously.

The festival was a great success. Casals was incredible. For the final concert, Sasha Schneider opened with a Vivaldi concerto, then Serkin and Eugene played the Mozart Two-Piano Concerto. Casals then conducted one of the most exciting performances of the Mozart G Minor Symphony I'd ever heard. The concert ended with the Beethoven Choral Fantasy, with Serkin as soloist. Serkin played like a devil; he seemed possessed by an irresistible drive that was hair-raising. The audience went absolutely mad. Everyone there understood what was happening musically and historically, and they were very much part of the evening's soaring excitement.

My wife and our two children had come with me to Israel. Vera was involved with many things that were important to us—philanthropies and friends. And the children, little Shira and Michael, were talking and growing at an astonishing pace.

The recitals played by the trio were warmly received by the Israeli critics. We had finally broken in our musical act, so to speak. But Lennie's cervical disc and Eugene's sudden onset of tendinitis in a thumb—he was unable to control its contractions—made further performances impossible.

When Eugene and I returned from a State Department–sponsored concert in Teheran in 1961—an exhausting trip involving long layovers—Eugene went to see a doctor, who promptly banned him from playing. His thumb in a cast, he flew back to New York, which meant that he could not play three scheduled special orchestra concerts. I had to rehearse both the Beethoven and the Mendelssohn concerti for a concert in Ein Gev, and conduct the Beethoven F Major *Romance* and the Mozart G Major Concerto. Casals conducted the Beethoven Fourth Symphony in the second half. How fortunate that nothing had gone wrong with me!

After that true beginning of the trio in Israel, I went on to Europe for a solo tour. Many one-night stands: Florence, Rome, Lausanne, Chaux-de-Fonds, Geneva, Zurich. My family caught up with me in the cities where I knew I'd be spending some days; we didn't want the children subjected to the rigors of those one-nighters. It was during that European tour that I flew to London and talked in the airport with Sol Hurok about Itzhak Perlman.

After Lennie's disc and Eugene's thumb had healed, the trio returned to making music. We were, it must be admitted, three very different people. What bound us together was our love of music. Lennie was a well-built, very good-looking man, about five feet eight, and a driven neurotic. His first wife had died of cancer, and now he was married again, to a beautiful woman named Xenia. He was a very successful teacher, knowledgeable, patient, but he couldn't get away from his nerves. He had to practice so many hours a morning, every morning. At four o'clock in the afternoon on the day of a concert, he had to have a steak and whatever came with it. No other food. Invariably, he was at the hall an hour before the concert, when he'd begin with a series of little exercises to warm up. But he always played through his nervousness, went right through it to the performance, which was unfailingly brilliant.

Eugene, slightly portly, as was I, was a superbly trained, deeply sensitive, learned and intuitive musician, as well as a voracious reader. When we played together, he never came to a rehearsal without being completely prepared. His analysis and knowledge of a score were always first-rate, and he'd bring to a performance not only musical insight but also a remarkably quick flexibility. He played the piano as if he were holding a violin bow. Musical phrases spun themselves from his fingers. Also, he was quite meticulous about the way his martinis were made. And he was an avid and knowledgeable baseball fan, particularly of the Detroit Tigers. He, too, needed a warm-up period.

Both Lennie and Eugene were always a little angry with me over my relaxed attitude. I could go onstage without a warm-up.

Some months after we returned from Israel, we played the Beethoven Triple Concerto in New York, at Carnegie Hall, with Alfred Wallenstein conducting the Symphony of the Air. After a warm and serious response by the critics, we decided to do a limited number of recitals every year in North America and Europe. Neither the Cortot-Thibaud-Casals nor the Rubinstein-Heifetz-Piatigorsky trio had played together for extended periods of time or undertaken tours.

Our tours took us, in 1962, to the Montreal World's Fair and to the Edinburgh, Lucerne, Menton, and Aix-en-Provence festivals. We played in Chicago's Orchestra Hall, Boston's Symphony Hall, Paris's Théâtre des Champs-Élysées, and London's Festival Hall. In 1963, we performed at the White House. During the year of Beethoven's bicentenary, 1970, we spent six months together, playing thirty or so works by Beethoven in London, Paris, Switzerland, Buenos Aires, Carnegie Hall. We played the first recital in the Concert Hall of the newly inaugurated John F. Kennedy Center for the Performing Arts in Washington, D.C. We traveled to Japan, where we played in Tokyo and other cities. Our tours took us to four continents.

During that period, we recorded the complete Beethoven trios and two piano-and-cello sonatas; Eugene and I began recording the ten piano-and-violin sonatas. We also later recorded the two Schubert trios, the two Mendelssohn trios, and the three Brahms trios. In later years, whenever we'd meet after fulfilling our commitments as solo performers, it would require only a few measures of playing together to start up the engine that gave the trio its artistic life.

Though we were three very distinct individuals, we were not three people playing; we were one trio. I was playing with two partners who were strongly endowed with enormous technical control and musical ideas. That made for a very special partnership and gave the trio the quality of brio that was unique about us. The large dynamic range that we could use at any time, from an orchestrated massiveness when we were going hell for leather to the intensity of a *pppp* that remained in the air with a floating urgency—all of that came through because we always brought to our playing the knowledge and the recognition of that ecstatic moment of unity between the music, the performer, and the audience. We always looked for that moment as soloists, and we brought our search for it to the service of the trio.

We were three equals. In fact, both Eugene and Lennie brought more depth and knowledge to our group than I did. As a result of my work with the trio, my search in the more profound areas of music—

the chamber-music repertory—was making greater and more deeply satisfying demands of me than might have come from my working on the details of a concerto by Wieniawski or the Lalo *Symphonie Espagnol.*

The first time we played at the White House, in 1963, Pierre Salinger, Kennedy's press secretary, had to be away, preparing for one of the presidential trips, so there was little opportunity for him to brief the president about the subtleties of a trio performance, especially with regard to the equal status of all the artists in the group. At the conclusion of the performance, when people were applauding, Kennedy rose, as was the custom, and said, "I want to thank Isaac Stern and his two accompanists." That didn't go over too well with Lennie and Eugene, and I wanted to sink through the floor. Kennedy invited the three of us upstairs to a private get-together after the concert, and the general reception and the receiving line. We joined him for a last drink and a chat, and he was charming. By that time, he realized that he had committed a gaffe, and he was especially gracious to Eugene and Lennie.

I needed the trio. We needed one another. Wherever we played, we were equals. In a letter I wrote in January 1970 to a concert organizer in Buenos Aires, I made it clear that his suggestion for the program—a violin concerto, the Brahms Double for violin and cello, and the Beethoven Triple for violin, piano, and cello—was "completely and utterly impossible," because it was unacceptable to me that Eugene and Lennie were being turned into "nothing more than a couple of accompanists in the final concerto, while I play throughout the evening. . . . Either we make a combination program of a piano concerto, the Brahms Double and the Beethoven Triple, or the Beethoven Triple alone. Otherwise we cannot really accept this concert."

For me, for all of us, the group was greater than the sum of its individual parts.

In the last fifteen years, it has become very chic and musically acceptable to play in a trio or a piano quartet even if one is a noted soloist. I'm proud of the innovative effect we had on the concert stages of the world.

Tragically, the era of the Istomin-Stern-Rose Trio ended in 1984 when Lennie died of leukemia.

SEVENTEEN

*D*URING ONE of the many times I participated in the Casals Festival, I had the opportunity to meet the governor of Puerto Rico, Luis Muñoz Marín. He was a tall, gregarious gentleman, a little portly, with intelligent eyes, a mustache, a ready smile. A man entirely without affectation, a statesman and a poet, he was deeply interested in the festival, proud of its presence in Puerto Rico. I told him of an idea I had to move the festival to Carnegie Hall in the summer of 1962, after it ended its regular season in Puerto Rico. The hall was newly air-conditioned, and the 1962 summer season would be the first in the hall's seventy-year history. What an event that would be: the Casals Festival in New York! But as it turned out, the idea was abandoned for lack of adequate financing.

Another individual with an abiding interest in the Casals Festival was Abe Fortas, a noted Washington lawyer, who had written Puerto Rico's constitution. He was a neat, quiet man, a well-dressed but never overdressed Southern gentleman. He knew how to listen; he could take a one-hour conversation and boil it down to its five-minute gist. He was a great reader and had a vast knowledge of the Bible, though he never flaunted any of it. Best of all, he was the kind of man you could take to a bar, a symphony, an opera, a ball game, a presidential dinner, or a hot-dog party—and he'd be at home, and everyone would be at home with him. At the time of the Johnson administration, he went on to the Supreme Court and much controversy. He was rather good at the fiddle. During the festivals, he'd join one or another of the quartets for some relaxed playing.

In the years that followed, we saw each other often, and he became my attorney. Abe was one of the most fanatically devoted amateur musicians I've ever known. He had a regular string quartet evening at his house every week, frequently with professional players. I was often in his home as a guest, and on every visit he would throw a dinner party and invite anyone I had a fancy to meet, including some people at the highest levels of government. He was deeply respected by almost everyone. As we grew closer, I arranged to buy him a good Italian violin that was not too large and was easily playable. He would never take any fees for acting as my attorney, which he did with extraordinary ability. One of the things I remember about his qualities as a lawyer was the soft-spoken, Southernly gallant way he would take a young lawyer and skin him alive in about three minutes if he dared make an improper or badly thought-out suggestion. Abe became a valued member of the Carnegie Hall board, employing his extraordinary analytic abilities to listen to discussions and boiling them down to the essence that one then used to make decisions.

He was Lyndon Johnson's closest personal advisor. I remember his telling me how Johnson talked to him about the Civil Rights Act in 1964, just before signing it. He asked Abe, "Is this the right thing to do?" And Abe said, "It's the greatest thing you *can* do." Johnson looked at him and said, "Then it's done."

Abe's nomination to the Supreme Court came much against his will and, even more so, against the wishes of his wife, Carolyn Agger. She wanted very much to live most comfortably and knew that Abe, who was not a wealthy man, could not guarantee their mutual comfort if he didn't complete a certain deal in which he was then involved, one that would bring in enough money to put them beyond the need to live off the salary of a Supreme Court justice. I was in their home the morning that President Johnson called and informed him of the nomination. I came downstairs in my pajamas and robe, and Abe told me about his nearly hour-long conversation with the president. He'd asked the president to delay the appointment until the business deal was completed so that he could earn his fee and be set for life, but Johnson refused, saying, "I'm sorry, Abe. I'm going on the air in one hour and appointing you to the Supreme Court." As Abe Fortas was just about the most loyal friend a man could ask for, he accepted the appointment, withdrew from the deal, and went on to the Supreme Court. A cartoon appeared the next day in the *Washington Post,* showing Abe holding his right hand up to take the oath of office, while his left arm is in a corkscrew from shoulder to wrist. It was quite accurate.

The scandal that followed sometime later regarding his acceptance of some gifts to influence an opinion was, I am certain, not Abe's fault. He and Carolyn had a lovely house in Georgetown and an elegant lifestyle. He drove a thirty-year-old Rolls-Royce, proudly and prancingly, and Carolyn ran a home that was always open to guests, good conversation, good wine, and, her particular favorite, old vintage bourbon whiskey. She was vigorous and very careful about her health, and had a hot-air enclosure built over their swimming pool in the backyard so that she could swim daily throughout the year. The scandal, I am certain in my own mind without having any solid evidence, resulted completely from the will of Carolyn Agger.

After Abe's death, in 1982, I discovered that he'd left me the violin that I had given him, requesting that I in turn give it to a worthy young violin student. He also left me his desk, a beautiful piece of furniture made out of an old square fortepiano, which he arranged to have sent to Carnegie Hall, to be used by me in my capacity as president. I'd never had an office in Carnegie Hall, and the desk was placed in the office of the executive director. But the recent tragic death of the executive director, Judith Aaron, has brought me into the daily administration of Carnegie Hall more than at any time in the past, and I now have an office there, in which I work at the desk that Abe Fortas bequeathed to me so many years ago.

WHEN John F. Kennedy was elected president in November 1960, there was a heady feeling among many that official attitudes toward the arts would soon change for the better. About nine months after he took office, my wife and I received an invitation to the White House. It read: "The President and Mrs. Kennedy request the pleasure of the company of Mr. & Mrs. Stern at dinner on Monday, November 13, 1961 at eight o'clock." It was to be the first musical soirée at the Kennedy White House; indeed, as far as I knew, it was the first White House evening concert ever. The guest of honor was Governor Muñoz Marín of

Puerto Rico. Abe Fortas would be there. I had been invited not to play the fiddle but to sit back and enjoy the evening as a guest. Pablo Casals would play. Eugene Istomin was there, too—also as a guest.

Kennedy was not the first American president I knew. I'd met Harry Truman through friends of his who had known him during his Kansas City years. He was on a visit there once when I played, and I was introduced to him. His daughter was for a time interested in a musical career, and he himself was a very down-to-earth man who liked music. There was nothing pretentious about him. I now think of him as one of the greatest presidents in the history of this country—certainly in the sixty years that I have been aware of the role that presidents play in our daily lives.

I met Eisenhower briefly at an Alfalfa Club dinner. The Alfalfa Club was a Washington institution, and the skits presented at its annual dinner roasted the mighty and the famous. Everyone came: senators, congressmen, journalists, Supreme Court justices, cabinet members. And President Eisenhower. They had invited me to play, and I'd said, "Of course." There was the usual receiving line and handshakes. Then they all went to have dinner. Zakin and I waited backstage; we were to play after dinner.

Dinner went on and on. A lot of wine and liquor was being passed around, and everyone was happy. A pop singer came on. By that time it was close to 11 o'clock. No one at that dinner seemed the least bit interested in serious music. Zakin said, "What're we doing here? Let's go. They don't need us. They won't notice whether we play or not." I said, "No, we have to stay. Let me handle this." Finally, someone announced us and we came out. There was applause. I said, "Ladies and gentlemen, before coming here tonight, I had someone call the White House to find out what was President Eisenhower's favorite music. And I was told that it was Bach." I saw Eisenhower nodding very firmly with a smile: definitely, yes, Bach. And everybody went, "Uh-huh." I wondered if he had ever in his life heard Bach. I said, "In deference to the president, I will play for you the Adagio and Fugue in G Minor for violin alone." Now, this was after that long dinner; most of the people there were half drunk. And Bach was very serious music. I played it, and they sat quietly. Then Zakin and I played some other things, and we finished. There was a good deal of applause. I think they were a little staggered by my not so little concert—but they sat still and listened. A few minutes later, as I was leaving, Justice Felix Frankfurter approached me and said, "Young man, anybody who's got the chutzpah to do what you did tonight I have to meet! Tomorrow in my chambers for lunch!" We got to know each other well, and met every time I returned to Washington.

Kennedy was the president I was to know best. Riding to the White House that November evening in 1961, I felt as though I were inside a golden coach drawn by four pure-bred white horses into the glitter of mythic Camelot. The dinner took place in the East Room. Kennedy was handsome, gracious. I was taken by his natural warmth, overwhelmed by his radiant charm.

I was invited back to the White House a number of times after that evening, to play as a soloist and with the trio. I knew Pierre Salinger because his mother, more than twenty-five years before, had taught me rudimentary French in San Francisco. He and I had become friends in Washington and then, of course, he became President Kennedy's press secretary. I remember I was in his office one day, trying to help in the creation of the agency that ultimately became the National Endowment for the Arts. Someone who knew very little about the arts had been chosen to head the new agency, because, it seemed, Kennedy wanted him near the White House for other things. I was on the telephone to New York when Kennedy entered the office. I said quickly into the telephone, "I'm sorry, I can't talk now, the president just walked in," and hung up. Kennedy looked at me, gave me his dazzling grin, and said, "What are you shilling for now, Isaac?" We talked for a few minutes, just some good-natured banter. I was struck by his extraordinary buoyancy. He seemed to be in a very positive mood, in spite of the way he was constantly being battered by the press.

About three weeks later, I flew west to play a concert with the San Antonio Symphony Orchestra. I arrived at the Dallas airport to catch my connecting flight, and as I was descending the stairway to the tarmac, I heard an attendant say, "Kennedy has just been shot." I walked into the terminal. Everybody was buzzing about what had happened;

this was only thirty minutes after the shooting. I remember thinking, The president has just been shot, how can they allow routine announcements of arriving and departing flights to go on?

I saw a shop in the terminal with some television sets, and I went in and said, "Do you mind putting on the television so we can see what's going on?" I watched for a few minutes and saw the reporters and the police and the ambulances and the people in front of the hospital. The man running the shop came over to me and said, "Are you looking, or are you going to buy?" It was only because the fiddle I was carrying was such a good one that I didn't slam it through the showcase.

I was supposed to fly to San Antonio for a rehearsal and a concert, and I didn't know what to do. I decided to call a friend of mine, a cellist with the Dallas Symphony Orchestra. I said, "Look, I'm at the airport. I have to spend a couple of hours here. I don't know if I'm going to San Antonio or back to New York. I don't know what to do. So come over, and please bring a bottle with you." In those days, no liquor was served at that airport. Then I called my wife, and we both began to cry on the telephone. My friend arrived with a bottle of bourbon, and we sat there talking and drinking.

Then we heard the announcement that Kennedy was dead. We looked across the airfield from the window of the café where we were sitting, and there was *Air Force One.* We sat there waiting, and watched it take off. Only later did I learn that on it was the president's body, Mrs. Kennedy in her blood-stained skirt, and Lyndon Johnson, who was being sworn in as president of the United States. I called the San Antonio concert manager and said, "You're not going to have the concert now, are you?" He said, "Oh, we must! We must! It's a full house. We've got to have the concert." I said, "But the president has just been assassinated." He said, "It doesn't matter. People will still want to come." So I said, "All right. I'll be there."

I arrived in San Antonio and went straight to the hotel. I got another bottle and sat in front of the television all night, watching. The entertainment programs were off the air. There was only quiet music and commentary and photographs of Kennedy and coverage of what was happening that night.

In the morning I went to the rehearsal. The streets were dead quiet. Everything was shut. Very little traffic. The few people who were on the streets walked along slowly. I went into the auditorium, and we started the rehearsal. I was due to play the Sibelius Violin Concerto in D Minor, but after the first three notes I stopped and said to the conductor, Victor Allesandro, "I'm sorry, I can't play this. I just can't play this kind of music now. I'll come to the concert tonight, I'll play something alone. And I promise I'll be back in the next few months. I'll make it up to you." He said, "All right." I went back to the hotel, packed my bags, was picked up by someone in a car, and, with my bags in the trunk, was brought to the auditorium. I came out onstage. Four thousand people were in the audience. I said, "There are many ways that people pray. Musicians pray sometimes by playing certain kinds of music. I will play some Bach." I chose Bach because there is in his music a pervasive sense of balance, a continuity of deep belief. Whatever he wrote, whether it was a religious choral work or a composition that was purely instrumental, one felt it was permeated with his faith, his devotion to God. For me, his music was always a catharsis; I play it sometimes quietly to myself when I am in a dark frame of mind. I said to the audience, "It will take about fifteen minutes. I will ask you please not to applaud at the end." I played the Bach Chaconne. As I approached the end, I was crying uncontrollably. I don't think there was a person in that audience who didn't feel a sense of personal loss with Kennedy's death. I admired him, respected him, loved him. When I finished playing, there was dead silence. I walked off the stage, put the violin into its case, got into the car, went directly to the airport, and flew back to New York.

The trio was invited to take part in the memorial service for Kennedy. The people arranging the service left it to us to decide what to play, and we chose the slow movement of the Schubert Trio in B-flat.

Kennedy's assassination was a profoundly historical loss for this country. Regardless of the shortcomings we now know he had, there was about him something that went beyond all his human weaknesses. And that was true of Jacqueline Kennedy as well. I saw her afterward a number of times; I was very fond of her. It was not so much the regality of the Kennedys, their courtly manners, that impressed me; it was their dignity. They preserved, and even very brightly burnished, the very necessary mythology of the office of the president. The country needed that very much. Now virtually every vestige of it is gone.

The incident in connection with Kennedy and the trio that I described earlier—after we'd played at the White House for the first time and Kennedy publicly thanked "Isaac Stern and his two accompanists"—points to a problem that some have had with me over the years: my rather outsize curiosity and willingness and ability to get along with all kinds of people have caused some to look upon me as the natural leader of any group of which I'm only an equal member, and caused others to feel that my personality is generally far too overbearing. In all honesty, there is little I can, or want to, do about my essential nature. I care passionately about music, and will talk and act in its behalf in my own way at every opportunity.

Years later, in 1966, I was asked to play in the Lyndon Johnson White House, at a reception for Prime Minister Indira Gandhi of India. A biography of me appearing in the program closed with this remark: "In his tours of the musical capitals of the world, Isaac Stern has served his country proudly and well as our unofficial musical ambassador." I was not at all offended by that description, true or not.

EIGHTEEN

*M*Y FAMILY had grown to five by the time of the Kennedy assassination. On May 21, 1963, our third child was born, a boy, whom we named David.

I was on tour in Russia when Shira, our first child, was born in 1956. When our second child, Michael, was due to be born, in 1959, the pediatrician, Dr. Jascha Rowe, was so busy bringing him into the world that he could call me only after the birth. But with our third child, David, Dr. Rowe got to me in time, and I was in the delivery room, gowned and face-masked. To be able to give his mother moral and physical support; to see this new lump of flesh emerge, turn from its fetal position, open its arms, give a cry, and instantly become a sentient human being—I will never forget that moment, nor forget the closeness it made me feel, not only to this third child but to the two others. It was a vision of nature in its rawest and most glorious moment. I urge every father-to-be to make every effort to realize that moment.

An artist's life is in a sense a very selfish one. Of necessity you think constantly and sometimes solely in terms of your need to fulfill your professional responsibilities, and that puts at risk the ordinary every-day life of your family. While I was away traveling, I would think constantly of the children. In California for a few days, playing some concerts, I spent some time with Danny Kaye, a dear friend. He was preparing one of his incredible Chinese dinners for us, and I began to talk to him about my family and how the children were growing up and I was always on tour. He said, "Isaac, the main thing for you is, when they're five or six, get them to an analyst. They'll feel angry and distrustful of you, because you're never home."

Vera and I tried hard to avoid letting that happen. When the children were sufficiently grown, we began to take them on some of my tours. They learned early on what travel entailed. They grew to understand how to live in hotels, their natural exuberance at times reducing a hotel's staff to a condition bordering on vassalage. They would attend rehearsals to the limit of their patience; they would often come to concerts; they would meet my friends. They had nannies, particularly after David was born, when a nurse-housekeeper came on, a Frenchwoman, Marthe Fougère, for whom David became a surrogate son. She cared for the children, took them for walks, tended to their needs. She was around them far more regularly than Vera or myself. She slept in a room next to theirs; if they woke in the middle of the night, it was she who saw to them. The life I chose, or was driven to choose, on that day long ago during the long bus ride back and forth through Manhattan—that life was not one that had me going to an office in the morning and coming home at night to a daily routine of problems, homework, and coping with teachers, sore throats, and toothaches. There was never any intention on my part to distance myself from the children. On the contrary, I wanted to bring them as close as possible to what I was doing and to how I lived.

There were some extraordinary moments. I remember once, in Paris, having to play an evening concert, and the two boys, who were still quite young, being sent off to bed. Vera and Shira went together to the concert hall. It was late when we returned to the hotel. We found the boys asleep in one bed, holding hands. The image of the two of them, asleep in that bed, their hands entwined . . .

Shira, being the eldest, watched over the boys like a mother hen. Once, when they were all somewhat older, my wife and I let the three of them take a train through France, with a countrywide rail pass issued for tourists. They got on and off, went to hotels and restaurants, wandered around. They were on their own, and absolutely capable of taking care of themselves. We went to Israel together early on. I would play recitals with Zakin and concerti with the Israel Philharmonic Orchestra. The children learned about that part of my touring life and what Israel meant to me. They came to regard Israel almost as a second home.

Because Vera was adept at many languages, French being one of them, and I spoke two languages other than English—not well, but with ease, my French much better than my Russian—and our nanny was a Frenchwoman, it made sense, when the time came to decide about the children's schooling, to enroll them in the École Française in New York. With the children in school and no longer able to travel freely, I was once again touring either alone or with Zakin.

A newspaper once carried a brief story about my wife having gone to the customs office in New York to pick up a package I had mailed from Australia. The customs inspector asked her to declare its worth. Vera said, "To me, a million dollars." The package was a tape recording, and its actual declarable value was fifty cents. That was one of the ways I regularly communicated with her and the children when I was on tour.

On one of the early tapes, sent in December 1961, I hear myself saying, "Hello, everybody. I'm talking to you from Belgium. Actually, at the moment, I'm lying in bed rather late at night, almost in the dark, just sort of closing my eyes and pretending I can see all of you while I'm talking. By the time you receive this—Michael, listen to Daddy, yes, come over here, don't run away, come over, sit down, that's it, now you listen. And, Shira, don't push him, hold him so he's real close to you and you're both together and you can hear what I say. Sit there with Mommy. That's it. Now, sit together. Fine. Now, Michael. First of all, it's past Michael's birthday. But just to have it on record, just once more, from Daddy." And I sang "Happy Birthday" to my two-year-old son, concluding with the words, "I love you," and the comment, "It's a good thing I never tried to be a crooner. . . . Anyway, Michael, that's a happy birthday from Daddy. And, Shira, a big hug and kiss, and an 'I love you' just for you. All for you, special. Mommy told me that you're going to school now, and you're beginning to learn things in French. And I want to hear all about it myself from you. You know, you have to tell me lots of things that have been going on since you got home, because I don't know what's been going on all the time. And, Shira, you and I are going to sit down alone, and we're going to have a long, long, long, long talk. And you'll tell me all about school, and the teachers, and what you do and what you learn and about the other children, and what you've been doing at home and who you've been seeing. And it's just going to be very, very lovely. And I want to send a big hug and kiss to Babushka [Vera's mother] and to Granny [my mother]. . . . And say hello to all our friends who come in. Just say, 'Daddy said hello, and he's coming home soon.' And then we'll all be together again. So here is a kiss for Michael, a kiss for Mommy, and a big kiss for Shira. Now, children, that's enough for this time. I want to talk now to Mommy for rather a long time. So give her a kiss, blow me a kiss, and let Mommy listen to the rest of this very quietly. Okay? Bye, bye. See you soon. Bye, Michael. Bye, Shira. Bye, bye."

From Sydney, Australia, I sent a tape that began, "Hello, everybody. . . . This morning I had the enormous pleasure of hearing the wonderful tapes you all made at the birthday party. I tell you, it is just wonderful to sit here and hear all your voices. I could just see you sitting there, I could see the room, I could see everybody urging everybody else on and giggling and the microphone going off and on, and—Shira, you sounded wonderful. And I'm so glad you spoke to me and told me about everything and about the birthday party and about all your presents. How are you doing with the alphabet now? I hope you're getting used to it. It's very important, because it'll help you to learn how to spell words and to read. And then you'll be able to read my letters and write to me, too. I'd like that, wouldn't you? And it was so wonderful to hear Michael say 'Daddy' for the first time, clearly, even with everybody prompting him. . . . Shira, really, after all the presents I got you, you weren't satisfied and you talked about the watch. Now, Puchikl . . . we'll see. I'm not promising to bring you a real watch, because you're still only five. Five-year-old girls are big girls, but they're not quite ready for real watches. You know, real watches are pretty big, and they don't look nice on a small girl's hand. Your hand has to be a little bit bigger, so that the watch will look right. All the watches that are small enough to look right on your hand are just pretend watches. And that's why Daddy didn't get one so far. But I was happy to hear all your voices, and Granny and Babushka. . . . I was waiting for these tapes, I can't tell you. I've played them both through three times each. Just to listen and hear everybody talking and hear about all the events that happened. I tell you, it was such a pleasure to me. . . . I kiss you all and I miss you all and I wish we were all together in New York, and we will be before too long, because the time is passing awfully quickly."

Then, with the children out of the room, I told Vera how the tapes were really worthwhile, and I was happy to hear all the news about everything. "I have been working like crazy. The reason I delayed writing to you was that I was just flat-out every single day, with either doing rehearsals or the concerts or traveling. And the last couple of days in Sydney I simply pooped out. I was so tired I had to take time off. . . . I've gotten a little overtired with all these things to do and to rehearse and to play and to go to. And yesterday, when I really wanted to rest, I had to go to [a party at] the America Club. . . . And, in the evening, the American consul general gave a very posh dinner party, black tie and all . . . in my honor. It was one of those affairs that I couldn't get out of. As a consequence, I get tired, because it's constant running around. . . . Tomorrow I have to play a recital in Melbourne. The following morning, we leave early for the island of Tasmania, to play a recital. I get back the following day, Friday. I have a rehearsal with the Melbourne Symphony in the afternoon, play two concerti with them on Saturday. Sunday I go to Adelaide. I rehearse there Monday, play Tuesday, and Wednesday I fly to Perth. So, you see, this is not too easy a schedule. In fact, I'm averaging more than four recitals a week. With rehearsals and traveling and all the other things going on, it really keeps me hopping just a bit.

"Darling, I started a long letter to you, to answer all your points. Unfortunately, I got tired and I couldn't finish it. . . . I'm going to finish it in Melbourne tomorrow or the next day. And then I'll send it to you from there. I'm sorry not to have kept in touch with you for the last few days, but it's really been very hectic. I'm trying my best to keep track of everything. I had a secretary in here and got all the major mail out of the way. . . . Everything is cleaned out, in the business sense. And I will send copies to you of these things as I go along, so you'll know exactly what's going on and be informed. . . .

"To hear Michael say his first word, I tell you, was such a thrill. I played it for Shura [Zakin] this afternoon, and he grinned like a Cheshire cat. . . . I want to tell you how happy I was to get the tapes and what it means to me. There is nothing that we can do that keeps us closer than this, because I close my eyes and I'm sitting next to you and I can hear the whole thing. And that's the thing that's most important to me."

I did the next tape in Adelaide. "Hello, everybody. Hello. . . . We're playing [two concerti] in a huge auditorium that holds about three thousand people. . . . But let's forget about this for the moment. First, I want to say hello to everybody and to kiss you all and tell you how terribly much I miss you. . . . I've been a little bit despondent. . . . Shiritchka, I love to hear you talk on these tapes and to tell me everything and to talk about school and what you're doing and what parties you had for your birthday and what's going on with Michael and with Granny and with Babushka and generally how you feel and what you're learning in school and how your alphabet is going. And, by the way, how's your French? *Tu parles le français maintenant? Tu comprends?* I hope you can answer and say '*Oui, Papa*' when I come home, because you know, we'd love to hear you speak in French, too, and we hope you'll be able to speak very soon with Mommy and Daddy. . . . I hold you in my arms, in a way of speaking, and I kiss you and I wish you well and I hope we'll be together very, very soon and have lots of fun together."

Then, continuing on the tape, I said, "I must tell you something very peculiar. I got into such a trough of depression three or four days ago. I don't know what it was. You see friends and have a gay time here and there. We were going out and having dinner and lunch, as the case may be. . . . But with all this, I got tired of speaking to people. . . . I feel sort of useless, because there's so much that I want to be involved in again, and be a part of . . . our lives back in New York. And I feel so cut off. And, musically, I can't say that this is a very exciting tour. . . . So that any kind of excitement that I would have ordinarily playing a tour is already over with, and I'm just waiting to play the string out. . . . I don't want to sound too pompous or snobbish about it . . . but I'm a little bit tired of the whole business. . . . Playing four and five times a week, with rehearsals and traveling and packing and unpacking and the official receptions and the interviews and so forth, it's just a wear and tear, and I can't catch up. This is the first week I can begin to see a little daylight, and I'm just going to sleep and practice, do nothing but practice

Stravinsky and sleep, because I feel useless otherwise. Fortunately in Perth I'll have a little more time. I've refused all social invitations. I got about four or five different ones, and I sent letters out and said I will not accept any official or social engagements in advance. . . . If I have an hour free and I feel all right, and someone wants to have a cup of tea or a boy wants to play for me, I'll see how I feel at the moment. But I'm not making any more engagements in advance. I want to have time for myself. It really gets to be too much, and I'm just plain tired. . . .

"Abby Simon heard a young Polish boy, about ten, twelve years old, named Helfgott . . . in Perth, and is very excited about this talent. He thinks he's first-rate. They want me to hear him and see what can be done. They claim that this is really a rare talent and that he doesn't know beans about the piano yet, but that he has a spark and needs encouragement and support. So I'll see what happens when I get out there. . . . So much for my activities."

Business affairs took up the rest of the tape, which then ended with "By the way, those pictures . . . I carry all of them in my wallet all the time. Since when is Michael so attracted to the piano? He looked so serious at it! He looked as if he was really trying to do something on there. And the way he stands up. . . . It's a joy to see him. I wonder if he'll know me at all. We'll all have to learn to get used to each other again now. When I start talking about the kids, I just can't tell you how I would like to crush them in my arms and hold them and to be with you and to hold you and be near you. Ah, this is a long way away, I tell you. I better not get onto that subject or I'll start to feel bad again. Anyway, I do feel much better now. . . . So I'll finish this now. I've just finished another three-hour rehearsal this morning, and I have to play the two concerti tonight. It's two-thirty in the afternoon and I haven't had any lunch yet, and I'm still in my wet rehearsal clothes. I have to get back and try and get into shape for tonight again. And tomorrow morning, I have to pack, and a very good violinist is coming to play for me. Twelve noon I have to go to the conservatory and make a speech to the students and listen to the student orchestra, and then take the plane in the afternoon to Perth, arriving there late in the evening. So I'll finish this now. I send my love to you and to the children, to both

Mammas. . . . Tell them I remember them, and soon I'll be back, and it'll be just as if I was never gone."

Recently, in Vermont, I watched my now grown youngest son, David, down on his knees in a small bathroom, lovingly and carefully bathing his about-to-be-two-year-old daughter. Her little playthings were in the tub, and he was soaping her while she gleefully splashed around. Suddenly she noticed that if she put her hands down very fast in the water, it splashed up—and that was wonderful! She started splashing, and David got completely wet. And all he did was smile!

This is a kind of tenderness that I now regret not having been able to experience. In hindsight, it's probable that with thoughtful, special effort, I could—should—have done something more along those lines in the time that we did have together.

NINETEEN

*I*T IS ASTONISHING to what degree performing artists are clasped to the bosoms of people everywhere. And if you don't exploit that generosity wrongly, it becomes a tremendous personal, private wealth. I'm very grateful to be a musician. Sometimes, when I'm onstage, I feel this wonderful sense of joy at being able to play. I feel blessed. It's extraordinary to have spent a lifetime making people enjoy themselves, and gaining a collective warmth and friendship that has lasted over decades. To be wanted and useful is the ultimate fulfillment for any artist. That's the greatest satisfaction an artist can have.

I am very fortunate to be a musician. It's nice to have all the success. One appreciates being lauded and applauded and embraced. It reminds me of a story told about Serge Koussevitzky. After a performance, an elderly, blue-haired lady came backstage and said to him, "Maestro, there is no one like you, you are unique." He said, "Thank you, I know." Another elderly lady said, "You are the greatest conductor." He said, "It's possible." A third one said, "Maestro, you are God!" And Koussevitzky said, "Yes, but such a responsibility!"

For me, success brought with it all sorts of responsibilities.

The fight to save Carnegie Hall, for example, did not end with the passing and signing of the necessary legislation and the acquisition of the building by the city of New York. The hall had to become viable financially and culturally in order to justify its continued existence. To that end, I took six months off from touring and went into the hall nearly every day, tending to matters that had to do with the board of directors, building renovations, fund-raising, innovations in programming. I did not involve myself in the selection of artists who would perform on our stage; to have done otherwise would have ensnared me in an unending and unendurable conflict of interest. Over the years, I have scrupulously left that responsibility to the executive director.

A program innovation for which I was responsible occurred in 1964. It was occasioned by a mournful event: Pierre Monteux died in the summer of that year. His passing marked the loss of a major figure in the music of our time, and a terrible personal loss for me. He had asked me to play what was going to be his last concert before retiring from active touring in London, and to repeat the Brahms concerto, which we had played the first time we were onstage together, in 1937. I suggested that a concert by the London Symphony Orchestra scheduled for October at the hall become a Monteux memorial concert and be used to set up a Monteux Memorial Fund at Carnegie Hall.

Monteux's favorite contemporary pianist, Rudolf Serkin, agreed to play. Leopold Stokowski conducted. The great contralto Maureen Forrester sang an aria from Bach's *St. Matthew Passion,* with the Rutgers University Choir, directed by F. Austin Walter. Casals flew in to share conducting honors with Stokowski. I played the Chausson *Poème.* It was very fitting somehow for me to have been able to arrange a concert in Monteux's memory at Carnegie Hall.

I must add here that my teacher Naoum Blinder died the following year, at the age of seventy-six. He was almost blind in his last years. Unable to see music scores anymore, he could play only from memory. It was very difficult for him toward the end. Losing Pierre Monteux and Naoum Blinder was deeply saddening to me—they had both been so intimately involved with the beginning and, indeed, the developmental fabric of my life.

At times my sense of responsibility for Carnegie Hall led to some unexpected consequences. Artists who appeared in the hall seemed instinctively to know where to address complaints. The nagging problems that afflicted our new air-conditioning system caused Eugene Ormandy to write to me, in early 1966, that during a recent performance of the Philadelphia Orchestra at the hall, he had the feeling twice that he would collapse on the stage. Apparently, it had been 88 degrees outside and 100 degrees in the hall. "I made a decision," he wrote, "that I refuse to die on the stage of Carnegie Hall during a concert." And he requested that his name be removed from any Carnegie Hall concerts beginning next season until such time as the air-conditioning functioned effectively. My response to him acknowledged that we had a problem that entailed "an extensive re-engineering of our air-conditioning system which I will try to get through." And I added, "When we meet in February I will tell you about some exciting new plans that we have for the Hall in general." Indeed, he came back as originally scheduled.

One's feeling of responsibility rarely is able to stop at the frontiers of a single enterprise. In 1965, I was appointed by President Johnson to the newly established National Council on the Arts. That same year, I accepted the presidency of the America-Israel Cultural Foundation, which was a reincarnation of the Norman Fund, established by music lovers to rescue Jewish musicians from Europe, resettle them in Palestine, and help create a symphony orchestra there; the America-Israel Cultural Foundation, set up in 1957, assisted performing and creative artists. At the same time, I was playing an average of eight or nine concerts a month, as a soloist and with the trio. All that responsibility was leaving me with very little time even for sleeping.

A toll was finally exacted. I had never yet canceled a concert. I'd played with a fever of 103 degrees. I'd played in Australia after having stomach poisoning and finding myself unconscious on the floor. I'd played in Israel after fainting from dehydration. I played! That was my life. But in October 1966, I came down with an unexpected virus attack that kept me home. It took a major act not of my volition to force the first cancellation I'd ever had in thirty-one years on the stage. By November, I was completely recovered and back on my regular schedule.

I HAVE FELT a strong bond with Israel ever since my first tour there shortly after the 1948 War of Independence. Not quite two decades later, in the spring of 1967, came the tense weeks of Arab threats and the Egyptian blockade of Israel. It seemed certain that another Holocaust was about to ensue, this time to the people of Israel. Then the conflict, now known as the Six-Day War, broke out. During the early days of fighting, the trio was preparing to record the Ravel trio, but our minds were not on the music. Eugene, Lennie, and I found ourselves spending more time watching the television reporting of the war than recording Ravel. Finally, we gave up and just watched television.

While the war was still being fought, I decided to fly to Israel. I was scheduled to play a concert at The Hague, and I cabled the Dutch Orchestra, saying that circumstances in the Middle East made it impossible for me to appear. They cabled back that they understood perfectly. I then flew to Paris, where, with the help of Israeli embassy officials, I was able to get on an El Al flight to Israel. On board with me were Israeli Air Force pilots and tank commanders, reservists, collected from various parts of Europe.

The war was virtually over by the time I got to Israel. I found Jerusalem incredibly changed. Much of the rubble of war had been cleared away, and the city was now a major metropolis, with a far greater sense of its uniqueness than before. In the narrow streets and little alleys of the Old City I saw the way the people lived, and I realized that the Israelis were now confronted by a problem of such frightening complexity that I wondered how they would ever work out a way of coexisting with the Arabs.

I offered to play in the hospitals for the wounded. It was impossible to have a piano moved into the various wards, so I simply took the fiddle and walked from ward to ward. I remember playing for several soldiers who had been burned in tank fires. I'd play some Bach, some Mozart, some Kreisler—just a few lines of each—and sometimes I'd ask in a whisper what they would like to hear. A group of doctors and nurses began to follow me through the wards, listening to the music and watching the reactions of the soldiers. On another day, I went to play for soldiers who were hospitalized in a facility originally built for severely handicapped children. The corridors were small, and all around were little carts with wheels that the children used to push themselves along the floor. Among those adorable children, with smiles on their faces despite their handicaps, were wounded soldiers in jerry-rigged rooms, lying on cots with medical apparatus next to their heads. It remains very special to me, the memory of having been able to bring some peace to them, if only for a few minutes.

We had settled into the new Orchestra House, a two-story stucco building located in the Tel Aviv suburb of Ramat Gan. There were staff offices, reception rooms, and large rehearsal rooms, as well as a kitchen. Eugene Istomin and the conductor Josef Krips had also come to Israel and were staying in the last two rooms. Large portraits of Toscanini, Rubinstein, and Huberman hung on the walls; all three had played major roles, together with William Steinberg, in founding the Palestine Symphony (now Israel Philharmonic) Orchestra.

I took a trip to the north and rode up to the newly captured Golan Heights and along the entire Israel-Syria border area. We drove through the West Bank, former Jordanian territory, and saw seemingly endless rows of Russian and British tanks and half tracks, smashed or captured, and hundreds of tanks and burned-out pillboxes and fortifications. We flew down the Sinai Peninsula to Sharm-al-Sheikh and from there went on to the Suez Canal. Miles of destroyed vehicles littered the desert. I had the sick feeling that some giant had stepped on them. Just as we were about to take off from Kantara in our helicopter, a sortie by the Egyptians took place twenty miles north of us, a prelude to two days of fighting. But we did not notice it, nor were we told anything, and learned of it only afterward.

Lenny Bernstein and I gave a concert on Mount Scopus that became much celebrated; it was the first concert to mark the retaking of Old Jerusalem, and it was played under the worst of conditions. For the first half of the concert, a hot sun blazed on the stage. During the entire concert, a strong desert wind blew dust into everyone's eyes, onto my fiddle, inside my fiddle, between my fingers. Music stands fell over. In the distance, mines were being detonated by army engineers. In the front row were David Ben-Gurion, Golda Meir, Moshe Sharett, Yitzhak Rabin, Moshe Dayan, the president of the Supreme Court, and many other high officials in the Israeli government. Despite the difficulties, the concert on Mount Scopus was a deeply moving experience for me, and when it was over, I was thankful to have taken part in it.

By the end of July, I'd played sixteen concerts with the Israel Philharmonic Orchestra, three with Lenny Bernstein, four with Josef Krips, and nine with a young Israeli conductor named Eliyahu Inbal. And I'd given six master classes.

Israel was a transformed nation, proud of its swift, decisive victory, sobered by the war's cost. Many had lost family members or had seriously wounded friends. The country faced enormous problems with the absorption and administration of about one million Arabs in the newly occupied territories. There were no clear answers.

EARLIER that year, I'd been urged by some people in the United States to cancel my scheduled appearance in Athens that summer. The new government of Greece, which had taken power by force, was dictatorial, anti-Semitic, and anti-Israel. From Israel I cabled the Athens Festival that "extraordinary circumstances" urgently necessitated my remaining in Israel, and I was therefore canceling my appearance.

To a good friend in the Soviet Union, Vladimir Bony, I wrote from Israel that I'd been looking forward with much pleasure and anticipation to coming back to Moscow in October for a week's visit and two or three concerts, but the recent position taken by the Soviet Union during the Middle East war—rabid anti-Israel speeches in the United Nations; breaking diplomatic relations with Israel—made it impossible for me to play in the Soviet Union at this time.

I canceled my visit to Budapest, scheduled for September. To Dr. Fizdo, the concert manager there, I wrote that the official position taken by the Hungarian government vis-à-vis Israel during the recent Middle East conflict made it awkward, if not impossible, for me to maintain the warm relationship with colleagues and public that was so necessarily a part of my life in music. I added that, as an American, I was taking this action completely on an individual basis, and on my own initiative. No representative of Israel had ever suggested, I wrote in the letter, either officially or unofficially, that I take this step. I made it clear that my action was the result of the very close personal and professional ties I'd had with Israelis for the last nineteen years and that I was concerned with the problems that concerned them.

I went to Switzerland with the family for a while, giving me an opportunity to recuperate from the arduous past weeks. Then Zakin joined me, and we began our autumn tour.

I played at the Tonhalle in Zurich that September. In the audience was Ellen Weyl, the mother of Hans Baer, my oldest and most stalwart friend in Switzerland. Hans and I had met the first time I went to Switzerland, in 1949, to play in Zurich. He is a strapping six-foot-three, with the kind of build that would have made him a natural basketball forward, and is one of the most respected members of Switzerland's banking system. He and his wife, Ilse, have long been involved with the cultural life in Zurich. Ellen Weyl, a superb though nonprofessional sculptor, returned home after the concert and, working through the night from memory, fashioned a magnificent fourteen-inch-high bronze sculpture of my head with a violin. She had it carefully packaged, and sent it by boat to my home in New York.

While the sculpture was slowly making its way across the Atlantic, Zakin and I, having completed our European tour, flew back to New York, arriving in mid-September. Two weeks later, we left for a tour in Japan, Korea, Hong Kong, Okinawa, Guam, and Honolulu.

In the meantime, the sculpture arrived in Brooklyn, one day after the start of a dock strike. It sat in the boat for several weeks. The boat was then moved to a dock in Manhattan. Finally, the sculpture was cleared through customs and placed in a prominent location in my apartment, with a spotlight on it. The children were astonished and delighted to see their itinerant troubadour of a father looking so alive in front of them. A second cast of this sculpture is now in the Shorin Club Room at Carnegie Hall.

THE TOUR of Asia and the Pacific islands was fascinating, though fatiguing. I loved that part of the world, its customs and its beauty. Now I had to face the realities of the next tour in the United States and the preparations for yet another tour in Europe. By the last week of January, I was back on the road.

The few weeks I had spent at home, living a little more normally than usual with my family, helped convince me that I needed to get a degree of order in my travel and playing plans in the years to come. I resolved that I would travel six months of the year and take only those concerts that I knew would give me musical pleasure, rather than blindly accepting a fully booked tour. It took a bit of doing to convince my managers that this was the way I wanted my tours handled.

In the final days of January, I played Beethoven and Franck sonatas at a recital in Houston with Zakin, and Lalo's *Symphonie Espagnol* at a concert in St. Louis with the St. Louis Symphony Orchestra. On the evening of February 1, while playing a recital in Boulder, Colorado, I suddenly felt that something was very wrong. Friends in Denver who were doctors immediately gave me some tests and told me that they didn't like what they'd seen; there was a real possibility of a major problem occurring soon. They urged me to return to New York, accompanied by a nurse. I did as they asked and walked into New York Hospital, where I was met by Dr. Rees Pritchett, head of cardiology. He admitted me into the hospital for observation, and it was there that the actual heart attack occurred. I passed out on the floor. Luckily, Dr. Pritchett was ten feet away, down the corridor. It was a minor attack, but it did some damage. Pinchas Zukerman replaced me on the tour—as I had, in times past, replaced Heifetz when he canceled a concert in Cleveland, and Milstein when he took ill.

I was recovering at home when I came down with a rather violent case of the flu that resulted in serious pulmonary complications and another stay in the hospital. It was then that I decided to take the full advice of my doctors. Weeks of rest followed; I lost thirty pounds; I stopped smoking. I had a chance to be at home with my family over a longer period than at any time in the past ten years. It all turned into a blessing in disguise.

By mid-April, I was feeling better than I'd felt in twenty years, and on April 27, I returned to full concert activity, setting out for a month-long tour with the trio. Touring once again, I felt truly marvelous and enjoyed myself immensely. For stage people, returning to the stage is like coming home. That was where I belonged; that was where I felt best. On May 10, we played in Carnegie Hall.

I canceled a couple of concerts in England with the Israel Philharmonic Orchestra because it would have meant an overnight flight immediately after the last concert with the trio in California, and plunging directly into a performance. Responsibility for my own well-being dictated that I no longer engage in that kind of hectic activity. I intended to continue playing concerts for the coming thirty years rather than the next thirty days.

OVER THE DECADES, the single object I've felt the greatest responsibility for has been my fiddle. It's been a part of my very being; I've loved it. During a tour, I'd hold it, play it, guard it in a very special way. After a tour, I'd always have it cared for by a leading luthier.

Flying with my fiddle rarely presented a problem, until the year an FAA regulation suddenly made it impossible for me to hold it on my lap during takeoffs and landings. Flight attendants on Delta, Trans World, and Western airlines began to insist that I abide by the new regulation and place the fiddle in the overhead bin. (If memory serves, the bins in those years were open, not closed as they are today. One can safely and comfortably put a violin case there now.) The vision of my fiddle slipping and sliding back and forth in that bin, or surrounded and mercilessly pummeled by other bags, was intolerable. The attendants insisted there was nothing they could do about it: during takeoffs and landings, the fiddle had to be either overhead or in one of the crowded compartments in the front of the plane.

In early 1968, I wrote to the three airlines, asking that an exception to the FAA regulation be made in my case. To my joy, dispensations arrived from all three. While recuperating from the heart attack and the flu, I wrote to the airlines and expressed my appreciation to them for their understanding and cooperation. Having benefited from my sense of responsibility, my fiddle continued to experience takeoffs and landings while resting comfortably on my lap.

Other matters were not so easy to resolve. The year 1968 was a difficult time in the United States: civil rights and anti–Vietnam War demonstrations, unrest on college campuses, riots in many cities. Sometimes I was called upon to explain my country to friends in Europe, and in a letter to one I wrote that not all America was in a state of revolution, with armed battles tearing our cities apart. I admitted there were some terrible difficulties, there had been looting, forty to fifty people had been killed. But there were 22 million blacks in the United States, I wrote, and those who rioted and looted were not more than a tiny fraction of our 250 million citizens. There was much destruction, but two or three blocks can look like an entire city on television. Unfortunately, the violence occurred in the poorer neighborhoods where the unthinking, the young, the hoodlums, and the uneducated did more to hurt themselves than anyone else. There was no minimizing the danger or gravity of this time, I went on, and we hoped only that people of good will on all sides would learn a lesson and work together for some useful purpose now.

Demonstrations in the United States and convulsions in Europe were mirrored, at least to some extent, by conflicts I was experiencing that summer between my sense of responsibility to myself and to my audience. I had resolved to choose with great care where I would be playing in the future. As it turned out, that resolve proved difficult to realize.

In mid-August, one of the managers at the Hurok agency, Walter Prude, wrote to me in London, saying that they had "holds for the Portland, Maine symphony and Wichita Falls, Texas symphony." Did I want to keep to my ruling of "no more regional orchestras," or would I accept these? Apparently, someone at the agency had committed me to those dates as early as the previous spring, before being advised that I did not wish to accept orchestras in this category. Would I agree to these two exceptions? The agency would promise not to accept any further such engagements without my approval. In that same letter, Mr. Prude expressed concern over the weight I'd put on, and pleaded with me to take seriously the matter of my diet.

I wrote him back, stating that the business about the two "regional orchestras" was an embarrassment. We had discussed not doing such concerts much earlier than last spring, and I couldn't understand how the agency could have made such an error. I wanted the agency people to know that such concerts involved "a heavy burden of massive disinterest on my part." I added that if the dates should turn out to be a really serious problem to get out of, I would do them. But with great reluctance.

I was aware of the importance of bringing music into all corners of the country. For years I had played with passion to audiences in towns large and small. But I thought it was time now to let the younger violinists, who were at the start of their careers, play with those orchestras. I had honed my skills and cut my eyeteeth playing with orchestras like that during the developmental years of my career. I felt that that time had passed and that others should take advantage of the same possibilities to start to learn their craft under direct fire. I was beginning to realize that my span of years was not infinite, nor was my strength endless. I no longer wanted to give up time that I could use more profitably at home or under better auspices. I did not play in Portland and Wichita Falls.

Nor did I accept the invitation to play in the Soviet Union that was extended to me after the summer of 1968, the summer of the Soviet invasion of Czechoslovakia. That refusal had nothing to do with "provincial orchestras" and everything to do with international cold war geopolitics. In an interview I gave in Stockholm that fall, just before my evening concert, I said that events in Czechoslovakia had released a chain of passive defense among artists. "Recently, it was the Russian pianist Emil Gilels in Oslo. The orchestra refused to play. The Polish conductor Semkov was in Copenhagen. The orchestra refused to play. In all likelihood, a spontaneous 'freezing out' of Soviet artists has started." I pointed out that the first artists who had played within the framework of cultural exchange between the Soviet Union and the United States, based on the agreement signed by Eisenhower and Khrushchev in Geneva in 1954, were looked upon as having been hired by the politicians of the two Great Powers. But the fact was that we, the artists, weren't there because we felt that friendly relations had suddenly been established between the CIA and the KGB, but because we had the feeling that, as artists, we were standing on a narrow bridge of understanding. Speaking for myself, I had contradictory reactions. On the one hand, I told myself that I, Isaac Stern, should not take part in political actions like "good-will concerts." At the same time, I also told myself, "Isaac Stern, can you afford to do without the narrow bridge, the medium of contact?" In the end, an old truth worked: relationships among governments are not the same as relationships among human beings.

Czechoslovakia set our two countries back fifteen years. I simply couldn't bring myself to play in the Soviet Union—not as a demonstration against the Soviet Union but as a sign of solidarity with the Czechs. It was seldom the case that music entered politics, but often politics entered music. Though I would not then play in the Soviet Union, I hoped that the indignation among the Soviet authorities over my two cancellations—after the Six-Day War and after the invasion of Czechoslovakia—would pass in time, as all politically motivated high feelings eventually do, and the narrow bridge, the cultural relations, connecting our two countries would be rebuilt.

I returned to the United States at the end of October and, after a few days, began a tour that lasted until late December: Paris, Milan, Rome, Florence, Teheran. Days went by and so did concerts, one after another. Then an American tour, starting in early January. Then, again, a European tour: London, Lisbon, Madrid, Barcelona, Zurich, Brussels, Paris. After a restful July, I was back in Europe. And then on tour in the United States. We were by then one of the highest-paid groups in classical music.

Eugene, Lennie, and I were planning to take the trio on a world tour in 1970, in honor of Beethoven's bicentennial year. We had decided to make our own Beethoven festival, on a worldwide basis, playing all thirty-one piano chamber works. We would be in Buenos Aires, in Israel, at the Edinburgh Festival, in Paris, Zurich, and New York. No other group, at least in our opinion, was as well-equipped as we to do justice to this literature, both in the power to project the sonatas and in the unique identity of the trio. We also planned to record everything by the end of September 1970, so the music could be released in time for the New York concert and for Christmas.

In late December 1969, the trio greeted the new decade with a concert at Carnegie Hall. At the time, I was troubled by pain I'd been experiencing in one of my hands, which two doctors had diagnosed as nonrheumatoid arthritis, the result of either overwork or strain from carrying the violin or a bag, and which was being treated with paraffin baths and a mild dosage of painkillers prior to performances.

Also of concern to me were events in Argentina. The dictatorship there had instituted complete censorship over all the arts. I wondered about the trio's responsibility for the arts and whether, perhaps, we should be thinking twice about honoring our commitment to play in Buenos Aires that June.

TWENTY

*I*N THE SUMMER of 1970, I celebrated my fiftieth birthday and my thirty-fifth year as a concert artist. I'd been playing the violin from the age of eight; I'd appeared on the stage as a professional performer since turning fifteen.

A musician spends an entire lifetime discovering that no matter how much one has played, no matter how much one has worked, there is always more to find and more to learn. For a young musician, though, there are times when one is better off not knowing what lies ahead. At my first big concert, all I knew was that everything around me seemed exciting and my job was to concentrate and do my very best. One is helped on those early occasions by not having had enough experience to know how dangerous things can be. The older you get, however, the more you know; the more you know, the more demands you make upon yourself; the more you demand of yourself, the more you realize how much there is still to learn as a musician. Also, the older you get, the greater the likelihood that you'll find yourself caught up in matters that are not at the very heart of music itself, but without which it would be difficult, if not impossible, to live the life of a musician.

Early in the 1970s, I found myself deeply involved in the suddenly changing destiny of the concert organization that had been managing my career. The relationship I enjoyed with the Hurok organization was, almost from its inception, a deeply personal one: first, between me and Sol Hurok; and with Mae Frohman, before she died; and with Walter Prude, Shelley Gold, and Martin Feinstein. It was not like a business office. We not only worked together, we also ate and drank together; we were a large family.

Walter Prude was a very good-looking, elegant, graceful man from a fine family. He smoked cigarettes endlessly and liked to have a drink or two from time to time. He was the major figure in the Hurok organization, particularly at those times when Hurok didn't want it to be perceived as especially Jewish in character. Walter's wife was the famous choreographer Agnes de Mille, who gave to ballet a uniquely American flavor that it had never before achieved. He provided a distinctive touch of class to the organization and was quite effective in its dealings with ecumenical groups. And Shelley Gold was a bright and sensitive humanist, as well as a tough, knowledgeable music-business professional. He cared deeply for his artists and was easy to talk to about supporting new young talent.

At some point in the early 1970s, General Electric made an offer to acquire the Hurok organization. Hurok was getting along in age and wanted financial security. He had made and lost many fortunes over the decades, and now was at a time in his life when he wanted a safety net. A pet statement of his in those days, which he claimed to have heard from General Electric people, was "Expand or suspend." As he was in no position to expand his organization, because of his age and waning health, he felt that by accepting the life buoy offered him by General Electric, he would gain a measure of security and leave the possibilities of expansion to others.

I was aware of the negotiations between Hurok and General Electric and was very upset at the prospect of having the personal relationship I'd enjoyed with the Hurok organization for so many years dissolve into the soulless atmosphere of a major corporation. For all of us who played and performed, and for Hurok as well, making music was a way of life. I was appalled at the thought of possibly having to deal with people who'd never had anything to do with the world of music, who looked at music as a business and cared only for the periodic bottom line. My loyalty was to Hurok, and only to him. I did not want to give General Electric the right to my services.

In the end, however, after lengthy negotiations, General Electric did not acquire the Hurok organization.

In March 1974, Sol Hurok died suddenly of a heart attack while walking along a New York street. I played at his funeral service at

Carnegie Hall, one of the most difficult moments of my life. All but the uppermost tier of the 2,800-seat hall was filled with mourners from the world of music. Flowers covered his coffin, and when I finished playing, I walked over and put my hand on it. I had lost a second father.

At that time, I could have moved to any of the major managements, had I wanted to. But I stayed for a while with the so-called Hurok office after it was taken over by Maynard Goldman, who ran it briefly and badly. I finally left in 1976. There was a hiatus of a year or two when I remained without management and was playing out the tours previously arranged for me by the Hurok organization. Then Shelley Gold decided to pick up the pieces and reconstruct the Hurok office, and I rejoined it when International Creative Management bought it and made it an ICM division.

When Shelley Gold began the job of rebuilding the Hurok office, he called me. At that time, Lee Lamont, who'd had a lot of experience in the music world, was working as my assistant. Gold said, "Isaac, I know that Lee works for you and keeps everything in order for you, but I need her to restart the office. She knows the business, and I need her as an executive." I said, "Of course, there's no question." So she became an officer of the corporation and ended up, after the sudden tragic death of Shelley Gold, as the president of ICM Artists, Ltd., where she's now chairman of the board.

I'd met Lee Lamont when she was working in the Hurok office as an assistant to George Perper. For me, she'd been someone who was always there. She was formidable, imaginative, discerning, intuitive about certain things. She knew where the music business came from and how it worked. She had particularly good business relationships all through Asia. She worked hard, dressed neatly, traveled constantly, smoked incessantly. She drank twelve to fourteen cups of coffee a day and little alcohol. Her husband was a very active guitarist and club player in popular music. She was in her early forties when she joined Shelley Gold in his effort to rebuild the Hurok organization, and with both of them in leadership positions, I returned to the ex-Hurok, now ICM management team, where I've remained to this day.

A MUSICIAN who is married and cares about his family will likely find himself involved in matters that might seem, at first glance, even more distant from music than management and corporate maneuvering. During a period between tours, in 1971, I had a chance to take apart and digest my plans and dates for the remainder of 1971 and all of 1972. I was home for the Passover Festival that April and enjoyed a happy weekend with the children, talking, playing, and being very close together. It became clear to me that the next two or three years would be of utmost importance to them and to me as far as our life together was concerned. It was not only a matter of a few vacation weeks in the summer and again at the end of the year; more important was my personal participation in their problems and their day-to-day routine during the school months, and my presence at meetings, from time to time, with their teachers. Those formative years, I realized, would never come again, and a few concerts more or less in that crucial period of two or three years would make no material difference to my career.

I knew only too well the problems of my colleagues and the tragedy of their children's lives, when those vital years had been sacrificed to the needs or selfish desires of the parents—and then one day those same parents asked themselves, "What happened?" I was determined that would not occur in my case.

Conversations with the children made it evident that the middle of November of that year was a particularly important period, with school examinations, teachers' meetings, and some important decisions about their future education. In all good conscience, and given my feelings for my children, I could not leave all that to Vera alone, and I resolved to do something I'd never done before. In a letter dated April 13, 1971, to Michael Rainer of the Organisation Artistique International in Paris, I wrote:

> I have . . . decided to curtail a part of the already planned concerts in the latter half of November, specifically Rome, Venice and London. You do not have to tell me how difficult

this is.... I must ask this be done now. I do not intend to pull any fake illnesses at the last moment.... You will understand this is not a decision come to lightly—I have been struggling with it for some days. The biggest job was to put myself in perspective and to realize that I, music, concerts, all this will continue without much change whether I play a little more or less until the children have entered early adulthood and begun to form their own lives. The real difference will be that I will be happier as a man and therefore as a musician. And my children, in a world full of dreadful pressures today, may be able to use this time as a basis for family life for decades to come.

About one month later, Zakin and I began a tour that took us to Spain, Australia, New Zealand, and England. In London, I took part in the recording of the sound track for the film version of *Fiddler on the Roof*. Those three days were truly a labor of love, because I adored the musical. What a wonderful time I had using the violin to provide the background for that touching and beautiful story!

THAT JULY and August, the family and I found ourselves in a heavenly situation. The flutist Jean-Pierre Rampal, who owned a house on the island of Corsica, had suggested that I rent a house there. The house I took had ample bedrooms, a kitchen, a dining room, and also, as with all houses there of a certain quality, covered porches to catch what cool air came through in the night or early morning. The place was constantly bathed in sunlight. A lot of open space made for breezeways, which were essential, as the days were beastly hot and there was no air-conditioning. And as the local water was of dubious quality, we drank tonic water from morning till night—we consumed crates of tonic water. Good tennis courts. Local television. If you had a fairly decent radio, you could pick up shortwave broadcasts. That was my first real rest in almost three years. A tranquil spot, the air full of wild mint and eucalyptus, mountains behind us and to the sides, and an unpolluted Mediterranean Sea in front.

There was no telephone in the house. Considering the way I normally lived with that instrument—a half dozen or more in proximity; talking constantly to people all over the world—its absence was a problem. One had to make an appointment in the village post office to use the telephone there. The house was on a hill; you needed a car to get to the village. When telephoning, you had to keep in mind the various time zones of the people you wanted to call.

Rampal and his wife, Françoise, lived in a lovely house with his father, a wonderful old man, a native of Marseilles. Rampal was a tall, roly-poly, mischievous elf of a man, one of the most compelling performing artists I've ever known, absolutely passionate about playing and listening to music, involved with the meaning of every note. He virtually created the flute as a solo instrument in the twentieth century: there had been great flutists in the past, but generally they were connected with orchestras in one way or another. Rampal, too, had played in orchestras in his day, but until he came along, no one really had made a complete career as a solo performer standing onstage alone to play recitals, with a piano or a harpsichord accompaniment, let alone to perform concerti with orchestras. He revived an enormous amount of repertoire, particularly from the Baroque period, and sparked the transcription of works from the violin for the flute. Many twentieth-century compositions for the flute were written because of him and for him.

He was an insatiable devourer not only of music but also of food, about which he was very knowledgeable. And he was a fanatical photographer. He owned at least thirty cameras and knew how to use every one of them, and I got the impression that some of his cameras were almost as important to him as his flute.

His wife, a charming, attractive woman and a wonderful housekeeper and cook, had a great sense of humor and much patience for her husband's madnesses. The two of them were the very essence of a good French family.

We had some truly outstanding times that summer. I learned to eat *oursins*, sea urchins that attached themselves to rocks. One day I went with Jean-Pierre and his father down to the bay, where we climbed into a rowboat. We had a flask of Pernod, bottles of ice water, small spoons, three glasses, and some lemon. And goggles and knives. We went out in the boat, put on the goggles, and flung ourselves overboard. With our knives, we removed the sea urchins from the rocks and then returned to the boat, where Jean-Pierre's father cleanly severed the end of each shell, poured Pernod into the glasses, then cut it with the ice water, turning the liquid cloudy. We ate the fresh *oursins* with the small spoons and drank the Pernod in the boat on the water. We were there for hours. I learned how to float facedown on the water with goggles on, searching for the sea urchins. As I floated, my back was steadily exposed to the Mediterranean sun. When I returned home later that day, there was a cross-shaped burn over the whole of my back, which led to huge blisters and a high fever. I was ill for days. But the *oursins* were so good, and the Pernod superb! It had been a wonderful day.

There was plenty for the family to do together: swimming, boating, tennis. One of the strangest experiences we had there that summer was sitting on the balcony of our house in that idyllically self-contained corner of the world and watching on local television the rest of the world tiredly going through its daily routines.

It took a while to slow down my inner motor after so many months without a break. But I couldn't really cut myself off from everything for too long, and so I began to look through the mountain of correspondence I'd brought with me and proceeded to dictate my mail on tapes. I then sent them by airmail to my secretary in New York, who would type the letters and mail them off. In the midst of the swimming and the playing and the good food, and being with the family and the Rampals, I managed to take care of a sizable amount of correspondence.

There was a letter to Sasha Schneider about joining me in Israel at the end of the year to inaugurate a master institute for music-making. There were letters to concert managers in Finland and Australia about past and forthcoming appearances in their countries; to Lennie Rose about the performances of the Istomin-Stern-Rose Trio during the week inaugurating the opening of the Kennedy Center in Washington, D.C.; to an old friend from my San Francisco days, Henry Shweid, turning down a request to play with the San Jose Symphony Orchestra because of previously scheduled recording and television dates. In a letter to Colonel Harold Riegelman, a close New York friend who had helped immeasurably in the fight to save Carnegie Hall eleven years before, I wrote that I was thoroughly enjoying one of the most beautiful vacations I'd had in the past ten years, and that I really did not miss the telephone.

In truth, however, Carnegie Hall was never far away from me, no matter where I might be. In New York, some months before, I'd answered a letter from a gentleman who'd been quite disturbed by the improper grooming he'd observed on the part of certain people attending concerts in the hall, and I'd written saying that I, too, wished that everybody would take the trouble to come to the hall properly groomed. But, I added, we lived in a time when the words "properly groomed" meant different things to different people. I reminded the writer that while it was true that Carnegie Hall was operated by the corporation I headed, it belonged to the city of New York and had to abide by the laws of the city. And in New York, dress was not a basis for exclusion from any public meeting place.

As far away as I was from Carnegie Hall that summer, the place followed me—in the person of its then executive director, Julius Bloom, who came to Corsica for a few days so we could discuss matters relating to the hall. We talked at length—fortified with some good lobster and wine and goat cheese—not only about the development of the property that lay to the east of the hall, but about artistic and aesthetic plans for the coming four or five years.

And then there was the letter I wrote to Henry Kissinger, with a very personal request:

> It has been a long time since we last met. . . . I write you now from Corsica where I am on vacation with my family until the end of August. First and foremost to congratulate you on the extraordinary coup of your visit to China and the immensely able arrangements you made for the forthcoming visit of the President. . . .
>
> Secondly, I ask if it would be at all possible for you to help in a very long cherished desire on my part to visit mainland China and possibly play there. I have been intrigued by this

© *Arnold Newman*

Vol. 43, No. 11 **LIFE** September 9, 1957

A RED TOWER REPLACING CARNEGIE HALL

The building boom that has been making over the old brownstone face of Manhattan with new façades of gleaming aluminum, green glass and copper-tinted steel will reach a new degree of flamboyance in the skyscraper to be erected on the site of Carnegie Hall. When the famous concert place is demolished in 1959, a new office building faced in panels of bright red porcelain will go up in its place. To liven up the effect even more, Architects Pomerance and Breines have offset the building's windows in diagonal instead of vertical rows to produce a strange-looking checkerboard pattern. Set on stilts, sunk in a broad plaza, the $22 million building will rise 44 floors above 57th Street.

All this was saddening news to the music lovers who have come to cherish old Victorian Carnegie Hall. Built as a business venture by Andrew Carnegie, a lover of Scotch bagpipe music, it opened in 1891 with a program partly conducted by Tchaikovsky. It became home for the New York Philharmonic and a magnet for the great musicians of the world. When it is demolished, U.S. music will lose one of its most acoustically perfect halls. But there was some good news for music lovers. As the office building goes up, Carnegie Hall's activities will move to Manhattan's new Lincoln Square cultural center and into a modern auditorium adjoining the new Metropolitan Opera House.

CARNEGIE HALL will offer two more full seasons of concerts and recitals before building is razed.

RED SKYSCRAPER will be reached from the street → level by a foot bridge spanning its sunken plaza.

Life magazine article showing artist's rendering of office tower slated to replace Carnegie Hall, 1957

Isaac Stern, now 38, made his debut with San Francisco orchestra at 11

A Fiddler Saves Carnegie Hall

Just as Wreckers Were About to Demolish New York's Famous Music Hall, Isaac Stern Became Hero of the Hour

Arriving at the gala reopening concert after the restoration of Carnegie Hall in 1986, with Walter Scheuer on the left

*With President and
Mrs. John F. Kennedy . . .*

. . President Lyndon Johnson . . .

*. . . President and
Mrs. Reagan . . .*

*. . . President and
Mrs. George Bush . . .*

*. . . and President
Bill Clinton*

Fiddling around with Charlie Chaplin . . .

. . . and Jack Benny

With Midori and Pinchas Zukerman

With Yo-Yo Ma (at the piano), Emanuel Ax, and Jaime Laredo

Surrounded by fans after a concert in
Philharmonic Hall, Kiev, c. 1956

In Moscow, 1960

In Israel with (clockwise) Leonard Rose, Golda
Meir, Eugene Istomin, David Ben-Gurion, Teddy
Kollek, and Pablo Casals (with pipe)

Backstage at the Jerusalem Theatre
during the Persian Gulf War, 1991

On my seventieth birthday, with Mstislav Rostropovich (in tutu) and Gregory Peck

Yehudi Menuhin, Dietrich Fischer-Dieskau, Mstislav Rostropovich, Vladimir Horowitz, Leonard Bernstein, and me singing the Hallelujah chorus from Handel's Messiah, *at "The Concert of the Century" celebrating the eighty-fifth anniversary of Carnegie Hall, 1976*

Kennedy Center honorees, 1984. I'm sitting with Lena Horne; Gian Carlo Menotti, Arthur Miller, and Danny Kaye stand behind.

With Linda Reynolds Stern at the dedication of the Isaac Stern Auditorium at Carnegie Hall

With my daughter, Shira,
her husband, Don Weber,
and their sons (left to right),
Ari, Eytan, and Noah

*With my son, Michael,
and his wife, Jeanette*

*With my son, David, his
wife, Katta, and their
children, Talia (on
David's lap) and Sophia*

*Coaching young violinists at the
Shanghai Conservatory, 1979*

*A workshop with the Cambiata
String Quartet at Carnegie Hall*

*With Linda , on
our wedding day*

*With Linda in our
garden in Connecticut*

land and its people for many years but the lack of diplomatic relations made direct requests impossible. . . .

No one from the outside can know to what degree contacts of any kind are to be built up between the United States and China in the coming months, but were it possible for me to go, I would do everything to cooperate. . . .

What prompted my letter was the announcement that Dr. Kissinger had been to China and that President Nixon was going there. I knew that China had one of the oldest cultures in the world, with ancient traditions in art, literature, and music; and that, despite the greatness of its culture, its people throughout the centuries had perished by the millions of starvation and at the hands of warlords. Yet that country had somehow turned from bare subsistence into a land where everybody was clothed and housed and fed. It had gone from a country of misery and disunity to one of cohesion and direction, a singular accomplishment of Communist rule. I didn't really think of it as Communist, but as a government authority that made it possible for the Chinese to exist as a people. I was curious to see how that had happened. Only later, when I went there, did I learn that the Long March, which ended with the defeat of the armies of Chiang Kai-shek, created the People's Republic of China, and changed the history of that country, was, in fact, a movement that originally consisted of about four hundred people led by Mao Tse-tung. That the destiny of so many hundreds of millions of people could be changed by a small band of believers fascinated me and made me want to see the country and meet the people.

I had met Henry Kissinger at a White House dinner, where we shared a table. Because we were able to converse with ease and seemed to understand each other, it was natural for me to turn to him for help. I was always interested in being part of the inception of something significant. I had no illusion as to the importance of any role I might have in our new relationship with China; I just wanted to be a part of the beginning of it.

When I returned to New York that September, I had lunch with Dr. Kissinger in Washington, and he told me that it was too early in our

relations with China, and that there were indications of political insta-
bility in the Communist Party there. It was best that, for the time
being, I put aside the idea of going. Henry and Nancy Kissinger
became close friends.

ANOTHER country I did not go to that year—not because I couldn't
but because I didn't want to—was Germany.

My instincts were always to make music in the best way possible and
to use music as a natural gesture between human beings. During all
my decades as a performer, there was only one limit to those instincts,
only one boundary beyond which I would never let them take me: my
unwillingness to play in Germany and Austria. That determination
was reinforced by my visit to Auschwitz in the mid-1960s, and then
reiterated in 1972, in a correspondence with a leading German conductor, Kurt Masur.

Vera and I had talked often about her experiences during the Holocaust: her father arrested in Paris, murdered in Auschwitz; she, her
mother, and her sister hiding in terror from the Germans; her war
years in Sweden. On some of our early trips to Paris, she showed me
where she had attended school, where the Jews were herded together
after the mass arrests in July 1942, where they were brought for ques-
tioning, where they were selected for transport to the death camps.
Our children knew of their mother's wartime experiences; they knew,
too, that my decision not to play in Germany and Austria had preceded my meeting her and had nothing to do with my later knowledge
of her suffering and the terrors she experienced. It was completely my
own personal decision.

When I'd played in Cracow, back in the 1960s, I asked to be taken to
Auschwitz, and I'd met a survivor there, a woman. I didn't speak Polish
or German, her languages, and she didn't speak English or Russian, my
languages. We discovered that we could speak comfortably in French. I
walked through all of Auschwitz with her, room by miserable room.
I recall standing in front of a thirty-foot-long, twelve-foot-deep,
twenty-foot-high glass vitrine filled with women's hair. And then we
saw the remains of the gas chambers and the ovens that had been

dynamited by the retreating Germans. She told me of her time in Auschwitz, of what went on there. How she could talk about all those things while standing in that place, I'll never know. I no longer remember her name.

I remember reaching down, at her suggestion, and picking up some dirt and crushing it in my hand. It was filled with bone ash. For the next few days, I showered three or four times a day and washed my hands endlessly. I couldn't get myself to feel clean.

In his letter to me written in October of 1971, Kurt Masur asked if I would play in Germany. Because of a heavy tour schedule, I was unable to reply until mid-February 1972. I told him that I wished it were possible for me to accept within myself the assurance that I might live with what I would feel and think were I to renounce my decision not to appear on German soil. But, unhappily, that time had not yet come. I assured him that there was nothing personal, ever, in any of this. It was a matter of long-held and deeply felt principle that involved no rancor or anger toward any single individual. In the past fifteen years we have become good friends and have often made music together happily, but not in Germany.

TWENTY-ONE

*I*N THE EARLY 1970S, I was visiting about seventy-five American cities each year, and I knew the country pretty well. I felt that young Americans were underestimated; there were thousands who enjoyed attending concerts as much as they did football games and dances. Many youngsters had organized clubs that were devoted not only to music but to all the arts. They met every week, listened to records, attended concerts, and enjoyed social activities together, inspired by their common love for cultural activities.

Once in Philadelphia, during the intermission following my appearance with the orchestra, I gave a talk offering to help start such music groups, and emphasized my interest not only in performing artists but in lovers of music who might be listeners only and amateurs. The response was astonishing. There were hundreds of letters. I visited such groups in Minneapolis, Wichita, Rochester, Montreal, and other cities. Many of my colleagues—Arthur Rubinstein and others—were interested in those music groups; the possibilities inherent in them were stupendous. They constituted a pool for future teachers and performers, as well as a potentially vital and intelligent musical audience.

I was deeply interested not only in the overall American musical culture but most especially in American violinists. There was no lack of knowledge about the technique of violin playing, but we certainly could have improved our practical application of this knowledge.

In an interview about violin technique, I offered some advice about the instrument. I remembered how, when very young, I kept forcing my hand into positions and leaps that frightened me when I thought about them in later years. Though it had taken many years of experience to learn how to use my hands with the greatest efficiency, I believed that progress was still possible during the early stages of violin training, when, in addition to actual practicing, careful study could be directed to the best ways of overcoming difficulties. It was important for violin teachers to concentrate on transmitting a thorough understanding of the muscular control of the hands. The teacher needed to be concerned with the physical possibilities of the individual student. It was necessary for the young violinist not only to practice faithfully but to think constructively and to strive for the technique that best suited his particular hand. And about the matter of practice, no youngster could possibly feel enthusiastic over the drudgery that was the foundation of accomplishment. Only later, when the student became aware of an ability to create musical sounds on his own and began to experience the excited discovery that he was able to create something special, only then would he gain more interest in the work required of him. The child should practice to the extent considered minimally necessary by his teacher, but not beyond the limits of concentration. When concentration on the task in hand ceased, all practice value was lost.

When asked if I ever allowed myself to think ahead while actually playing in public, I explained I never played *without* thinking a measure or two ahead. I always had a mental impression of the next measures. For me there was always a key note in each passage around which I would plan my fingerings and shifts. And then set the passage. In my mind, as I played, I mentally had a picture of the way my left hand would set and where the fingers should be before and after this key note.

With regard to the bow arm, the general rule of thumb is that the bow should always be clearly and neatly parallel to the bridge with the distance between the bridge and fingerboard to be decided on the quality of the sound that one wanted to produce and the amount of bow pressure to get that quality. Generally speaking, this idea of parallel bow strokes is largely correct but must be adjusted to the length of each player's bow arm. There are some youngsters whose arms are so short that, if they tried to keep the bow parallel at all times, they would extend the two muscles that are necessary to have flexibility to keep control of the bow, the extensor and the flexor muscles that lead from the base of the middle finger to the elbow, and the base of the thumb to the elbow. Anytime these two muscles are extended in a straight line, they lose the flexibility necessary to control bow speed and bow pressure. These two muscles can easily be identified by forming a circle with the middle (longest) finger of the right hand and the thumb and pressing them together—you will feel those two muscles contract immediately. Their flexibility must be protected at all times to use the bow to its maximum power. Also, bow speed must be taught and learned to be used as a musical weapon. Far too often, the bow is allowed to travel thoughtlessly with great speed in the middle, leaving very little room either at the tip or the frog for the end of a phrase.

Young players very often are not taught that rotating the hand where the bow is held, and putting most of the pressure on the bow with the forefinger, inevitably forces the bow into the string. Instead, making the center of pressure the middle finger into a circle with the thumb, maintains a pressure which can control the whole bow without forcing the bow into the string and thus saving a scratchy sound from being a normal concomitant to the young player. For me, having the whole weight of the arm hanging down from that middle finger is what gives the most natural bow arm, the most natural control of the bow, and a consistency of sound. Also to be remembered is that, much as with tennis, Ping-Pong, or swinging a golf club, the follow-through is important. Any young person who also plays a sport will recognize that if he or she is handling a tennis racket, a Ping-Pong paddle, or a golf club and suddenly stops the stroke, the ball takes off erratically and goes in the wrong direction. The same thing is true for the control of sound on a violin.

Generally speaking, bow speed should be constant. Speeding up the bow either up or down can be used for musical emphasis for any given note or phrase without making an accent; simply speeding up the bow in either direction can create a gentle swell of sound when used properly. Also, the use of fast, light bowing, *flautando*, should also be learned to give air underneath a very quiet sound, *piano* or *pianissimo*, because it travels farther without being louder.

The other musical power weapon that is sometimes used indiscriminately is *vibrato.* The vibrato is the hardest technical discipline to teach because it involves several different motions. Normally, for me, a constant fast vibrato that comes totally from the arm with a fairly stiff wrist is neither varied enough nor strong enough to indicate vastly differing musical moods or musical emphasis. Indeed, there are, for me, two basic rules for vibrato: (1) When you hear a vibrato, it is too much, and (2) a vibrato should be constant, the performer choosing to use less or more depending on the musical direction, and absent only when needed for musical emphasis—in other words, a white sound. Not only is the vibrato very hard to teach, it is even more impossible to describe in words. I think it begins from the back of the shoulder, continuing down the arm and ending in a flexible wrist that can swivel the tip of the finger over the area of the note that is being played. Both the speed and the width of the vibrato should *always* be controlled so as to indicate quiet intensity, excitement, thoughtfulness, pensiveness, or passion—whatever the musical mood needs. The only simile I can think of is a twenty-four-foot bullwhip with a very thick handle and a very thin end. If you take that whip and make a light motion with the handle, the very end will make an enormous snap. For me, that is the same idea of the impetus and end result of a vibrato. This may be inadequate, but it's the best I can do in words.

Once again, to summarize for the advancing student, let me try to list some things that I think should be taught early on, not casually acquired after other bad habits have been allowed to set in:

1. An awareness of harmonic progression under each note that is played on the violin. It's never too early for a young player to learn the difference between the innocence of C major and the dark complexity of F-sharp minor and to learn the difference between E-flat and D-sharp, depending on the underlying harmony and what the direction of the resolution of that harmony is.

2. To choose fingerings that have to do with the musical direction that is chosen and to recognize the difference of string color—the open brilliance of the A and E strings, the darker color of the D string, and the deep sound of the

G string. A change of fingering to use the timbre of the strings for phrasing is never unimportant.

3. Bow speed. The bow should move steadily—not faster or slower at any time only because of the bad habit of not listening to what you are really doing. The ear must be trained to listen to the kind of sound that is truly being produced. And the performer must learn how to decide what kind of sound he or she wants and to use bow speed accordingly.

4. Vibrato. The vibrato is the voice box, the larynx, the vocal cords of any violin player. And again, knowledge, imagination, and thought about what can be done *between* each note is essentially important.

All of these basic building blocks, as far as I am concerned, are necessary for any student to understand that music is not made by playing those round little dots on a piece of paper, but what happens *between* each note—from where you are coming to where you are going. That constant ebb and flow is what makes a musical line. The control of that musical line makes the difference between a musician and a mere fiddle player.

Unless a child shows a truly remarkable talent at a very early age, he or she should not actually begin to work, I would think, on any instrument until the age of five or six. In any event, all young beginners should be shown how to use the Carl Flesch Scale Studies with all their variants: with thirds, sixths, octaves, tenths, and harmonics. Students should always be shown how to read the whole score of whatever they are learning, no matter how simple or basic. The idea of learning how a single horizontal line can be part of an overall picture with harmonies and accompaniments below is, I think, something that can never be shown too early to the student. To learn to memorize only the notes that one is playing without hearing their relationship to everything else that is going on is short-sighted and ultimately boring.

In the morning, when I'd first take up my violin, I would not play anything that would place undue strain on my hands for the first five to ten minutes; they, like me, needed a little time to wake up. Nor did I practice silent finger studies. Once past those early moments, my hands fully awake, I might turn to a new composition by a contemporary composer like Prokofiev, Bartók, Berg, Lutoslawski, Penderecki, or Dutilleux. Their music is considerably different from works by Beethoven, Bach, Mozart, Brahms, and Schubert, whose musical languages and voices I already knew very well. In the case of the classical composers, I simply had to learn how their already familiar voices were speaking in the specific work I was studying. But with contemporary composers, it was like learning a new language. They were pretty much saying the same things as their predecessors, but with a different accent, with inflections on different syllables. That meant taking the terms of reference I already had from classical music and applying them to contemporary musical language. Quickly and inevitably I found close correlations between the new ideas and those I had used as a learning process for classical music. I tried to grasp the sound of the contemporary language, the inner coherence holding the work together. Memory became instinctive for me; working long enough with a new language made it a familiar one.

I have frequently been asked what I did when I was alone in my silent dressing room just before a concert. I tried to take some deep breaths and quietly play something from the works I was about to perform, or, even better at times, a melody or a passage from something quite different from what I had to play that evening. For me, that was a little relaxation and lessened my stress of the moment.

WHILE driving through Vermont woods one July night in 1972, on the way to dinner with Sasha Schneider, I heard over the radio of the death of Göran Gentele, in a car accident in Europe. What a shock that was! I almost ran the car off the road.

Gentele had just been appointed general manager of the Metropolitan Opera. A short, slim man, always neatly dressed, with a lithe body and a spring in his carriage, he was filled with boundless energy and enthusiasm. Enormously well read in the arts, he had a special talent for putting together music and ideas. He was director of the Swedish opera and also directed in the theater. He knew the musicians, the writers, the dancers, the choreographers in Scandinavia and abroad. We often spent very happy days and nights in Stockholm going to concerts or the opera or the theater and regaling ourselves with the wonderful drink and herring of Sweden. Göran knew the classics and was eager to experiment with the contemporary, and I became closely involved with his coming to New York and his engagement by the Met. He and his wife, Marit, were in our apartment very often, and some of his important decisions were made there. One such decision was arrived at sometime around 2 a.m., after three hours of discussion between us: he resolved that he himself would direct the opening night of *Carmen* at the Met. His death shockingly obliterated most of whatever joy that summer might have held.

Some weeks later, when the family and I were on a cruise in the Mediterranean, on the S.S. *Renaissance,* during which I played chamber music with many friends, there came the news of the murder, by Palestinian terrorists, of the Israeli athletes at the Olympic Games in Munich—and that small happy interlude, too, was destroyed.

The ineptness and mediocrity exemplified by the November elections in the United States that year made one look with some pleasure at the realization that 1972 would soon be over. But one specially happy event took place before the year ended, and that was the bar mitzvah celebration of Michael, our first son. It took place at the Jewish Theological Seminary in New York, as part of the regular Saturday morning service for the students. Michael read the Torah and Haftorah portions. The Torah section was the story of Joseph and his brothers. Michael not only read well but knew the meaning of the Hebrew and understood what he was saying. It was a moment of great pride for us. The service was followed by a small reception in the room next to the student cafeteria. There was no extravagant lunch at a hotel, no grand ball, no safari to Africa—just a few close friends and a donation to the student scholarship fund of the seminary. Shira, a lovely young woman, was considering a career in medicine, with the intention of becoming a pediatric nurse. And little David was growing healthily and adorably, with a gentleness that was touching. It was a happy family day.

TWENTY-TWO

E SPENT July 1973 in our rebuilt home in Connecticut. I was trying to relax after the winter and spring of work and travel and, at the same time, catching up on the many things that had accumulated during the months of my absence. My mother was vacationing in Europe. Shira was on a kibbutz in Israel, picking fruit from 4 a.m. to noon and packing it in a warehouse.

I was no longer a member of the council of the National Endowment for the Arts, nor a member of any of the advisory panels, but few seemed aware of that. People kept writing to me, requesting grants for their projects—one physicist wanted to investigate tone production on the violin and the variants made by hair, rosin, and string thickness—and their letters required answers. I was, of course, still involved with Carnegie Hall, even to the point of being drawn into the problem of the noise issuing from the subway that ran under the hall. The rumble of the subway was appalling, especially during the quiet moments of a performance. (Some of the noise would be alleviated in 1986, when the hall underwent a major renovation.)

I also let it be known that I would not be in Paris that September for the performance of Schoenberg's *Moses und Aron,* which was to open the opera season and to which I had been invited, because the dates fell on the eve and the day of Rosh Hashanah, the Jewish New Year. Though I was not religiously observant, I did forgo all public appearances during the High Holy Days out of respect for the feelings of my coreligionists.

In early August, the family and I flew to Israel for the opening of the Jerusalem Music Centre, which had been a dream of mine for many years. Participating with me in the opening celebration were Sasha

Schneider, Lennie Rose, and Pablo Casals—a young and spry ninety-six! For the rest of August, we played music with young people, ages fourteen to twenty. At one point during that month, I spent five and a half hours interviewing Casals. We talked about his early years in Paris, the summers of chamber music and tennis games he played with Fritz Kreisler, Eugène Ysaÿe, and other great artists who were his close friends; about the tours when he performed one concert a day and two on Sunday; about his memories of Anton Rubinstein and Pablo de Sarasate; about his first concerts in St. Petersburg around the time of the 1905 failed revolution. A warm, meandering conversation, with the Jerusalem sunlight filtering into the room. And I remember we were still talking when the door opened—and in the doorway stood Golda Meir and David Ben-Gurion, who had come over together to greet Casals. A memorable meeting!

In September, I flew to Europe and the family returned to New York. I was in Paris on Yom Kippur, visiting a friend late in the afternoon, waiting for the end of the day of fasting, when the first news came of the attacks on Israel by the armies of Egypt and Syria.

At first, I thought it would all end quickly, with the Arab armies routed, but the days passed and the news grew worse. By then I was in Strasbourg. I remembered the 1967 war, when I'd wanted to get to Israel as soon as the fighting had begun but couldn't, and had arrived about five days after it was over. I called home and spoke to Vera. "I think I'm going to have to go."

There was a long silence. "I thought you would feel like that," she said. "Go. But take care of yourself. And don't do anything that you don't have to."

I was scheduled to play the following day in Rotterdam. Knowing the kindness shown by many of the Dutch to the Jews during the Nazi occupation, and their support of Israel over the years, I decided not to cancel the concert. But the next week's concert in Yugoslavia, a long-standing opponent of Israel, I could not have canceled with more pleasure.

There was a problem, however: the American ambassador to Yugoslavia was expecting me; it was necessary that I inform him of my intended cancellation. I tried to get through by phone from Paris, but the French were having one of their usual strikes, and the international phones were not working. I asked the American embassy in Paris to telephone the cancellation over their wires. I did not tell the concert managers in Yugoslavia that I was ill or had another commitment; I told them directly that I was on my way to Israel.

I then called the Israeli embassy in Paris and spoke to the ambassador, telling him that I wished to go to Israel and asking to be put on the first available flight. Two days later, at 5:30 in the morning, I flew out of Rotterdam aboard an El Al jetliner. The plane made a number of stops in Europe, picking up supplies and reservists. We landed in Tel Aviv close to midnight. The city was blacked out. To see a city the size of Tel Aviv in total darkness! It was eerie.

The next morning, representatives from various orchestras came to the hotel where I was staying to discuss with me what I might do. Concerts were still taking place, but at an early hour, to enable the audiences to return home before dark. But there were problems about getting to the concerts: most of the buses and private cars were being used to transport soldiers. I came on television that night after the news broadcast and gave my first performance, as a way of letting the people know that I was in the country and participating to the best of my ability in the war. From the television studio, I went to the Mann Auditorium, where I arrived as the scheduled concert was coming to an end. I came out onstage and proceeded to play with the orchestra—without rehearsal.

During the following days, I played more than a dozen times, morning, noon, and night: free concerts, at two-thirty in the afternoon, when people could attend. Entire families came, with children and babes in arms. Soldiers passing through the city on the way to their units would drop in, doctors on leave, El Al flight attendants. One flight attendant told me she had worked a straight twenty-six hours, flying people in and out of the country. "You have no idea what it meant to have music for an hour and a half, and just bathe the insides in something other than the horror we have to face every single day."

One day I arrived, with the Israel Philharmonic Orchestra, at a large air base where Phantom jets were about three minutes' flying time from the Golan Heights. The base commander said to us, "We've never done this before, but we'd like to see what might happen."

There was a little hall on the base with a stage.

The commanding officer said, "Don't play anything long, not a whole symphony."

The orchestra and I climbed up on the stage. I said to Zubin Mehta, "What did you bring?"

He said, "I brought Tchaikovsky, Mendelssohn, Bach."

I said, "It doesn't matter to me. Whatever you start, I'll finish."

At the beginning, there were more performers on the stage than people in the audience. Planes were arriving and leaving all the time. You could hear the roar of the jets. If a plane was hit and managed to make it back, it was repaired and ready to be flown again within hours. The mechanics lived a few meters away from the aircraft they serviced. Food and changes of clothing were brought to them. They were on constant alert.

No one knew what music might mean to anyone on that base.

We began to play. Soon there were ten people in the hall. Then twenty. Then seventy. Very quickly, the hall was three-quarters filled. I saw men in gray dungarees entering, staying awhile, and then very quietly leaving. Later I discovered they were pilots on alert. Once an entire group of them left together. We kept on playing and, minutes later, heard the roar of aircraft taking off. We were still playing when they returned, all of them. They came back into the hall and sat there listening to us play, and when we were through they brought us over to their planes, where we all stood around, talking.

The most shattering experience was in the hospitals. I remember arriving at Hadassah Hospital in Jerusalem and being met by a man who had been wounded the day before on the Golan Heights. He had lost four fingers of one hand; the bandaged wound was still seeping blood. There was a gaping hole on one side of his face. He happened to be a music buff and had heard that I was coming and insisted on getting up from his bed and greeting me at the door.

I went into the wards and talked with some of the men. Orderlies wheeled about sixty or seventy men into a corridor and improvised a little stage and a microphone. I had no accompanist, and, I must admit, it took a bit of ingenuity to figure out a version of the Mendelssohn Violin Concerto that could be played alone, without an orchestra, in five to ten minutes—the time allotted by the staff for this group of wounded men. I managed it by humming some of the parts. Then I went into other wards.

At one point the head of the hospital asked me if I would accompany him to some of the most severe cases. I said, "That's what I'm here for. You tell me what to do." He said that entertainers who had been to the hospital until then were not allowed into the wards of the very badly wounded, but he'd heard that I'd played for injured people before.

We went into a room. I saw four men, burned almost black from head to toe. All were suspended so their bodies would not be in contact with the beds; two were facedown, two faceup. Two had been in an antiaircraft unit that had shot down an Egyptian plane; it fell in flames onto the gun, killing three men; these two had survived. The other two were tank men, whose tanks had been hit by the new and, until then, unknown Russian-built antitank missile that could be operated by even the most technically inept of soldiers.

I bent down to talk to each of them, to ask if I could play. Each said, "Would you, please? But before you do, ask the others."

I stood there in the semidarkness; apparently, with burn cases, the doctors didn't want much light in the room. Nurses hovered over the men, monitoring the tubes to which they were connected. I started to play some Bach, quiet, contemplative, inward-directed, soothing. When I finished, there was dead silence. I thought that perhaps I should leave them with something livelier, and I began a piece by Kreisler, *Schön Rosmarin,* and as I was playing, I could see that one of the men who was on his stomach was raising his head slightly so that he could see me. I motioned with my head to tell the nurse to step out of the way, which she did. There was a space between his bed and the wall, and I bent down and played directly to him for a while. Then I went to the other beds and played to each of the remaining three men.

Afterward, on my way back from the hospital, with my head and heart full of that experience, I thought how those hours that I'd spent there pointed up the need felt by the Israelis to retain those aspects of civilized life that have kept humankind together all through its history; that never before had the cultural elements of their society been so vital to them, so basic to their existence, as during this terrible war. I was also convinced that the Israel I had known until then was finished, that it would emerge from the war a new country. It would have to look at itself in very hard terms, harness all the intellectual, moral, and artistic strength it possessed to keep itself the unique and different nation it was in that part of the world.

In the last eight or nine years I have been increasingly concerned, at times deeply saddened, by public attitudes rarely seen so openly before: Israelis obdurately, vehemently, and violently arrayed against one another. I wondered how Jews in Israel, having known about being demeaned, humiliated, and physically attacked, could in turn humiliate and abuse others who are, for better or worse, their permanent neighbors. I wondered that they did not look at themselves and say, "If not peace, then what other alternatives are there? To kill or be killed? To have the young come back dead or wounded?" I believe passionately that a genuine resolving effort is the only thing that can turn Israel into the nation we all would hope it to become and save us from more nightmares like the Yom Kippur War. With the astonishing results of the 1999 election, I have renewed hope for a positive future. I would gladly settle for a strictly administered cease-fire. "Peace" comes from living together, not from a signed document.

I played in other hospitals. Once a wounded soldier said to me, "I want to thank you for coming." I looked at him and said, "*You* are thanking *me*?" I felt abashed. I always came away with a sense of deep embarrassment whenever I was thanked for having gone to Israel to play in a time of war.

I played a benefit concert with the Jerusalem Symphony conducted by Mendi Rodan in the Jerusalem Theatre. The tickets cost practically nothing, but everyone who came had to bring something to be sent to the soldiers at the front lines: battery-operated radios, sneakers and socks, instant coffee and canned milk—whatever the army said the soldiers needed. A huge pile of goods began accumulating in the area between the stage and the audience, and on all sides people sat not only in the regular seats but on chairs and boxes, listening to the Beethoven Violin Concerto as we played it for them.

I remember visiting Mayor Teddy Kollek in his office in Jerusalem, and then Prime Minister Golda Meir. I sat with others in Golda Meir's office as news kept coming in from the southern front about General Ariel Sharon's attempt to split the Egyptian armies; the concern was whether his daring attack would be outflanked by the Egyptians. Golda was very nervous. Finally, the report came in that Sharon had achieved his objective. I can still recall the ecstatic smiles and the huge sighs of relief that went around the room.

I spent about eight or nine days in Israel. Just before departing, I called my family from the airport. The two boys, home alone, answered the phone. I heard them asking, "Daddy, where are you?" They thought I was still in Europe; Vera had not told them that I'd gone to Israel.

I said, "I'm in Tel Aviv."

David, the ten-year-old, said, "Daddy, you must be kidding."

Michael, who was thirteen and a half, said, "Are you out of your mind or something?" Then, after a brief pause, he said, "You know, come to think of it, that's not a bad idea."

The next day Shira started a fund at Dalton for the Tel Hashomer Hospital in Israel. More than two thousand dollars was raised.

At the end of October, I was in Paris, playing Prokofiev, Leclair, Mozart, and Spohr with Pinchas Zukerman, for whom I'd once taken upon myself the rather audacious task of writing a personal letter to General Moshe Dayan, asking that the young musician's army duty be postponed so his musical education in New York would not be interrupted.

By mid-November, I was back in New York, and on November 18, I played Mendelssohn and Brahms sextets on the stage of Carnegie Hall, with Itzhak Perlman, Pinchas Zukerman, Jaime Laredo, Lennie Rose, and Sasha Schneider. But I could not forget the war. I spoke about it that December at a luncheon meeting of the America-Israel Cultural Foundation: Tel Aviv in total darkness; the afternoon and early evening concerts; the visits to the air base and the hospitals; playing to the wounded; and the way the badly burned soldier, lying on his stomach, kept raising his head to look at me as I played Bach and Kreisler.

THAT YEAR was made even more dismal by the shattering sudden death of David Oistrakh, on October 23, at the age of sixty-six.

He was the gentlest of human beings, and a giant violinist. There was in his playing a beautiful control at all times, whether in fast passages or long, slow phrases. A sudden burst of virile strength and the gentle caress of a soft nuance, the smooth, sweet tone unfailingly produced at all parts of the bow, at all levels of sound, never forced, never ugly. And always that wonderfully pure intonation that was invariably harmonically accurate as well. Those were the hallmarks of his playing. As for himself as a person—his life in the Soviet Union might have been expected to embitter him, yet I never once heard him utter an unkind word against a colleague, nor gossip about anyone's failings and weaknesses. He was truly a golden man.

$\mathcal{B}$Y THE MID-1970S, Shira was at Brown University, and our oldest son, Michael, at Harvard. I was deeply involved in matters that had little to do directly with my own music-making—matters relating to Carnegie Hall and the new Jerusalem Music Centre at Mishkenot Sha'anannim: meetings, phone calls, fund-raising. At the same time, I was trying to practice enough to make forthcoming concerts acceptable at least to my ears. A most pleasant distraction was the honorary doctorate I received from Yale University in May 1975, in a ceremony marked by pomp without pomposity. The enthusiastic reception by students and faculty was heartwarming.

Numerous requests were coming my way by mail, some odd and others rather interesting. Among the more pleasant ones was an invitation to participate in a book of letters honoring Gregor Piatigorsky, whom I regarded as an artist of legendary accomplishment and a great teacher who had inspired young cellists for decades—and I said precisely that, and more, in the letter I wrote. He was one of the great cellists of the second half of the twentieth century—the first names to come to anyone's mind when one spoke of cellists were Casals and Piatigorsky. I had met him in Los Angeles soon after Alexander Zakin joined me as my regular partner at the piano in 1940. Zakin had known him in Berlin back in the mid-twenties; they had been students together at the Hochschule, and close friends. Piatigorsky was six feet four inches tall, handsome, and well-educated, someone for whom I had the greatest respect and affection—for his talent, his humor, his urbane knowledge of the world. He had made Beverly Hills his home, and whenever Zakin and I were in Los Angeles, we would visit him. We were able to use his studio as a rehearsal space—it had a wonderful piano and extraordinary paintings by Soutine, Léger, Dufy, Matisse, Picasso, to name only a few, as well as vodka and sandwiches. There was also a chess table, because his wife, a member of the Rothschild family, had been women's chess champion in the United States and went on playing chess all her life. There were many moments of musical happiness with Grisha, as we called him. We would play chamber music in California and, in later years, we gave concerts together, playing the Brahms Double Concerto for violin, cello, and orchestra. At one time we played a tour with the major orchestras of the United States. His natural talent was so enormous, he didn't especially like to practice a great deal. Arriving to play a concert in Seattle, he was asked by the organizers when he wanted the rehearsal with the conductor and if he would need a room to practice in before the rehearsal. He said, "Practice? What do you mean, practice?" They mentioned some famous artists who had recently been in Seattle to play with the symphony and had demanded a quiet place where they could rehearse. Piatigorsky said, "Well, some people have to."

One particular memory strikes me at this moment. Many members of the audiences who have heard me over the years might remember that sometimes I come out from the wings through the violin section to take my place as soloist at the center of the stage, and I hold my violin up, my left hand practically at eye level so as to clear all the music stands and the backs of the players in the violin section. I learned that from Piatigorsky, who, when we walked onstage together, was worried about his cello because of the size of the instrument and the need to maneuver it through a narrow corridor of orchestral musicians. He would hold it at shoulder height, straight ahead, as he walked—a magnificent gesture and a lesson to. me in the need to establish a certain character of one's own when coming onstage. For those reasons, and many more, I participated with great pleasure in honoring Gregor Piatigorsky.

There were letters requesting an acknowledgment of artistic appreciation—my imprimatur, as it were—for the high qualities of the School of Music of Indiana University; from the Tulsa Philharmonic Orchestra, which was celebrating its silver anniversary; from Southern

Methodist University, whose artist in residence, Alexander Uninsky, an old and treasured friend, had suddenly died. There were many others. Travel, the need to practice, and fatigue kept me from answering them all.

Similar requests had been addressed to me as far back as the early sixties, among them: to endorse the luthier and violin maker Carl Becker and to offer a statement about my early warm musical relationship with the 92nd Street YM & YWHA. Then there was the request from *Esquire* to select "one place in the world to visit or spend a vacation, or live in for an extended period." (I told them I had been to too many beautiful and desirable places and couldn't pick any one of them over the others.) And the rather challenging request from *Playboy* for comments about the sources of creativity, to which I replied at some length, explaining that I regarded performing artists not as "creators" but as "re-creators," who filtered the ideas given them by the creative genius of the composer.

One of the strangest requests came, in 1962, from Alice S. Morris, literary editor of *Harper's Bazaar*, who wanted to know if I would let myself be included in a forthcoming issue featuring the bed. A number of notable people were to be photographed in bed; the essay, by the French writer and satirist Jean Dutourd, would deal with the unique relation to the world that one had from one's bed. My response to that one was: "In bed?? My dear Miss Morris! Cordially yours, Isaac Stern."

THERE ARE very few violins without some cracks that have been repaired in the past. Rarely does this have anything to do with the intrinsic value of the instrument, unless the damage has been so extreme that it has considerably affected either the sound or the appearance of the instrument. Very few of the great violins that artists play are as absolutely perfect as when they were made in the eighteenth century. We play them, small cracks and all.

The violin is a demanding taskmaster. The older I got, the higher became my standards. That was especially the case when I was studying a new composition. The difference between "creator" and "re-creator," between composer and performer, has remained intact for me all through the years. Still, one quality is absolutely necessary for both creator and re-creator, be it author, playwright, poet, painter, musician, sculptor, choreographer, or performing interpretive artist. That quality is perception—the ability to see further, to feel more, to understand more deeply than what is apparent to the average observer. In a sense, the difference is that between one who stands gazing at a sunset, seeing its colors and giving wings to his imagination in whatever art form he chooses, and one who merely observes the sun going down, feels the air turning chilly, and goes off to find shelter.

So much of creativity is God-given and inexplicable. Like music itself, it can be described but never explained. Mozart wrote five violin concerti. Between the first and the last there was a maturity of ideas and a depth of understanding that span half a lifetime. Yet all five concerti were composed by him in about nine months, from the end of his eighteenth year into his nineteenth year! Can one explain the source of that creativity, or that of one of the most brilliant compositions of the Romantic period, the octet written by Mendelssohn when he was only sixteen? And, at the other end of the age spectrum, how are we to explain Verdi's writing some of his greatest works after the age of seventy?

The only thread that seems to run through all these artistic accomplishments—and, similarly, in the other arts—is the imaginativeness of that mind, the ability to see below the surface, to see with clarity what is only dimly perceived by others, and to accomplish with seeming ease what is apparently impossible for the less talented.

In the 1970s, George Rochberg and Krzysztof Penderecki were commissioned to write violin concerti for me. I remember the rather frenetic air that accompanied my learning and playing the Rochberg Violin Concerto. In April 1975, I was apologizing to the historian Isaiah Berlin for my seeming bad manners in not getting in touch with him while in London earlier that year, explaining that I'd flown to Paris for an urgent conference about UNESCO, at the request of the American government, while ill with laryngitis. I had tried without success to call him from Paris, had gone on to Geneva, had tried to call him from there, then from a motel at Charles De Gaulle Airport, and kept getting busy signals—and therefore was unable to inform him that my original plan to spend time with him at Oxford would have to be canceled, because I had to get back to New York as quickly as possible to prepare for the world premiere of the Rochberg. Rochberg had studied at the Curtis Institute and now taught at the University of Pennsylvania, where he had been writing the concerto, and now it was done. I worked on it ten to twelve hours a day. It was forty-four minutes long, with five movements and an almost continuous violin line from the beginning of the work to the end.

The premiere took place in Pittsburgh early in April 1975. I played it with the Pittsburgh Symphony Orchestra under Donald Johanos. I then performed it again, in Chicago, with Georg Solti conducting, and in New York, at Carnegie Hall, with the Pittsburgh Symphony Orchestra.

While learning the piece, I had thought it remarkably effective but found myself wondering at times if the intrinsic material and its somewhat lengthy and melodramatic treatment would hold up on the field of battle—that is, the stage. But the work was quickly and warmly received by the public and by the critics—for which I was profoundly grateful. It was well written for the violin and, happily, after I arranged to play it in many of the major cities in America and Europe, it has been taken up by many of my younger colleagues.

Afterward, Rochberg wrote me, citing from his journal to the effect that "something . . . fundamental took place simultaneous with the birth of the concerto, with its public coming to life. Something was released which drew everyone involved very close together. The work created a living bond. It gave joy and pleasure; it released a sense of life and music which everyone shared. . . . It's not simply the fact of the incredible responses . . . of all the audiences. . . . It's what the responses signify—life responding to life. . . . Is this not what we call music is given to us for: to create a new and special energy and joy . . . ?" He thanked me graciously for my part in the work—". . . untiring, always ready to give and give more. . . ." The fact was, I admired the piece and was proud to be the first to present it to the world.

Two years later, on April 27, 1977, I played the world premiere of the Penderecki Violin Concerto with the Basel Symphony Orchestra, under the direction of Moshe Atzmon. The concerto was an enormously complex work, which I had to learn in fewer than six weeks. But it was wonderfully evocative both for orchestra and for violin, a highly personal statement made with craftsmanship and an inner musical need that I found immensely moving. It remains a major composition of the twentieth century.

My manager in Switzerland, Walter Schulthess, who was also a composer, had a wife named Steffi Geyer, who was a member of an orchestra in Zurich. He came to me one day and said that his wife was very ill and asked if I would come and visit her. Having known her well and liked her, I immediately said yes and went to his home. She told me then that when she was a young girl (and from others, I understand that she was a beautiful young woman violinist), she had a relationship with the young Bela Bartók. As a kind of love letter to her, he sent her the first movement of a violin concerto, which had never been published. What had been printed was a work known as "Two Portraits for Orchestra" and this "love letter"–concerto movement was one of those portraits. Now that Bartók was dead and Steffi Geyer felt she was not going to live very long, she wanted to have it published, and played by me. Of course I agreed immediately and thanked her for this singular honor. I immediately called Eugene Ormandy in Philadelphia, with whom I was to play the following season, and told him about it, and he agreed to present the world premiere. The time between my receiving the manuscript from her and clearing it with the Bartók family, who controlled all of his works, was an extended period, and, in the meantime, they promised that the first performance, should it ever come to light, would have to be in Switzerland. I had understood that it would be in Winterthur, but I have been told by those who have checked the records that it was done in Basel by a violinist named Schneeberger. Following that premiere there, which went relatively unnoticed, the concerto movement was given to printers, the additional printing of the orchestral parts was done, and in the season of 1957–58, I performed the American premiere with the Philadelphia Orchestra and Eugene Ormandy. We recorded it as well, and subsequently played it in many cities around the world. It has since become a staple of the violin and orchestra repertoire.

Also in connection with Bartók was a question someone put to me concerning an apparently questionable decision of mine at the end of a concert: I had chosen not to play any encores. Why?

I responded that the Bartók Sonata No. 2 with which I had ended the concert was probably the single greatest work for violin and piano written since the last sonata of Brahms. In the concert, the Bartók had been preceded by Schubert's Fantasie in C, a rarely programmed piece because of its immense difficulty. Few listeners were aware of the enormous technical problems the soloist faced in the performance of the piece; in fact, it was the lack of obvious difficulty that one sought in working out that particular composition. The Bartók Sonata No. 2 had a very special place in my heart and mind, and due to its enormous power and brilliance, it had to come at the end of a performance, because anything following it would have paled musically. I was convinced that after the Schubert and the Bartók, the audience would be utterly drained. I certainly was, so I played no encores.

DEEP SADNESS marred 1977 for me. Zakin, my companion-in-arms for thirty-three years, was ill. For the past two years, he'd had to use a cane; we wouldn't leave the stage until half the concert was over, because it was too difficult for him to walk back and forth. But I wouldn't let him go, until one day he said to me, "I can't, I can't anymore."

After we stopped playing together, he rapidly became more and more ill. He had terrible curvature of the spine, and then—I'd never seen it before—Alzheimer's. His mind went almost completely. He was able to recognize people and things, but he couldn't make connections, he couldn't put people or events together. He really could not speak. It was a very painful and difficult time.

Israel celebrated its thirtieth birthday in the spring of 1978. The year before, I'd helped Teddy Kollek, then mayor of Jerusalem, organize the Independence Day concert, which was a great success. I was by then firmly convinced that the work of the America-Israel Cultural Foundation, together with the efforts of our friends and colleagues in Israel, had become increasingly important in an atmosphere where the political situation was a continuing tense ebb and flow in search of peace. Never before had Israel's intellectual and artistic strengths been more clearly needed as foundations for future peace. Surely those strengths would be counted one day as vital factors in the recognition of the value of peace by the peoples of that region.

ONE OF the longest and most extraordinary careers in music was that of Vladimir Horowitz, who was invited to give a recital at the White House that February. President and Mrs. Carter were gracious hosts; the atmosphere was joyous, the mood relaxed and most fitting for the musical importance of the occasion.

When it came to people in high political office, I had no illusions as to how much influence my views on important issues of state would have upon them. I was not convinced that having a performer speak substantively to people in politics or commerce after a performance was very effective. Most people tended to put performers in somewhat gilded compartments; they would listen with great interest to any comments the performer made with regard to his specific field of endeavor—music or any of the other arts—but would give only polite, cursory attention should the performer venture into the "real world." Even when I played at Chequers and, afterward, spoke directly with Prime Minister Heath and his guests, there was a touch of smiling condescension about the way they listened to the "entertainer" involving himself in matters far beyond his competence. On the other hand, a sit-down lunch or a meeting over drinks—not involving the performer as an entertainer—was generally far more effective, especially if there was a certain amount of awareness beforehand that the performer's experience in the world gave him something of value to add to such a conversation.

LIFE AS A SOLOIST was heady and draining. I was on tour during almost all of 1978, and at one point someone asked me for my opinion about John Corigliano, who had been a strong, reliable, and warmly cooperative colleague as concertmaster of the New York Philharmonic

Orchestra. The request started me thinking about the similarities and differences between a solo performer and a concertmaster.

It seemed to me that an alert and sophisticated concertmaster could add immeasurably in the preparation of a concert performance by understanding quickly what the soloist wanted to do and transforming that into action for the first-violin section, thereby influencing the playing of all the string groups. With rehearsal time always being shorter than ideal, speed was of the essence. The good concertmaster translated into practical application, quickly and quietly, the slightest nuance of the soloist, the smallest change of phrase or bowing or fingering. That sometimes saved a lengthy conversation between the soloist and the conductor, who would otherwise have to stop the orchestra and explain the changes. An effective concertmaster could bring about such changes even while the orchestra was playing.

Sometimes soloists were not properly prepared to play the enormous range and complexity of the orchestral repertoire. A good concertmaster not only knew the repertoire and made it his business to learn the compositions with which he was not familiar, but also was the right arm of the conductor in translating the interpretational ideas into performing practice and leading his section strongly enough so that there could be no doubt, down to the last player at the last stand, of how any particular passage should be played.

As for the difference in temperament between the soloist and the concertmaster, being able to play even extraordinarily well in a group did not necessarily mean that a given performer had the personal power and stage magnetism to stand up alone and dominate an audience by his performance, even though his playing could be musically and technically of the first order. Being a soloist was very much a matter of special temperament and superconfident bravura that was quite different from the qualities necessary to being a first-rate concertmaster, who after all had to be an enthusiastic colleague rather than an independent, risk-taking leader.

Probably it was those qualities of a soloist that led me to urge Carnegie Hall on to its own path of independence and risk-taking. Some have said that I changed the general nature of the concert business. I certainly made every effort to effect major changes in the nature and direction of Carnegie Hall. I wrote a detailed and rather lengthy memo in 1978 concerning the immediate needs and the future possibilities of the hall:

It has become clear that Carnegie Hall must very quickly decide where, when and how to risk a certain amount of money in stimulating imaginative programming, programming that will either go elsewhere, be "purchased" by more advantageous contracts or not appear in a major auditorium in New York.

An example of the first instance above: The English Chamber Orchestra with Vladimir Ashkenazy as soloist and conductor to Lincoln Center for an average fee of $13,000. As Mr. Ashkenazy regularly sells out his own recitals at Carnegie Hall at a gross of $22,500 and has been gaining an increasing reputation as a conductor, the risk to us would have been rather small, but this attraction was not even offered because of the necessary timidity shown by our staff and because we have not a predetermined direction with money to match and must depend on a case-by-case presentation; a process I suggest now as too slow, professionally unmanageable and dangerous to our prospects.

The Pittsburgh Symphony, as well as several other orchestras, is going to Lincoln Center for their concerts instead of their preferred and traditional venue at Carnegie Hall because of a contract offering them a minimum guarantee of $12,500 as against ours of $2,000 plus a possible profit sharing. Several other orchestras now planned for next season's series of the IFVO [International Festival of Visiting Orchestras]; i.e., the Toronto Symphony, the Moscow Symphony and the German radio orchestra are all unable to accept our usual contract as outlined above and individually sustain the added losses to an already large deficit that travelling always inflicts on a musical organization. . . .

We have not begun to tap the wealth of artists appearing at the Hall regularly every year and to form with their appearances and in combination with all the various managements the single most prestigious, most authoritative and attractive subscription series anywhere in the world. . . . In other words, we should stake out our claim, visible to the whole profession, of what we can and will do. I am certain that once we show a serious intent, backing that intent with concrete proposals in which we take a financial part, the top areas of artists and the managers will come to us with proposals. . . . What we must do now is show them how this can work to our mutual benefit and how, in the long run, it is as much in their interests as it is in ours. For example, the creation of a series of such power would make it possible for Carnegie Hall, in conjunction with various managements, to introduce *every single season* two or three extraordinarily gifted but still relatively unknown young performers who will be the staples of the profession five to ten years from now. . . .

I urged that a musical organization be created through which plans could be formulated and substantive funding sought; that an outreach program be established in the city's boroughs; that talented young people be given an opportunity to participate in our in-house American Symphony Orchestra; that these young musicians be guaranteed a decent annual salary sufficient to retain their loyalty.

The concluding words of the memorandum:

> The first one to succeed in putting together a viable organization would almost by necessity command the entire field and make difficult, if not impossible, any other major organization. *We must be first!!!*

It wasn't just the artistic side of Carnegie Hall that preoccupied me—how to move musically into the future—but more mundane matters as well: staff salaries, maintenance costs, reconstructing that grand old building so it could dwell comfortably in the modern world of music. A major fund-raising effort was begun. At times I felt I was back in the early years soon after the saving of the hall, when I had stopped touring for six months and spent every day tending to details large and small in an effort to turn what had been saved into something viable and truly alive.

THE SUMMER OF 1978 was made joyous by the celebration of Leonard Bernstein's sixtieth birthday; the winter brought news of the death of Golda Meir.

Lenny was the dominant figure in American music—as conductor, composer, and performer—ever since his Vesuvian entrance on the music scene in 1943. Most composers and performers on the concert stage and in the theater had been touched by his talent, and most of all, by his love affair with music. I remembered the decades of our being together, of making music together, of talking together; the years of performances here and abroad; the many recordings; the conversations on the state of music, the world around us, our hopes and our work.

Sadly, that was a time of great personal anguish for Lenny: his wife had died of cancer the year before. Which made it even more important for all who loved him to be with him, in actuality or in spirit, to make it clear to him how deeply he was valued as a man, as a friend, and as a musician.

The death of Golda Meir was profoundly saddening. She was one of the giants in the establishment of the modern state of Israel; no one defended the land and the people with more fervor. I was asked to join the American delegation that flew to Israel on the White House plane with President Carter's mother, but I couldn't go because of unchangeable commitments—particularly, a major benefit concert.

Sometime later, I learned that in her last conscious hours, she saw the film *Music from Jerusalem* on television in Israel. The film, made in 1973, showed behind-the-scenes activities at the Jerusalem Music Centre: students playing, and Sasha Schneider, Yefim Bronfman, William Steinberg, Claude Frank, and I teaching; and Pablo Casals, then ninety-six, conversing with David Ben-Gurion, eighty-seven—for both of them, their last year. I was told that after seeing the film, Golda

Meir remarked that it had given her one of the happiest hours she had ever experienced.

THERE LIVED in our apartment building a couple named Dr. Sheldon and Helen Atlas, with whom Vera and I had become close friends. Dr. Atlas was an accomplished chemist, with many discoveries that had major commercial applications and that had brought him into close relationship with a number of foreign countries, including Russia and the People's Republic of China. He was also one of the chief consultants on plastics to NASA and the American space program. Helen Atlas was editor of a dance magazine and much involved with the ballet. They were generous hosts and supporters of the arts, especially young talents. Many artists of renown today were once taken care of personally and financially by the Atlases, whose house was always open to everyone in the ballet and to visiting artists from the Soviet Union.

On one occasion, Dr. Atlas had become friendly with the then Chinese ambassador to the United Nations, a man named Huang Hua, who later became foreign minister. Dr. Atlas had been to China several times at the invitation of the Chinese government, to advise in the field of plastics. He knew of my interest in China, and one day he called and invited Vera and me to join him and his wife at their apartment; the Chinese ambassador to the UN would be there, with his wife.

It was a private dinner. In the course of the evening, I mentioned to Huang Hua my interest in China and my desire to visit. His wife asked me what I did, and I said I was a violinist. She said, "Oh, do you play professionally?" and I said yes, I played some concerts. She said, "Well, if you continue to work hard and if you believe in what you do, I am sure you will one day develop yourself so you can enter a good orchestra and earn a good living."

I did not comment—one of my rare moments of diplomatic silence. I should add that this is the correct version of the encounter, though it is told slightly differently in the film *Isaac Stern: A Life.*

Out of that evening came the invitation, through Huang Hua, to visit China. The official invitation, from the People's Republic of

China, came in March 1978 and proposed a date later that year. I tried to reorganize my schedule, which had been set since the previous year, and found that it wasn't possible. I wrote Huang Hua, who was by then back in China as its foreign minister, suggesting that the best time for me would be the latter part of June 1979, for a period of two or three weeks. I added that in return for his generous granting of the visit, I would like to be able to make music for the people of China and play a few concerts with my associate, pianist David Golub, in recital and, if possible, to meet and also perform with the Peking Symphony Orchestra. "Professional encounters," I wrote, "are, after all, the very best way to get to know each other and make friends." I further informed him that my wife and children were very eager to join me on such an exhilarating trip. In point of fact, the whole family had let it be known that if I didn't take them along, they would never speak to me again.

The trip was finally set for the latter part of June 1979.

Then a close friend, a businessman named Walter Scheuer, suggested that I consider taking along a small camera crew to make a record of the trip to keep as a family archive. The family was very opposed to the idea of a film crew coming along on what they had considered a private family visit, but in the end, Walter Scheuer, entirely at his own expense and with no clear notion of what would come of such an enterprise, brought along not only a film crew but also a director, Murray Lerner. In June 1979, we left for Japan, where there were a few days of concerts and recitals in Tokyo, Osaka, and Kyoto.

David Golub was a tall, thickset young man with a pleasant countenance. For some time, I had been looking for a performing and traveling colleague to take Zakin's place. The moment he sat down at the piano in my studio, everything that came out was pure music. His body language was at ease and at one with the music he played; there was a naturalness to both his physical posture at the piano and the way the music emerged from his hands. I engaged him on the spot.

On June 18, we arrived in Beijing.

TWENTY-FOUR

*C*ERTAIN OTHER orchestras and artists—the pianist Walter Hautzig, for example—had been to China before, but I knew of none that had made a tour of the country, certainly not to some of the cities we were to visit. In that regard, the trip to China was reminiscent of the one I had made two decades before to the Soviet Union.

There was a difference, however, between the two trips: the Soviets would not have permitted us to enter their country with our own film crew. Of course, the Chinese knew that we would be under their control every step of the way; we could not go anywhere without authorization. Still, they were aware that our intentions were entirely friendly, and they wanted good publicity. In general, it seemed to me that they had about them a worldliness I had rarely found among the Soviets. In addition, we had what the Chinese call "kwan-shee," the only way I know to spell it phonetically. In plain language, it means "Who do you know?" Of course, our official host was the foreign minister and this gave us extra attention and entrée wherever we wanted.

On the flight from Japan, I had mentioned to Vera that it might not be a good idea to converse in Russian, as we often did, while in China. Among those in the welcoming committee that stood waiting as we disembarked was a Chinese orchestra conductor, Li Delun, who was to be the conductor of the concert I was to play with the Peking Symphony Orchestra. He greeted us in Russian. It turned out that many of the Chinese musicians we were to meet had studied in the Soviet Union.

I told the members of the welcoming committee that I had come with the intention of meeting the people of China; that this was less a concert tour than a hello through music. I was using music as a kind of passport into the country.

The easiest way to learn about another country was to meet the professionals in one's own field. I had accepted an invitation to play with the Central Philharmonic, the major orchestra in Beijing. The agreement was for me to simply play in rehearsal with members of the orchestra and perhaps do a recital at a conservatory. No formal concerts were planned; I wanted no paid concerts on that trip. And though we intended to come out of China via Canton and Hong Kong, I did not want to play a concert in Hong Kong, because the weather would be very hot then and, also, I was reluctant to be tied down to a specific date should our trip in China be extended or shortened for any reason.

As I entered the rehearsal hall in Beijing (at that time, the city was still called Peking), I found it jammed with people who, it quickly became apparent, knew music. Also immediately apparent was the rather limited approach of both the conductor and the orchestra to Western music; they were unaccustomed to playing with varieties of color and passion. There was a distinctly stiff, technical, old-fashioned approach to the way they played.

The immediate problem was how to deal with the conductor without causing him to lose face in front of his orchestra. Before the rehearsal, I spent a few minutes alone with him, going over the salient points in the music. In the presence of the orchestra, I made it clear—with a smile, a joke, a friendly gesture—that I was not trying to be a big shot and had not the least intent to cut the conductor down. To the contrary, I was trying to build them all up; there was a difference, and all orchestras can sense it. In the case of the Central Philharmonic, both the conductor and the players recognized immediately that when I asked them to do this or that, I was not teaching them how to play; I was making them feel individually capable of accomplishing more than they were doing now.

As it turned out, I played a full concert with the Central Philharmonic, gave one recital in Beijing and two in Shanghai, taught master classes in the conservatories of both cities, listened to many young people play, and talked with dozens of the older music teachers and professors. The concert with the orchestra in Beijing was an enormous success and was followed by a series of banquets, during which toasts were offered to the great relationship between the People's Republic of China and the United States of America. In all the food that was served—not bad but not terribly memorable—the one missing item, which I craved the most, was Peking duck. As luck would have it, I received a call one day from the American embassy: it seemed that none of the diplomatic staff—or, indeed, the entire diplomatic community—had been able to obtain tickets to either of my concerts, because they had been sold in advance to the Chinese; would I come to the embassy and play for at least an hour. I said of course, and went and played for an hour and a half—and discovered later that I'd missed the one banquet at which the Chinese had served Peking duck.

At each of the music conservatories I visited in Beijing, I heard players with an extraordinary level of talent. They could all play the notes with astonishing dexterity, but they didn't understand the music. They wanted to play the fast, flashy, loud, difficult compositions, display their technical virtuosity. They hadn't had sufficient time or instruction in basic musical values that were part of the old European tradition, and they also thought that technique alone would get them the best jobs. I tried to show them that technical excellence was a necessary part of good music-making, but that it wasn't everything; I talked to them about emphasizing the mind, about playing each note with the ear and the heart.

Some of the players were quite young. I remember a boy cellist and a boy pianist with remarkable abilities. I felt I could help best by encouraging them, by giving them and their teachers a sense of musical direction. And I especially recall an incident with a young girl violinist, who played before me on a stage in an auditorium filled to capacity with a warm audience clearly knowledgeable in Western music. She was about ten or eleven and had on a pale blue dress and a red scarf. To me, children are open flowers—you have to treat them hands on. When I asked her to stop playing and to sing the music instead, I didn't know if she could sing; nor did I think about her possible loss of face. I saw how shy she was and sensed her hesitation, but that lasted only a second or two. She sang the passage in a sweet, feeling voice, and then I asked her to play it that way. And the change was so obvious that the audience burst into applause.

Had she been unwilling to sing, had she begun to cry—I would've hugged her and asked that she do something else. There was always a way to handle it. They were all so eager and willing, and you related to them as one human being to another rather than as an international violinist to a little Chinese girl. You looked at the child and you knew quickly whether there was any real talent that could be touched or opened up. You could never really know how much it could be opened, but if you saw that there was nothing there, you didn't try. Anybody who knew his craft would be able to recognize immediately if there was a possibility of doing something for or with a new talent; you went for it. I'd done that before. She was a sweet child. And she had talent. There was something about her eyes and the way she carried herself, a certain tension, a certain nervousness, a certain shy grace. It was one of those moments of risk that I would take without thinking. And it turned into one of the memorable events of the trip.

We traveled by train, van, and boat, in all about twenty people: my family, David Golub, Wally Scheuer and the film crew, our guides. In Xi'an, we saw the early stages of the archaeological excavations in which a small army of life-size clay figures was being uncovered, soldiers symbolically entombed with their dead emperor, to protect him on his journey to the next world. We were not permitted to take pictures, and so the film crew stood idle; but the temptation proved irresistible, and every once in a while I'd open my jacket and the camera hanging from my neck would go click-click. I got a few good photographs of that astonishing sight.

In Xi'an, it was hot inside the hotel. There were air conditioners, but for some reason they were in boxes *outside* the building, and all the windows were wide open to the blazing summer heat. We had gone there simply as tourists, but that didn't deter a group of musicians in the nearby conservatory from showing up at the hotel and asking if I would listen to some of the local players. A nearby movie house was cleared of its patrons, and three or four people played for me, among them a young man of considerable talent. The training and artistic level displayed by the others was somewhat primitive, but I was as encouraging as possible. They'd had poorly trained teachers, and it was almost impossible for them to obtain funds and permission for foreign study. I often wondered during that trip if anyone I encountered would ever be able to leave China to study music abroad.

We traveled by train alongside rice paddies and villages and rivers and through vast, fertile plains. As we approached Kweilin, we transferred to a boat—our guides had reserved the entire upper deck for us. The hills came directly to the river's edge, as if a hand had clawed the side of the mountain down to the water. A truly wondrous sight. There were fishermen on the river. They looked up at us and kept on with their fishing and housework. They lived on their boats. For the trip back, we rode on land in air-conditioned vans. That was special treatment, and we knew it.

We knew, too, that no Chinese could visit a foreign hotel without passing the police who were stationed there, and so they made no attempt to visit. Only someone whose visit you expected would be permitted to enter your hotel; you had to inform the plainclothes people in advance and request that the visitor not be stopped. Shira and the boys found Chinese their own age among the musicians and befriended them, but there wasn't much time for socializing; we were kept busy seeing the country.

In Kweilin, we attended a vaudeville show: gymnasts and balancing acts and two remarkable Chinese comedians performing sound effects of trains and birds. That was certainly one of the happiest nights we spent in China.

David Golub and I were to play a recital in Shanghai, the most cosmopolitan city in China. We found there a surprising awareness of Western popular culture: people knew of John Denver, Dolly Parton, various rock groups. The city had a lively air of openness and informality. What it did not have—as David and I discovered when we arrived at the auditorium where the concert was to be held—was a good piano.

The piano in the auditorium was literally unplayable. We were informed that it was the best piano in all of Shanghai. I told the concert hall manager that there was a very good piano in Beijing and I would call certain government officials and get it shipped to Shanghai overnight by plane and truck. The manager suddenly remembered that there was another piano in Shanghai after all, and he arranged to have it brought to the auditorium. It was playable—barely.

The concert was a great success. There was a warmth about the audience, an eager receptivity. Golub and I felt it on the stage as a palpable force.

On one of our days in Shanghai, we all went to visit a local physical-training center known as a sports palace. The people there seemed quite young. A hurly-burly of activity—Ping-Pong, jousting with long sticks, gymnasts doing all sorts of astonishing feats. The utter concentration of those young people! There was clear evidence of organization and training from very early in life. That discipline was carried into musical education as well. We visited the conservatory in Shanghai, which only the most talented attended, chosen in nationwide competitions. Incidentally, the conservatory building was, in the pre-revolutionary days, the quite graceful and dignified edifice of the Jewish Community Center. With the revolution, all of the members of that community dispersed to Japan, Hong Kong, or the United States. One out of every fourteen applicants made it into that school. They began at the age of ten and lived at the school. Each student studied one major instrument, besides other subjects. China, we were told, was trying to modernize itself in all aspects of its national life, including music.

I found Chinese music to be as close to Western music as any other non-Western music I knew, if not closer. The Chinese violin—the pi-pa—for example, was taught and played with the same phrasing that I used when teaching classical music. Chinese music was pure music, which was not so of Japan, where music largely served to accompany either words or movement. True, it was not the kind of pure music that a symphony or a quartet or a violin solo was. Nor did the Chinese have a music infrastructure: there were no concert facilities, no theaters or gathering places strictly reserved for music. But in China music was an ancient tradition; some of their pi-pa players were masterly, but they were accustomed to playing for a few people in a room inside a teahouse. China was without a tradition of great performances or concert halls. And the very idea of Western music had been terribly mangled between 1966 and 1977, when the extremists in the Communist Party, the group known as the Gang of Four, instituted what has come to be called the Cultural Revolution. Apparently, Mao had begun to fear that an external cultural virus might destroy the Chinese Revolution, which was then only forty years old, and so he moved to thwart all inquisitiveness and destroy all outside influence—to isolate China from the rest of the world and to rule by simplistic, didactic doctrines that could be understood by everyone. Anything connected with the West—including Mozart, Beethoven, and violins—was regarded as having been contaminated by Western devils and could in turn contaminate the culture of Communist China. Music teachers were imprisoned, beaten, humiliated, starved. Many committed suicide.

But things were very different by the time we arrived; the mere fact that we had been invited to travel inside the country was a measure of that difference. Of course, a three-week visit did not turn us into experts on China, but it was clear that, at least culturally, the Chinese were freer than they had been before, and that their inquisitiveness was increasing from day to day. They were trying to make up for the losses incurred during that awful time; they were trying to reconnect to Western music.

Chinese songs sounded somewhat like the music of Dvořák; there was a certain affinity between them, regardless of the pentatonic scale. Their music placed an emphasis on emotional impact, on the instrument imitating the human voice, so for them Western music was not that far a jump. That they hadn't heard a great deal of it didn't seem to matter much; they reacted instantly when they did—wildly, ecstatically.

I remember once telling a group of students that their instruments were there for the music, and not the other way around. Every time you took up your instrument, you were making a statement, the player's statement: a statement of faith, a statement that this was the way you wanted the music to speak through your instrument. I had the distinct feeling that most of them understood exactly what I was saying.

All the family was having a wonderful time. We had made arrangements to leave China from Canton on the hydrofoil to Hong Kong, and I'll never forget our translator standing on the dock and all of us hugging her, with tears in our eyes. She was crying like a baby as the hydrofoil slowly pulled away. We watched the shoreline fade. The translator was still standing on the dock.

We bounced happily all the way to Hong Kong. When the hydrofoil docked, we were greeted by two Rolls-Royces from the Mandarin Hotel, where we were to stay. The kids went from the dusty backward atmosphere of China to the glittering wealth and comfort of Hong Kong. The first things for them: showers, hamburgers, and Cokes.

The governor of Hong Kong, whom I met a day or two later at an affair, invited us to meet him at Government House. We talked at length about our three weeks in China. Shira and the boys had heard about the boat people from Vietnam and asked the governor if they could see them. After the difficulties in China and now the sybaritic wealth of Hong Kong, they felt it would be wrong not to witness what another part of Asia was experiencing.

I arranged, through the office of the governor, to visit a camp where the boat people were being held. We arrived just as a boat loaded with Vietnamese refugees was pulling in. It was literally stacked with people, layer upon layer of dazed, half-starved men, women, and children. Shira and the boys stared at the scene: Asians stumbling out of the boat, looking around. There were police on the dock. Later, I spoke in French with Vietnamese in a refugee camp and listened to them tell me about their fears of the North Vietnamese, their difficulties with the Hong Kong Chinese, their utter dread of being sent back to Vietnam.

We were in Hong Kong about five days, and then we flew home.

To have visited China was to have experienced an entirely different world from the one we knew. But it was a world of human beings, toward whom we came to feel great warmth and with whom we ultimately shared a common language—the humanity of music. In the end, Mao could not prevail against Mozart.

ALL THE TIME we were there, save for the visit to the excavations at Xi'an, the film crew assembled by Walter Scheuer was diligently making a record of the trip. There was only one instance of a staged scene. I went one day to listen to Chinese musicians playing Stephen Foster melodies on Chinese instruments. They were exquisite, stunning. The film crew was somewhere else, and I sent for them, and the musicians played again and were filmed.

Not only was nothing staged for the film crew; there was also no logic to what was being filmed. The director had no apparent story line in his head and no script. He was shooting wild, capturing things as they happened. We were fortunate in that the Chinese trusted us. When Bob Hope came in for a show, his people got into trouble of some kind, and the authorities confiscated some of his film. All of our film footage made it out of China.

The uncut film was sent by air back to the United States, and arrived safely. There was more than sixty hours of it. Then Walter Scheuer and the director had a falling-out, and the director left. No one seemed to know what to do with all that film. I introduced Walter to a man I knew named Alan Miller, who was both a moviemaker and a trained musician. Alan viewed the film again and again, trying to find a single viable line on which he could build a feasible story, a coherent film. It took him a year of viewing. He finally emerged with about eighty-eight minutes of film. I looked at it and cut four more minutes, sections that I thought were not polite to the Chinese. For example, the incident over the piano in Shanghai—I'd been fit to be tied, and I'd shown it, but I didn't want to embarrass the director of the auditorium, so I cut some of it. When we were done, the sixty hours of raw footage had become a documentary film of eighty-four minutes, now known as *From Mao to Mozart*.

From start to finish, the film was financed by Walter Scheuer. He knew nothing about filmmaking, producing, or distributing, and proved it many times over by making every possible error and inventing a few new ones that have become part of the lore of modern filmmaking. But what he had then, and continues to have to this day, is an extraordinary generosity, a love for other people, and a desire to help make the world a better place. We have known many generous people in our lives but very few as selfless and totally good and decent as Walter Scheuer. He was pushed around a good deal, but he kept on showing it to people and getting people interested. Slowly, it began to move. It played in a theater in Paris for six months, and in Zurich for four. It began to appear in small art theaters in the United States, to excellent reviews. Then he submitted it to the Academy Awards.

The night it won the Oscar for the best documentary of 1980, I was sitting quietly with Sophie and Leonard Davis in their Florida home, watching the Academy Awards with some interest but not much excitement; I didn't really expect that our little film would net the prize. As the nominations for best documentary came up on the screen, I began to feel a little more excited. And when the announcement came that we had won, I let out a shout loud enough to be heard from Florida to New York and California.

MY MOTHER died in December 1979, five months after the trip to China. Her last weeks were terribly difficult for her to endure and for the family to watch helplessly. The final serenity she needed came too slowly and with great pain. She died at home, taken care of by her family, and was put to rest next to my father, in earth bathed by sunlight and with soft words spoken by her children and grandchildren.

TWENTY-FIVE

*I*N THE OLD DAYS, the public relations department of the Hurok organization would send out a press packet in advance of my arrival at a destination on my tour itinerary. The packet distributed in 1949 contained news and feature stories about my early years in San Francisco, my musical accomplishments, my more recent travels. Anecdotes, quips, quotes, reviews.

One of those stories has me beating Jascha Heifetz at table tennis— three games out of five. (This would have been nice, but it is factually inaccurate. With my awe and respect for this giant in the history of violin playing and my knowledge of how he felt about his own abilities as a Ping-Pong player, I carefully arranged to win only one out of five, letting him just beat me in the other four. I was a better player, but I darn well wasn't going to show it off at that moment!) It says that I enjoy outdoor tennis, swim a great deal, and devour the sports page. Football and baseball are said to be "my dish." On the road, the story continues, an average day for me and Zakin runs eight to ten hours; we perform more than one hundred concerts a year. "As the train pulls into the station, they settle their gin rummy scores and get ready for practice sessions that last three to four hours. At night, of course, he has to put in a couple of strenuous hours to please the customers."

The story quotes me as saying, "Let me play the fiddle as well as I can. What is equally important to me is to live like a human being. If I can show people that a musician needn't be a crackpot, that he is fundamentally no different from the next fellow, that music is not a luxury but as natural as reading or arithmetic—if I can do that then I've really done something."

I was twenty-nine when that somewhat colloquially worded puff piece was written in 1949. In 1980, at the age of sixty, I would have said much of it again, and added words about the very special experiences of enjoying both a private family—raising my children—and a public family—teaching music to young students.

More and more I felt, as I approached my sixtieth year, that the greatest wealth one could accumulate was one's own family and a few close friends. Michael, our elder son, was then in his senior year at Harvard, majoring in American history and with his professional future yet to be determined. David, our younger and taller (by one inch at six-foot-two) at age seventeen, attended Dalton and was still living at home; he was eager to enter Yale, to study—of all things!— music. I had tried to discourage him from seriously entertaining that outlandish goal, but it seemed that surroundings and influences had something to say in the way his young mind was growing. I didn't think he would be a solo performer, but he was certainly capable of turning into a gifted and knowledgeable musician. He had the ear and the mind; he was a very good student and a happy human being.

Shira, our firstborn and, at age twenty-four, in her third year of postgraduate studies, was on her way to becoming a rabbi. She had attended Brown University, and while there had been strongly influenced by a member of the faculty, himself a rabbi and a professor of Jewish studies, toward a life in Judaism. Neither I nor her mother was elated with that choice; indeed, I have it on unimpeachable authority that when Shira first told us about it, I flew into a rage. In no sense could we have been considered practicing Jews. We were very much part of an international public life; our friends were musicians, painters, dancers, writers. But Shira was saying to us, "I am me, and I have to be different." She knew that her brothers had musical talent, and sensed I was closer to them than I was to her. In light of that, she would do what she felt she had to: she would become her own person and enter a world far away from professional music. Basically, she already had shown an extraordinary gift for compassion for the very young, the very ill, and anyone in need. She is a born teacher and counselor. In later years, she would on occasion allude to how hurt she had been by the favoritism she believed I showed her two brothers because of their musical talent. I didn't think it was true then, and it is certainly not now, but one cannot always see into the hearts and minds of one's children and understand how they perceive their relationship with their parents.

In fact, I never wanted my sons to become professional musicians, never encouraged them in that direction. To learn to play an instrument, yes; in our circles, no child could be considered educated without knowing music—it was unthinkable. But children often go their own way. Michael, while excelling in history at Harvard, was also playing the violin and the viola with chamber music groups. One of his playing partners, an older student, was Yo-Yo Ma. And by the time Michael graduated, in the spring of 1980, he had decided to become a conductor.

So the boys were headed toward lives in music, and Shira was studying for a life in the rabbinate. Vera, that year, in her attractive and capable way, continued happily directing our lives with a firm hand and staying involved in the doings at Carnegie Hall and the America-Israel Cultural Foundation. Life was never dull for us, especially the year I turned sixty.

I THOUGHT often of the students I had met on the trip through China, especially the girl violinist in the pale blue dress and red scarf, and of the students I was encountering on my celebratory sixtieth-birthday tour of Europe and Israel. There were things I could show them, technical things, and things I tried to elicit from them—not so much *how* but *why* they were playing a piece of music in a certain way. Too often there was simply not enough time—a growing frustration of mine with master classes: you tore the students down and then had to leave before you could recast the broken parts. I tried to continue teaching beyond the master-class setting, in letters, in talks to music groups, in interviews—wherever a opportunity presented itself. Music students were turning into a worldwide family for me, the counterpart to my very private and beloved family back home. I was thrilled to be able to play and make recordings, and happy that there was documentation of my playing, but I hoped that in the future there would be a record not only of my good performances but also of how and why I got to those performances. It was becoming my dream to be able to articulate that to students and to young teachers of music.

I met with students everywhere, while on tour and at home in New York and Connecticut. A teacher would contact me. Or someone I knew would make a spur-of-the-moment call: they'd heard a gifted person. If I had the time, I'd say yes, come on over. If the player was not very good, I'd get to my point quickly, and in fifteen minutes it would be finished; there was no point in wasting time on someone who was not going to be receptive. But in the case of a fine player, one who, for example, was preparing for a concert, he'd go home and think about what I'd said and begin to listen to every note he was playing. He would not play his next concert the same way he'd played the previous one. Often I'd say to young violin students, "If you have any question in your own mind about how a phrase should go, put down the instrument and sing it. Then listen again to how you sang it and where you took a breath, and try to do the same thing with the violin and bow. Eight times out of ten we sing the phrase naturally and properly, and that is what you should try to do with your instrument."

I would urge them not to listen to violin records. I'd say, "Listen to a quartet, but with the score. Know the score before you listen, and read the score while you're listening. Listen to the Budapest String Quartet play the Beethoven quartets—you'll hear the score being written right in front of your ears. If you want to hear what beauty can be, listen to a great voice singing German lieder. Or listen to a first-rate performance of a Mozart opera. Hear how voices are used, how they change with each word. Notes are our words. And we have to use them in the same way that most people use words when they speak, and as individually as most people, who will sound differently while saying the same thing."

Again and again I said to young students, "First of all, learn to look at yourself and say honestly, 'I'm not trying to impress the listener; what I really want is for the listener to hear how beautiful is the music the composer wrote. I want the listener to feel how much I love this music. I want to convince the listener that this music is very important to us, necessary for us, as human beings.' "

I was hearing about thirty students a year. Some went on to really good careers. At the same time, I was also responding to students who were writing to me from everywhere. In one response I talked about music and the imagination:

> Your teacher . . . was quite right in telling you to use your imagination when you are playing music. Whether it should be a literal story or simply an idea of form or content makes no difference really, because, as you study more and more, and read about it and learn to analyze it, you will find it less necessary to have pictures of an event in your mind; rather the music itself will speak to you in its own language and you will begin to learn to have a dialogue between your understanding of the music and what the composer has written. Whatever you use to excite your imagination in playing or listening is worthwhile, because inevitably it will lead you in the direction of music which is, indeed, a way of speaking. It does not speak in words, it speaks in images which each of us creates in his own way and it is the only way to get into the inside of the music to find out how many ways there are of speaking in the same phrase.

In a more practical vein was my response to a cry of outrage from the aunt of a talented young violinist whose recital had been ignored by the critics:

> Not that it will make you feel any better in this case, but I can tell you that an artist like Shlomo Mintz, who had already made an international name for himself . . . made his Carnegie Hall debut—his first major New York recital—and not a single critic came. . . . There is no way that anyone, manager or artist, can insist on or force the papers to cover a given recital. . . . Pinchas Zukerman's first two New York Carnegie Hall recitals were not reviewed either. The only answer I can give you or your nephew is to say that if he has a real talent and determination he must continue and he will

be heard and he will be reviewed. Real good talents can never be denied, and one concert is not a whole life.

What I really wanted to do, my most cherished, private dream, was to make Carnegie Hall into a musical conservatory dedicated to the highest possible accomplishments in the art of musical performance and training, a center that would be the goal of every gifted youngster in the world. It would be a tough place; those chosen would be trained rigorously. They would be helped, honed—until they came out masters who would pass on to the next generation what music was all about.

No single event in my life triggered a decision about teaching as such. For a while, an anecdote circulated to the effect that early in my career I'd been told by Jascha Heifetz that I had all the talent and ability to become a virtuoso, a highly accomplished musician and performer, but if I really applied myself and expressed my talent to the fullest, I might become good enough to teach. The truth is that no such conversation between us ever took place. There isn't a fiddler alive who does not, quite accurately, consider Heifetz the premier violinist of the twentieth century, but he was hardly the most generous or compassionate of men; he did not really give of himself to younger players; he was not a great teacher.

I began to teach in part because I felt an instinctive distaste toward the kind of instruction that bred mechanical perfection. I never played with automatic dexterity—my mind worked constantly while I performed. It was a dangerous way to live, but infinitely rewarding. Every moment had meaning. There could be no real performance without inner tension, and every performer had to find his own way of resolving the tension. I'd learned about that from my own teacher, Naoum Blinder, in my beginning years in San Francisco; he taught me how to teach myself, and I've never ceased to be grateful for that. In later years, I was influenced by respected and dedicated colleagues and teachers like Rudolf Serkin, Gregor Piatigorsky, Nathan Milstein, Leonard Rose. And I cannot not mention all those other musicians who left their mark on my formative years, each in his or her own way: Pierre Monteux, all four members of the Budapest String Quartet—

Joseph Roisman, Alexander (Sasha) Schneider, Boris Kroyt, and Mischa Schneider—Myra Hess, Pablo Casals, Maureen Forrester, Kirsten Flagstad, Lotte Lehmann, Jan Peerce, Richard Tucker, Lily Pons, Elisabeth Rethberg, Elisabeth Söderstrom, Jussi Björling, Arthur Rubinstein, Vladimir Horowitz, Arturo Toscanini, Bruno Walter, Otto Klemperer, Fritz Reiner, William Steinberg, Charles Munch, Eric Leinsdorf, Sir Thomas Beecham, Eduard van Beinum, Leonard Bernstein. And this is only a very small, partial list. In other words, I learned from listening to, knowing, respecting, and having affection for great artists whom I had the occasion to meet and be with over the last sixty-five years of the twentieth century. I feel it is my responsibility, my duty, to pass along the excitement that these cherished talents gave me to the next generations of performers.

Of all these, two influenced me most about the importance of teaching and learning for teaching: Sasha Schneider and Pablo Casals. The years I spent in their presence, playing music with them, learning music from them, being close friends with them, provided me with the highest of models for the infinite value of leaving a legacy of music.

THE LEGACY would be false were I not at the same time candid about myself. I didn't think, as I edged closer to my sixtieth year, that I was really the kind of success musically that I'd have liked to be. There were many things I didn't do well, and there were pieces, such as the Paganini concerto, I could no longer play. There were other things I had not done enough of. I was hoping that God would grant me time, in the next fifteen or twenty years, now that I'd made my mistakes and done my experimentation, to concentrate on the areas I thought were important musically, and which would be my final musical statement.

That meant that through many years of trying, I'd found the things I thought were right and wrong, and I now had to do what was right. There had been people I'd hurt, people I'd overlooked, moments I'd rather not have had to think about when I'd been foolish, stupid, excessive, arrogant. I'd have done far better if I'd lived more healthily, exercised more, eaten less. But I loved food and drink. I loved tastes and textures. I loved living. That was the power source of my playing.

When I played music, the feeling was very sensuous. Perhaps I should be called a sensualist. I love feelings and I love gratifying the senses. I would find it difficult to be abstemious.

Whether I was capable of the same carefree pyrotechnics of thirty years before didn't make any difference. What had happened was that my music-making had deepened—and *that* couldn't be touched. That could only get bigger. As long as I could hold a fiddle decently and make a good sound, I would always be able to make and teach music. That was my resolve as the summer of 1980 brought me into my sixtieth year.

TWENTY-SIX

*I*T WAS a joyous celebratory year, the year of my sixtieth birthday, filled with public and private happiness. In Paris, during May and June 1980, there took place a festival of eleven concerts, in which I played thirteen concerti with two orchestras and six maestros. I also played a group of one-hour programs that featured smaller pieces for violin and chamber orchestra, and offered a series of string seminars with the string sections of the two orchestras with which I'd played as soloist. I worked an average of sixty to eighty hours a week for seven weeks. It drained me completely, but it was an alive time; I was more alive than I'd been in years.

In July, the month of my birthday, I played in England twice and then gave a series of concerts in Israel. I remember arriving at my birthday party at the Tel Aviv Hilton in an open, sputtering 1930 Ford while a Dixieland trio in the backseat played a noisy version of "When the Saints Come Marching In." Later, at the party, a pretty violinist stepped out of an enormous birthday cake and proceeded to play some of my favorite melodies. One of the concerts I gave in Israel was to an outdoor audience of 15,000 listeners, with the Israel Philharmonic Orchestra led by Zubin Mehta. There had been no time for rehearsals. We just walked onstage and played the Mendelssohn Violin Concerto and Kreisler's *Schön Rosmarin*. It all came out sounding as if it was the easiest thing to do. *That* was craftsmanship. And good luck.

I opened the New York Philharmonic season in September, in a televised pension-fund concert conducted by Zubin Mehta and with my friends Pinchas Zukerman and Itzhak Perlman. In October, I played five concerts with the National Symphony Orchestra at the Kennedy

Center in Washington under Rostropovitch, Ormandy, Mehta, Rudel, and Slatkin. At one of those concerts, Roslyn Carter rode onstage in a magnificently decorated golf cart. A birthday gift suggested by Abe Fortas. Given another sixty years, I still could not have come up with that as a possible present. I had it brought to my home in Connecticut, where I used it in my wanderings about the place, thereby happily making sure that I didn't exercise unduly or lose too much weight.

In the first week of November, I played concerts at Carnegie Hall, and in the last weeks I was back in San Francisco, where my life with the fiddle had begun some fifty years before. I played four concerts with the San Francisco Symphony Orchestra in its new home, Davies Symphony Hall.

Some critics were saying that I might then have been at the very peak of my career had I not devoted so much time and energy to talent scouting and other causes. But they left me unmoved. Perhaps if I had stuck only to the fiddle, only to practicing with the fingers, I might have been playing a little better, I might have accomplished a little more musically—but to what purpose? I hadn't lacked for public success. So I missed a few notes sometimes. Was that really a big deal? I had the joy of being surrounded by young people who had become world figures and by others who were coming up. I had a whole world of family, and in that sense I was one of the richest men in the world.

I was also hearing murmurings about the nature of the relationship between myself and my young protégés and others: the "Kosher Nostra," some were calling us, a fellowship that bordered on clannishness and outright favoritism. I rejected that odious term as the grumbling of outsiders always looking for a reason to explain why they weren't inside. People in music, especially professional musicians, thought that I ran Carnegie Hall. The fact is that I never ran Carnegie Hall nor do I try to now. The Israelis who appeared at the hall made it on their own; I arranged not a single one of their appearances. Indeed, two of my closest colleagues and dearest friends, Eugene Istomin and Leonard Rose, great artists with highly successful worldwide careers, did not appear with any regularity at Carnegie Hall. Decisions as to who should appear on the Carnegie stage are always made by the director of the hall. He or she would inform me when the decisions were made—

but not prior to those decisions. And that's the way it remains to this day.

The profession of the solo performer is both simple and cruel. There is no way you can create a career for someone without talent, and no way to stop a career of someone with talent. As if to illustrate that, there came to my attention in the early eighties an eleven-year-old girl named Midori, who had been born in Osaka, Japan, and was studying in New York at the Juilliard School of Music. Accompanied by her mother and her teacher, she arrived at my home one day to play for me—and I found myself listening to one of the most extraordinary talents I'd heard in the last forty years. She was a tiny figure of a girl, with enormous control and thoughtfulness, and an astonishing repertoire already committed to memory. I determined to take a personal interest in her development.

The last concert I played that year, the year I turned sixty, was the Brahms Concerto, with the Los Angeles Philharmonic Orchestra, conducted by Zubin Mehta at the Chandler Pavilion. I had to admit to myself, when the year was over, that I was pretty much exhausted. I resolved to spend a portion of the next year on sabbatical: no travels, no tours, no concerts.

But the reduction in the number of concerts seemed hardly to affect the pace of my activities; it only redirected them—toward Carnegie Hall. In the meantime, our film, *From Mao to Mozart,* after winning the Academy Award, was making its way into theaters throughout the United States and Europe, and reactions were coming in. The compliments and the attention were simply astonishing. Nothing I'd done in all my years as a performer had elicited such a public response. More than four decades of travel, work, and thought seemed to have been eclipsed by the eighty-four minutes of that film. It was being rapturously received everywhere. Alan Miller's superb editing, which revealed the core of what we'd tried to do in China, had turned raw footage into a world-class film. All of us involved with it were, of course, delighted by the Academy Award and the film's subsequent chance for commercial success. We hoped it would earn some money; we'd agreed that everything it made by way of royalties would be given over to Carnegie Hall to be used for young performers.

The hall had been central to my thoughts and activities for the past twenty-two years. Its activities and centrality to the American contribution to the civilized life of our time were unchallenged and growing ever wider. A fund-raising drive had been initiated to raise $50 million for the renovation and rehabilitation of the outer and inner shells. All of us who were involved with the hall had resolved that it was now necessary to prepare this grand old lady for life in the twenty-first century.

Gifts, generous gifts, came from many individuals and foundations. One especially interesting gift came from Denmark, where, in celebration of the tricentennial of the Jewish community, I played a concert with the Danish Radio Orchestra, for which I would not take a fee. In return, the community pledged to make a sizable contribution in Danish lighting for the refurbishing of the Carnegie Recital Hall. There were many ways of buying my favors.

By mid-1985, we had raised close to $35 million and were twisting arms for the last $15 million. Despite all dire predictions, it seemed we might succeed.

FROM THE euphoria of joyous birthdays and successful accomplishments to the sadness of loss—some seemingly easy to bear though painful, others profound and searing.

On the evening of January 23, 1982, I was in my suite at the Ritz-Carlton Hotel in Chicago, preparing for a recital the next afternoon. I decided to phone my former accompanist, Shura Zakin, to wish him a happy seventy-ninth birthday. I held my violin and bow in my left hand as I phoned, because I wanted to play to him. The ringing telephone went unanswered. I called three or four times over a period of more than an hour, always with the violin and bow in hand.

At one point, I put the bow down while still holding the violin in my left hand, and reached for the telephone once more with my right hand. As I leaned over the end of the couch to the side where the telephone rested, my foot slipped and I fell backward, landing with my right hip on top of the bow and shattering it completely in the middle.

It was a dreadful moment, not just because of the value of the bow; more important, the bow had a special quality and balance that suited

my hand most beautifully for certain major works in the violin repertoire. No two bows are identical in balance, weight, or sound; each has
uniquely individual characteristics and needs to fit the hand and the
playing habits of the performer. That particular bow had been a part of
my approach in performance for all the years I'd owned it, and had an
agility, sound, and attack that were especially suited to my way of playing. It was completely unrepairable. A painful loss.

But infinitely more painful was the illness of the dear friend whom
I'd been trying to reach by telephone. Shura Zakin and I had been
musical and personal companions for nearly forty years. Our personal
and musical lives had become completely entwined. The musical bond
was so close that true freedom, coming as it did from a highly disci-
plined base, made it possible to breathe, to phrase, to weave musical
lines back and forth, because we knew each other so intimately. We
would listen so carefully to each other's playing that every hint of
a nuance from the violin or the piano brought instant response and
collaboration.

Zakin had been confined to his home for some years, barely able to
walk except for a few faltering steps, and not always aware of his surroundings. I used to visit him from time to time. It was difficult for
him to carry on a coherent conversation. His wife, Isabelle, was caring
for him, even to the point of helping him on with his clothes. How
painful it was to see him that way, in such a state of deterioration. He
was paying a sad price for a long life.

Added to that sadness was the death of Jascha Heifetz, in 1981, at the
age of eighty-six. He'd played his last live performance nine years earlier. There had been reports, after he'd stopped his public appearances,
that he'd experienced so much pleasure—the devotion of countless
admirers, the favor of royalty, and great wealth—that he'd simply
become bored. More likely, once he sensed he was losing the ability to
come up to his own standard of perfection, he would not play in public. One of the most astonishing things about Heifetz was that no matter how fast he played, it never sounded speedy. He could go like the
wind, but every note was under control. And whenever he played—
and the same was true of Kreisler, Milstein, Oistrakh; all the very great
ones—you could hear the harmony below. Even though he was

playing horizontally, you could still hear the vertical harmony. That was something very special, to play harmonically in tune; to accomplish that, you needed an enormously accurate ear and great finger technique. And you had to have in your mind a clear sense of the total harmonic and melodic and contrapuntal picture. Heifetz had that. For string players, he was the single most dominant influence in the twentieth century. It was clear beyond discussion that no other violinist had quite *this* mastery, *this* control, *this* constant flow of polished fire. He was one of the four or five giants in the 350-year history of performance on the violin. In the last fifteen to twenty years of his life, he had become ever more reclusive. He was not one to make friends easily, nor would he go out of his way to help a young violinist onto the ladder of a career. He must have been very lonely in his last years. An incalculable loss.

No MATTER where I was during the eighties, no matter what I was doing, there seemed never an end to the politics of music. A strange wind was blowing through the intellectual scene. The emerging dominance of fundamentalism was becoming one of the great dangers to many Western nations. In the case of the United States, it was possibly a little less immediately dangerous because of the natural good sense that we Americans tend to exhibit over the long run. Still, so much harm could be done in the meanwhile, especially to the arts.

Some historical background might be useful here, for the record. The first National Council on the Arts came into being in 1965, in part as a result of conversations that I had initiated with President Kennedy, Mrs. Kennedy, and Pierre Salinger. After President Kennedy's assassination, I spoke further about that idea with Pierre Salinger and Abe Fortas. Abe, not yet on the Supreme Court, was then my lawyer and a close friend. Through Abe, who was President Johnson's closest personal advisor on a daily basis, the idea of the National Council on the Arts was revived and brought to the attention of the president. I remember very clearly being asked to see President Johnson and his sitting me down and saying, "Isaac, I don't know from beans about the arts, but you and Abe tell me this is a very important thing to do, and so I think it's important, and I will back it. And I promise you I will keep my cotton-pickin' hands off it."

A short time later, Abe and I were discussing who should be chairman of the Council, and he asked me to call Roger Stevens, who was then head of the Kennedy Center, and offer him the position. From the time that Roger Stevens accepted the chairmanship, it was he who activated everything, brought us all together. And what a group that first NEA group was! It included Albert Bush-Brown, René d'Harnoncourt, Paul Engle, Philip Hanes, Jr., Oliver Smith, George Stevens, Sr., Minoru Yamasaki, Leonard Bernstein, Anthony Bliss, David Brinkley, Warner Lawson, William Pereira, Richard Rodgers, David Smith, James Johnson Sweeney, Elizabeth Ashley, Agnes de Mille, Ralph Ellison, Father Gilbert Hartke, Eleanor Lambert, Gregory Peck, Otto Wittmann, and Stanley Young. And me, too. Most important, Roger Stevens protected us from the attacks and pressures to which we were subjected by Congress from time to time.

Once, during the Reagan era, there was some hitch in the appropriations for the National Endowment for the Arts, for which the Council served as the advisory body. By chance, I was invited around that time to an informal dinner with the president at the White House; just two tables, eight or ten people to a table. The president was telling everybody about his recent experience of having been shot, how he'd felt, how long it had taken him to recover. He was in a jovial mood. After dinner, we gathered in another room for light talk and drinks. We were sauntering about, chatting. I went over to President Reagan and said, "Mr. President, perhaps I'm taking advantage of a private moment, but I wish you would give some attention to the appropriation for the National Endowment, because there are many people in the arts who have made plans and contracts and commitments for the next few years on the basis of the expectation that what had been voted on would actually be forthcoming." He listened and said, "I'll make a note of it." I remember Henry Kissinger coming up to me and saying angrily, "Isaac, you had no right to talk to the president like that under these social circumstances." I said, "Oh—h—h." I hadn't known the rules.

I have no way of knowing if what I said did any good, but about a week later the appropriation suddenly became unstuck and was signed by the president. I think it is possible, and certainly probable, that someone else will, very properly, come up with the credit for that action by President Reagan.

In the fundamentalist atmosphere of the eighties, the arts became the targets and victims of right-wing religionists and budget-cutting zealots. I argued endlessly that education in the arts was not an elitist luxury but the basis for any civilized society. I spoke before interest groups, state legislatures, committees of Congress. The more I encountered the fundamentalist mind—Christian, Jewish, or Muslim—the more convinced I became that it was a threat to the way of life I held dear.

JUSTICE ABE FORTAS died in 1982. For some years, he and a young woman named Bella Linden had worked together in legal matters. They were not only professional colleagues but also close personal friends. I was introduced to her as a most able and astute person who could be of great value as a friend in music and a legal advisor.

Bella was intelligent, very quick in understanding almost any problem, and enormously informed in finance, copyright, and estate law. Opinionated and, as she put it, "sometimes wrong but never in doubt," she also had no compunction about asking advice of others who she thought knew more than she. In legal confrontations, she was a cross between a pit bull and a stalking tiger, always in a quiet and very controlled fashion. She adored music and the theater and was a constant concert-goer; a gifted gardener; a collector of ladies' frilly shirts, early American and English china, and early American art. And, at the same time, she was a great lover of Yiddish, which she spoke in the most educated and literate way. Despite all these faults, I asked her to become my lawyer some years after Abe died, and she agreed.

IN DECEMBER 1984, I traveled to Washington, D.C., for the Kennedy Center Honors ceremony. Danny Kaye was another of the recipients, along with Lena Horne, Gian Carlo Menotti, and Arthur Miller. It was a dazzling evening, with a private celebration ceremony at the White

House, led by President Reagan, and the public ceremony at the Kennedy Center, hosted by Walter Cronkite. A few weeks later, in early January, my family and I left for a Caribbean music cruise. Shira, now a rabbi and married to a rabbi, Don Weber, was busy with her own life and had elected to remain home. She was pregnant with our first grandchild.

At the end of that month, newspapers were reporting that I would be giving a concert for peace in Hiroshima in June 1985, the proceeds of which would help promote the construction of a peace center commemorating the tragedy that had taken place in Hiroshima's sister city, Poland's Oświęcim (Auschwitz).

Between the end of January and that concert, I toured all through the United States and then went on to Madrid, Paris, Manchester, Oslo, Dublin, London, Philadelphia, Hong Kong, and Taipei—arriving in Hiroshima in the second week of June. I was nearing my sixty-fifth birthday. Somehow the fingers still knew what to do if I practiced quietly and concentrated. The only difference between then and my earlier years was that I now had to concentrate a little harder. So I did.

The event at Hiroshima was called "A Recital for Peace." David Golub had gone on to a separate and subsequently highly successful musical career, and my new accompanist was Paul Ostrovsky. The concert took place at Hiroshima Yubin Chokin Kaikan Hall, on June 10. I took no fee; all the proceeds were donated to atomic-bomb victims in Hiroshima and to the peace center in Kurose Town, next to Hiroshima city.

In a brief talk I gave after the performance, I said: "All countries, beginning with the most powerful on earth today, must believe that it is not only possible but an absolute necessity to find a way to live together without threatening each other's way of life." I said that war was a disease that had to be stamped out of the minds of men, that the concept of a superior nation or a superior race as a natural way of life only led to a natural way of death, and that I believed there was enough power in the human spirit to weld us together in a mutual desire to enjoy the fruits of our planet and to have faith in the continued promise of peace for our children and grandchildren.

Afterward, Paul Ostrovsky and I toured Japan, Korea, and Australia, playing eight concerts in twenty days, including travel time and laundry. I was back home in early July.

The trip to the Far East had been exhausting. I was hoping to relax in the Connecticut house and spend the next two months preparing two world premieres—concerti by Henri Dutilleux and Peter Maxwell Davies—and *Kammerkonzert* by Alban Berg, which I had not played before. But then came a most startling event.

I'd returned home from the Far East on Saturday at 1 a.m., and the very next day, at 5 p.m., Shira gave birth to a boy. He'd decided to arrive three weeks ahead of schedule, perhaps having picked up his grandfather's predilection for moving rather rapidly from point to point. He weighed in at seven pounds and was born on the seventh day of the seventh month, the month of my sixty-fifth birthday. His name would be Noah Lev Stern Weber. Vera and our two sons, Michael and David, were delirious with pleasure. A beautiful, healthy baby. My first grandchild! I held him with special excitement while making more idiotic sounds than the child himself. I couldn't help wondering if he might one day pick up a musical instrument and begin to play. Surely he would be educated in music.

My two sons had, of themselves, chosen to make their lives in music as symphony orchestra conductors. Michael had graduated from Harvard and begun to study with Max Rudolf, conductor of the Cincinnati Symphony Orchestra, with whom I had a very warm, close relationship. When Michael had told me he wanted to become a conductor, I called Max. He asked me, over the telephone, what sort of person Michael was, how he was in school, was he a follower or a leader; rather searching questions. Max Rudolf was one of the most educated musicians I'd ever met, with a profound grasp of the total history of music and its place in society. He had a superb private music library. About five foot nine, fairly thin, with a hawklike beak and twinkling eyes, he was happier reading and thinking about music than doing anything else. He was also a gentle human being. He agreed to see Michael. At the time I called him, he was in his summer home in Maine, and Michael drove up and they met. Before long Michael had a closer relationship with him than he'd almost ever had with me. I think that Max became the grandfather Michael never had; certainly I always thought that Max felt that way about him. He studied with Max for five years at the Curtis Institute in Philadelphia, and he helped edit and write the revision of Max's second book, *The Art of Conducting*. When Max died, he left much of his library to Michael.

Michael had conducted his first professional engagement in Florida in June 1985, and then had gone on to the Monteux School in Hancock, Maine, where he was to stay for six weeks, until the end of July. The birth of Shira's son interrupted his stay and brought him south for a few happy days with his new nephew.

David had gone from the Dalton School in Manhattan to Yale, because, as he put it, "they have the best undergraduate music course that I can find." After graduating from Dalton and before entering Yale, he studied for a year in New York with a wonderful piano teacher, Herbert Stessin. At the same time, he also worked as an usher at a YMHA, where he could hear some of the finest concerts in the city. And he attended concerts at Carnegie Hall. He bathed himself in music.

At Yale, he studied with several people and, as a conducting student, came under Otto Werner-Mueller, a highly trained, quintessential Central European musician and a very good teacher. He was very helpful to David, who soon became conductor of the Yale Bach Society and began to conduct the Yale Orchestra. At one concert he conducted, I played as his soloist. I also played on the fourth stand in the symphony that ended the concert with his girlfriend, Katta, who later became his wife. What a prideful experience that was for me! The summer Shira gave birth, David was just back from a ten-day course in Stuttgart, working with one of his Yale professors on the *St. Matthew Passion*.

That was a happy summer, the summer I turned sixty-five. All the family together, marveling at the miracle of the new baby. The sense of joy he brought to all of us, the sense of continuation of the family!

TWENTY-SEVEN

*A*ND THERE WAS a sense of continuation, too, about my own life. Not in all things, perhaps—my tennis game wasn't what it had once been—but certainly when it came to my life in music.

Much of that feeling of continuation in music came from the two new concerti I was learning that summer. Dutilleux, the composer of one of them, spent two days at the Connecticut house in August, and we went over the entire score. It was a beautiful and quite difficult work, demanding a fine orchestra, a world-class conductor, six or seven rehearsals for the orchestra, and a cymbalum player. I was certain it was worth all the effort I was putting into learning it.

Dutilleux is a most gentle person, shy, graceful, and completely unostentatious. I loved working with him. He dedicated the work to me, which, according to Dutilleux, meant that I was granted the right to all first performances. Radio France had commissioned him for a work a long time before, and paid him—if one wanted to call it that—20,000 francs (the equivalent of just over $5,000 in 1984), an utterly ridiculous sum for a major work by a world-renowned composer.

In November 1985, I premiered the Dutilleux Violin Concerto in Paris, with Lorin Maazel leading the Orchestre National de France. The concerto was a great success. We then recorded it. The following year, I played it again, in Montreal, Boston, and New York. I also played in Baltimore and on tour with the Baltimore Symphony, with David Zinman conducting, where they coined a name for the concerto as we traveled around—the "Due-to-you" concerto. Over the years, much to my delight, it has entered the violin repertoire.

In June 1986, I premiered the Peter Maxwell Davies Violin Concerto—in Kirkwall, Scotland, on the island of Orkney, the home of the composer. We were surrounded by the sea and the rocky terrain and by birds wheeling overhead—the timelessness of nature putting flesh on the bones of the composer's vision. Four days later, I played the concerto again at the Royal Festival Hall in London, with André Previn conducting the Royal Philharmonic Orchestra.

There were, of course, other things as well. I set a rather punishing recording schedule for myself: all the Beethoven sonatas for piano and violin; and the Alban Berg concerto for violin, piano, and thirteen wind instruments, with Peter Serkin as the piano soloist and Claudio Abbado conducting members of the London Symphony Orchestra. I played about sixty concerts that year and flew about 200,000 miles. One flight I took, from Denver to Chicago, was, it seemed to me, rather thoughtlessly delayed on the runway, while small plane after small plane was given permission by the tower to take off. I sat there watching my forty-minute connection from Chicago to Montreal evaporate. The captain radioed ahead and had the Montreal flight wait for me. That was more than mere politeness on his part; it was thoughtfulness of the first degree. I had told him that I had a rehearsal in Montreal that evening for a new work, which was having its North American premiere that week, and that I had to get there on time. I made the connection, made the rehearsal, and played the work: the new Dutilleux.

I continued teaching, too—personally and by mail. One day a letter arrived from a violin student in Shanghai; an American had given him my address. He had once listened, in secret, to my tape of some Bach; Western classical music was forbidden at the time. He wrote that he'd heard about the film *From Mao to Mozart* but hadn't seen it; the film wasn't being shown in China. Shanghai, he wrote, was a city of ten million people—with only three violin teachers. People were more interested in science than Western music. He asked me at what age one should start learning the violin, and I suggested that six to nine years of age was a good time, because the hands were still soft and the muscles well-knit, and you could count on the student for a certain amount of concentration. I also informed him that there were several copies of *From Mao to Mozart* in China, at the Ministry of Foreign Affairs and elsewhere, and told him how to arrange to view it. I saw no need to inform him that I'd kept in touch with several of the people in the film. A girl who had played the Brahms Violin Concerto was now studying in London and playing with several orchestras, and a professor of music who had been imprisoned during the Cultural Revolution had recently visited New York. As a matter of fact, every young performer in the film *From Mao to Mozart* has left China to study: some have started good careers, some have joined good orchestras, and others are teaching.

Part of my teaching involved explaining choices I made for my concerts, in particular when I played new, unfamiliar composers. I remember defending Bartók to an angry concert-goer, who had been profoundly bored by a Bartók composition I had played. He let me know about his feelings in a letter, and I explained that solo performers chose music in which they believed. Bartók, in my view, was the natural and unassailable important continuation of the great musical tradition that went from Beethoven and Brahms into our time. Indeed, I added, many today considered Bartók a rather old-fashioned composer.

And to those of my younger colleagues who would listen—Pinchas Zukerman, Itzhak Perlman, Miriam Fried, as well as my conductor sons and others—I urged that they now go to Germany and perform there. I had always felt that the biases of elders should not be passed on to younger people. In no way did my personal feelings about playing in today's Germany diminish my respect for those who lived and labored there in an area that was the rich mother lode of the Central European musical tradition that had nourished us all.

And so the traveling, the playing, and the teaching went on. My sons had begun their careers. Shira, working as a mother and a rabbi, was pregnant again. Vera was very busy with the America-Israel Cultural Foundation. Sadly, some strains had developed in our marriage.

In 1986, I played a recital with Marvin Hamlisch at the Public Theater in New York: Kreisler and pieces from Jerry Bock's *Fiddler on the Roof*. I was also playing recitals now with Yefim Bronfman—a magnificent young musician whom I regarded as one of the leading talents of our time—and chamber music with Emanuel Ax, Yo-Yo Ma, Jaime Laredo, and Cho-Liang Lin. My joyous continuation in music.

THE CONTINUATION was suddenly interrupted in the middle of 1987.

I was having trouble with my heart. For some time now I'd been popping nitroglycerin pills while pushing away the memory of my 1968 heart attack. In June of 1987, I needed to go to Israel to play a number of benefit concerts. I never canceled benefits: too many years went into the planning, too many people depended on the proceeds. I promised my doctor, who had urged me not to go, that I would stay in touch with him. I flew to Israel.

I wasn't playing well. It wasn't only the pain; at times I felt faint. After the second concert, I went to see a doctor friend of mine in Israel. He checked me and said, "You're going to have trouble." I said, "I know. I'm going home immediately after the last concert, in two days." He said, "All right," and gave me more nitroglycerin.

After the last concert, I flew to Paris, where I boarded the Concorde to New York. I called my doctor from Kennedy Airport. He said, "Don't go home, come right to the hospital." I sent my fiddle and bags back to the apartment. After the tests, my doctor said, "I think you're going to have a bypass operation tomorrow morning." And I said, "Goddamn it!" and rammed my fist against the wall. I was angry. I knew that the bypass surgery had to happen eventually: all the pain, the shortness of breath, the feelings of fatigue, the nitroglycerin pills. Still, I was really furious.

Early the next morning, they prepared me for the surgery. The nurses were a little upset because I insisted on keeping my glasses on so I could watch things on the monitor. Always curious! As I was going under, I said, "I'll see you afterward, I hope. If I do, I'll be happy. If I don't, that's my problem."

I was fortunate in that the surgeon, Dr. Wayne Isom, who was head of cardiac surgery at the hospital, loved music and knew that if a certain artery was used for the bypass, there was some remote chance that my fingers might be adversely affected. The procedure he planned avoided that possibility entirely. Of course, at the time I had no idea what they were doing; only afterward did I realize what a piece of dead meat I was on the table. There I was, being cut up, while my heart was beating from one machine and my lungs were breathing from another and my body temperature was being cooled to near freezing for the surgery.

It was a triple bypass. I had all these staples in my chest. I lay in bed in my hospital room, watching the Oliver North trial on television, from morning till night. It was a great way of not paying attention to myself.

I discovered later how angry at me my children were. How could I think so little of them to have taken such a chance with my life? I told them that I had done what I had to do. I had given my word that I would perform those benefit concerts in Israel, and I had to live up to my promise.

The recovery was fairly rapid. Three months after the operation, I was on tour in Hong Kong and Japan, then the United States and Europe. Happily, the bypass surgery was not only completely success-ful but left me feeling younger and far more energetic than I'd felt for the past few years. I used that newfound energy in March of the fol-lowing year to speak before the Washington State Senate, urging sup-port for the $7.7 million budget request for the Washington State Arts Commission. I said:

> The arts are not casual, social adornments to society; they are basic to the way we live. The fetus in the womb of the mother has a heartbeat. . . . When that child comes out and that little form suddenly opens up and goes "Aaaa"—it is making its first sound. Now you put the heartbeat and the sound together and that's your first music, and that's why music is basic to the way we live . . . and why all people every-where have a reaction to the power of music—all kinds of music. The more you have a chance to listen to it, the greater becomes your appreciation—your need for living with music.

I talked about the history of the National Endowment for the Arts, how we started with barely $3 million, how we warded off repeated attempts by members of Congress to cut the current budget of $150 million. I reminded them of the cities that were being brought back to life through the construction of centers for the arts:

> I don't have to give you figures on what artists, music organizations, and theater groups can do for you. You have enough lobbyists lining the walls here to give you all the figures. Just listen to them. . . . We have the greatest wealth in the world in our young people. That pool of talent is what will make this country work in the decades and the centuries to come.

On December 11, 1989, I played my last concert of the eighties, at Carnegie Hall, with Cho-Liang Lin, Jaime Laredo, Michael Tree, Yo-Yo Ma, Sharon Robinson, and Emanuel Ax: the Brahms Quartet in A Major and the Brahms Sextet in B-flat Major. The joy of making music was somewhat beclouded by the increasing difficulties Vera and I were experiencing with our marriage. Shira had by then given us two new grandsons, Ariel and Eytan, so I was a triple grandfather as well as a triple bypass as we entered the final decade of the century.

TWENTY-EIGHT

ONCE IN THE SIXTIES, I was playing in Sarajevo during a summer music festival and in the audience sat Marshal Tito, the Communist president of Yugoslavia, together with the presidents of the various Yugoslav republics. Suddenly there was a power failure and the lights went out.

The darkness was so total that I was unable to make out my hands in front of my face, nor could the pianist see anything. After two or three minutes, I heard the audience growing restive. I began to play a piece by Bach for solo violin. Most violinists can do that, play without seeing fingers or the bowstrings. The audience fell silent. I played until the lights came back on.

I've played in rain, in cold, in blistering heat, in fiercely blowing winds, in darkness that was the absence of light, and in darkness that marked the end of lives that were dear to me. I played at the funeral of Sol Hurok. I played with sadness in my heart after the death of Shura Zakin, my wonderful colleague with whom music-making had been a joy for almost forty years. And I played with a sense of mortal grief after the death of Leonard Bernstein. Shura and Lenny—both suddenly gone in 1990.

I was in Philadelphia, having just played with the Curtis Institute Orchestra—a benefit for them in preparation for a concert two days later at Carnegie Hall—and as I came offstage, my son Michael told me of Lenny's passing a few hours before.

Many of his close friends had known that he was ill and that his physical stamina had been sharply reduced. But when you love someone, you can steel yourself against the pain, and you always hope that maybe there will be a miracle. It wasn't to be. We had spent so much time together, talking, playing music, walking on the streets of Venice and Paris. I thought back to that concert in Rochester, New York, in 1947, the first time that he and I appeared together. We played the Prokofiev D Major Concerto and the Bach A Minor Concerto, and we were planning to play that program again at Avery Fisher Hall the next April. He was not only a colleague but a very close friend for forty-three years. What I remembered most clearly about him was his mind, that enormous sponge with an insatiable appetite for all kinds of knowledge. His love of being challenged by the Double-crostic in the Sunday *Times;* his love of words. He cared for his fellow man and for his friends. As is often the case with genius, he was at times deeply ambivalent both personally and professionally, equivocal in some of his relationships and torn between his dual passions for conducting and composing. I had been with him in Connecticut a couple of times three or four weeks before, and he'd played for me the last movement of the work he'd just finished revising about a month before: one of the most beautiful moments in all the music he'd ever written, a memorial to his friends who had gone. It was very difficult to use the word "was" when thinking about Lenny. Not to be able to pick up the phone and say, "Lenny," and hear his voice at the other end. I was certain other lights would come along, but not like his. He was unique in this century.

There was little doubt about it in my heart: playing music and teaching music were some of the ways I defied the darkness. And most especially when I played as a soloist with orchestras conducted by my sons.

Those were among the most joyously celebratory moments that marked my seventieth year. I was playing less now, but enjoying it more. Nor was I feeling in any way patriarchal. I had turned gray, but didn't walk—or, I hoped, play—with deliberate steps. I had no intention of hanging up my two Guarneris. True, it was taking me a little longer to run the four-minute mile. And my concert schedule was down from a high of nearly one hundred to around sixty-five a year. But I was playing more chamber music than ever before, frequently with younger colleagues—Emanual Ax, Yo-Yo Ma, Daniel Barenboim—and recording a great deal: Mozart, Schubert, Vivaldi, Rameau, Brahms. I was playing where, what, and when I liked to play.

In July of that year, I was a guest at a gala dinner in my hometown, San Francisco. My son David, who had married in May, came with his wife, Katta. And my son Michael was there with his fiancée, Jeanette. The next day I attended a free outdoor concert at Stern Grove, given by the San Francisco Symphony Orchestra for my seventieth birthday. It was rather a smallish party, with only 20,000 people in attendance. I didn't have to play a note. Michael and David were present, but did not conduct. On the stage were Gregory Peck, who spoke, and Mark Peskanov, Jimmy Lin, Jaime Laredo, and Gil Shaham, who played a tribute together. Old pals like Alexander Schneider, Jean-Pierre Rampal, and Mstislav Rostropovitch and newer colleagues Cho Liang-Lin, Yefim Bronfman, Robert McDonald, and Sharon Robinson all stood in with the orchestra. And David Zinman conducting them all, laboring joyously and endlessly to put it all together in the most wonderful way. What a special privilege to have friends show their warmth and affection that openly and gladly. I am blessed.

There were festivities in Europe, too. At the Évian Festival, my son David conducted a French youth orchestra in a Mozart concerto, with me as soloist. In London, Michael conducted the London Symphony Orchestra when I played the Beethoven Violin Concerto.

In every performance I'd given over the years, there had always been a moment when all time stopped and everything was suspended except the beauty of the musical line hanging in the air. You knew it was transitory; you knew it wouldn't ever happen quite that way again. So you savored it, you tried to remember it. I loved being onstage, and that love was raised to tearful ecstasy as I played Mozart and Beethoven with my sons.

There was much written about me in the press that year—about the saving of Carnegie Hall, the first tour of the Soviet Union, the creation of the National Endowment for the Arts, my young protégés, my teaching, the tour of China, my role as cultural ambassador. A high air of grandeur seemed to hover over my name. In truth, I had little taste for glitzy glamour and preferred to remain accessible and part of the crowd. I liked people: the taxi drivers, the porters, the vendors. Also, I believed that a healthy measure of self-deprecation was a useful antidote to overdoses of self-esteem. In a full-length mirror, I'd see a portly five-foot-six figure, gray-haired, wearing glasses, a roundish form that had led me once to remark to the people seated on the stage for a sold-out concert, "Pardon my back," and then, after turning and facing the audience, "Pardon my front." Not much glamour and grandeur there; it was my music that I took seriously, not myself.

AND I TOOK loyalty very seriously, too. All my life I've remained loyal to friends who had faith in me during my early years: musicians, conductors, managers, the company with which I'd recorded music for more than five decades through all its various corporate permutations. There was kinship and comfort in my relationships with all of them. They were part of my natural center.

For example, Zubin Mehta. Ever since his early leadership in Montreal, then his many years with the Los Angeles Philharmonic, the Israel Philharmonic, and the New York Philharmonic—for all these more than forty years—we have been the closest of friends and musical comrades. Countless concerts, benefits, recordings. To play with Zubin is to know ultimate support and mutual musical fervor.

Now I was a loyal, severe, and compassionate friend to a new generation of violinists. In the year 1991, when some were lamenting the crisis in conducting and the dearth of great tenors and the meager presence of supreme artists at the keyboard, there was astonishing virtuosity on the violin, the most difficult instrument of all: Itzhak Perlman, Anne-Sophie Mutter, Gidon Kremer, Maxim Vengerov, Gil Shaham, Midori, Joshua Bell. Some saw me behind much of this flourishing of string players: a sort of Svengali known in violin circles as "the godfather," snapping up gifted ten-year-olds, funding their education at Juilliard with Dorothy DeLay, who, when they were ready for the world, picked up the phone, called Lee Lamont at ICM, and urged her to listen to them play. Completely untrue, but so they thought.

Well, a youngster with great talent merited the loyalty and the learning of the older generation that he or she would one day replace. I was simply giving back what friends in the past had once given me.

And loyalty to Israel remained—not only to the students I was engaging in chamber-music classes, but to the entire Israeli people. I didn't go to Israel at the start of the Persian Gulf War, because there was nowhere I could play: the threat of gas attacks by Scud missiles had forced the Israeli authorities to prohibit all public assemblies. But some days after the outbreak of the war, when I was informed by phone that gatherings would be permitted in small halls that could be quickly evacuated, I said I would come over. I flew there and played five concerts in three days, and arranged to play a final concert in Jerusalem on a Saturday night. The date was February 23, 1991. I knew that I needed to leave Israel later that night, because I had to be in Montreal the next day for a rehearsal. The concert was set for 6:30 p.m.

At 6:55, the orchestra and I, with Zubin Mehta conducting, were in the middle of a Mozart concerto when suddenly Zubin put down his hands and said to me, "There is a problem." Then someone came onstage and announced that an air-raid alert was in progress, and though the hall we were in was sealed and protected against gas, would everyone please put on their gas masks anyway and remain calm.

Zubin, the orchestra, and I went offstage. We knew that it took between four and seven minutes from the time of the warning until the missile came down somewhere. We waited for the missile to land. This was the first night of live music in Jerusalem since the war had begun, and now the audience was sitting there with masks on. I sensed they were becoming nervous. It felt strange waiting aimlessly for something to happen. The restiveness in the audience was increasing—one could feel the rustle of fear and unrest throughout the hall. At that moment, it seemed to me that the most obvious thing to do was to take up the violin and play. So I walked out onstage without a mask and calmed them down with some motions of my hands and said, "Listen," and I began to play the Sarabande from the D Minor Partita for Solo Violin by Bach.

Everyone grew quiet. It was the eeriest, most bizarre experience, to look out and see an audience of gas masks, to feel the effect of the music as the people became still, to wait for the thud of the missile. We knew the Iraqis wouldn't aim their missiles at Jerusalem, with all the Muslim holy places and the Arabs who were there. But we also knew how inaccurate those missiles were, how far from their intended targets they sometimes landed. That was one of the most heart-stopping moments of my life. And still I went on playing. I had picked that music because it was quiet, contemplative. A very distant explosion was heard as I played, and we learned later that the missile had fallen halfway between the concert hall and Ben-Gurion Airport. When I finished and walked offstage, I was completely overwrought, as were Zubin and the members of the orchestra. Then the alert ended, and we were informed by the military that there was no evidence of gas, and we all walked back onstage to continue the concert.

There was a roar from the audience. They jumped to their feet. I finished the Mozart concerto with the orchestra, then played a Brahms sonata and one encore with a gifted young Israeli pianist, and drove like a low-flying missile to Ben-Gurion Airport, with Zubin madly at the wheel. I made the flight by twenty minutes and was at my scheduled rehearsal the next day in Montreal. As we flew over the Atlantic Ocean the pilot announced the beginning of the Desert Storm ground attack in Iraq.

It was important for me to have been in Jerusalem at that moment, to do what I did, to express my continuing loyalty to Israel and my faith in what humankind could do well. Besides, the time to be a friend is in a time of trouble. How many times could you say to yourself that you were somewhere at a moment when you were really needed? People made far too much of my playing during a Scud attack. A great act of courage? Nonsense! I was there to do something very specific: bring comfort through music. It was really a blessing for me under such circumstances to feel useful. We'd all had enough of destruction. I wanted to balance it—to defy it—with music.

My loyalty to Carnegie Hall remained undiminished. We raised that last necessary $15 million, and an additional $10 million to cover unanticipated costs. I remember describing the hall in a letter to Frank

Sinatra in which I thanked him for his personal gift to me of a sumptu-
ous double packet of tubed Cuban cigars plus a handsome cutter. That
was in 1986. The hall, I wrote, looked "a little bit like a fish which has
just been taken out of water, gutted, beheaded and all the scales
scraped off." But, I assured him, "what we have started already seems to
prove the correctness of all our plans and hopes."

Frank and I had met at a benefit concert in New York and become
good friends, with mutual respect and affection between us. I once
had the opportunity to stay in his wonderful home in Palm Springs,
and discovered that he was an innate musician who understood and
respected what musical performances meant in the classical as well as
the popular field. He also loved to whip up marvelous spaghetti sauce
and share a drink or fifteen with friends. Over the years he became one
of Carnegie Hall's staunchest allies and quietly generous supporters.
And some years later, in place of the gutted, beheaded, scraped fish I'd
described in my letter to him, there stood a grand building returned to
its original concept, a vibrant monument to the wonders of music,
many different kinds of music.

I'd played all kinds of music on the stage of the hall—with one
exception. The only music by an enormously talented composer that I
consistently could not play, in Carnegie Hall or anywhere else, was the
Schoenberg Violin Concerto. Lenny Bernstein had once wanted me to
play it with him—he called it Schumann with wrong notes—but there
was something in it to which I could not bond.

And I never liked rock music; it was always for me the music of
angry young people. But I loved jazz, loved its presence at Carnegie
Hall. I was brought up in the jazz era. I remember walking down 52nd
Street in New York and going into those rooms that held all of forty
people. You needed a fan to get through all the smoke. And listening to Art Tatum, Cleo Brown, and Artie Shaw; and to Duke Elling-
ton reaching out beyond jazz into new realms of music; and to the
others—great musicians. How I loved those sounds in the new life of
Carnegie Hall.

There were new things going on as well in the Jerusalem Music Centre, where every other year or so I would spend two weeks of a summer, teaching. I had always disliked the term "master class," with its

connotation of subservience, and we now called those classes "encounters." More than a mere change in terminology, the new name was intended to reflect a shift in relationship, a meeting between greatly experienced professional musicians and younger musicians rather than teachers and students.

The various ensembles came to Jerusalem from Europe, the United States, and Israel. In 1996, there were four piano trios, a string trio, a piano quartet, a string quartet, and a duo. The young musicians ranged in age from fifteen to thirty, and had all had some stage experience as ensembles. They'd been selected, out of about thirty-four groups that had applied, to spend two weeks in Jerusalem, with myself and a number of my colleagues, all of them world-class professional musicians and experienced performers. To name just a few: Jaime Laredo, Michael Tree, Yo-Yo Ma, Sharon Robinson, Emanuel Ax, Yefim Bronfman, Joseph Kalichstein, and Henry Meyer. I am grateful to them for their generosity and tenderness in joining together in Jerusalem, and many of them, and more, at Carnegie Hall. We now give these "encounters" every other year in Jerusalem and at Carnegie Hall, and are adding some in countries such as Japan, Holland, and Germany. And we have plans for others in Europe and the United States in the upcoming years: a prospect of work and association that delights me more than I can say. The younger musicians, during their time in Jerusalem, would be exposed to 250 years of collective master-musician experience.

The older musicians would not play. We didn't want the younger ones to imitate us; we wanted them to learn how to teach themselves. On occasion, one of us might pick up an instrument to demonstrate something; I wasn't too keen on that, either. Some of the younger players, it turned out, were remarkably gifted. I was not afraid of their talent; on the contrary, if I found someone with talent that exceeded my own, it made me happy.

It was all a whirlwind of activity for me. I was often asked to speak before state legislatures about the need to maintain budgets for the arts. Lobbying, traveling, playing music, listening to young people, guiding them, trying to kindle lights in their hearts, raising money for Carnegie Hall, talking to groups about the arts and about music education; and awarded the Medal of Freedom at the Kennedy Center, in December, on the worst possible day of 1992, with storms raging up and down the East Coast and mobs at the railroad stations, and getting to Washington after ten hours on the trains and three hours of sleep following a New York Philharmonic gala in my honor, all a bit taxing; and being in Washington as Itzhak Rabin, Shimon Peres, and Chairman Arafat stood together with President Clinton in an extraordinary moment of history that brought tears to the eyes of everyone in the audience; and an honorary doctorate from Oxford in 1993; and, four years later, on January 28, 1997, the gala Carnegie Hall Tribute and the book of letters honoring me that came from friends near and far—it was difficult through all of that *not* to think of myself as some kind of a political animal. In fact, loyalty to music was what united the disparate parts of my life. I am, for better or worse, a musical activist.

I CONTINUED to travel and play, but not more than four or five months of the year and only to places where I wanted to go. I was playing more and more chamber music and recording Brahms and Fauré quartets with Emanuel Ax, Yo-Yo Ma, and Jaime Laredo, and Brahms string sextets with Jimmy Lin, Michael Tree, Jaime Laredo, Sharon Robinson, and Yo-Yo Ma. Those days were so full of joy and special music-making. I was also in the midst of making recordings of all the Mozart sonatas with Yefim Bronfman, one of today's giants of the keyboard. The two of us had recorded all the Brahms sonatas "Live in St. Petersburg" when we were there in 1992, after the fall of the Soviet Union—the first time I'd been back to Russia to play in twenty-five years!

I was seventy-three years old in 1993, and spent the latter part of that year playing concerts in Hong Kong and Japan with Bronfman. From Japan we flew westward across Europe to England and Oxford. I had two close friends at Oxford, Sir Isaiah Berlin, the philosopher and founding president of Wolfson College, and Sir Claus Moser, warden of Wadham College. Oxford was offering me an honorary degree, which coincided with Sir Claus' retirement. We happily played a concert in his honor. I stayed at Headington House, Aline and Isaiah's home.

The actual doctorate ceremony had certain traditions, which touched me deeply. I was dressed in the appropriate gown and stayed in a side chapel until a warder knocked ceremoniously on a door and I was officially invited to join the procession into the Sheldonian Theatre. I stood where indicated and listened to a highly praising speech, of which, since it was in Latin, I was thoughtfully given an English translation. At the proper moment, I went up the steps to the stage, bowed my head, had the appropriate colored sash and the Brueghel-like cap—which is probably the most beautiful mortarboard anywhere—put on. High tea was offered to me by Isaiah Berlin, a very ceremonial moment with more than one hundred guests.

That evening at the Sheldonian Theatre, Fima Bronfman and I played a recital in honor of Sir Claus. For the end of the program, we had prepared two surprise encores. As we left the stage at the end of the printed program, I quickly put on the robe and cap with which I had been honored in the afternoon and walked back onstage wearing it and carrying my violin, much to the amused enjoyment of the public, particularly our close friends. Unbeknownst to them, we had prepared two encores, both involving Sir Claus. The first was a movement of a Mozart sonata that he and I played, with Fima Bronfman turning the pages for him. After that ended to happy applause, we walked out once more, I without the violin and went up with Sir Claus to the stage where I sat in the page turner's chair and he and Fima Bronfman played a four-handed encore. The whole evening was especially happy for me and all concerned, particularly for Claus, his wife, Mary, Isaiah, Aline, and many friends who were there with us. There *are* moments in life which one never forgets

Isaiah Berlin was an idol of mine and probably the finest mind I have ever encountered. We shared many moments of happy conversation, discussing everything from music to politics to people to gossip at his home, on the telephone, or in letters. We met in London, in Oxford, in Jerusalem, in New York, wherever it was possible to be together at the same time. I loved him deeply and I miss him.

Vera had become president of the America-Israel Cultural Foundation (I had remained as honorary chairman of the board), and was heavily engaged in heading up the fund-raising campaign to help Mayor Teddy Kollek win reelection in Jerusalem that November. Our marriage was by then deeply troubled and the source of much sadness and conflict for us both. Michael and David had fine careers as conductors: David largely in opera, and living in Paris; and Michael guest-conducting all over Europe and with a growing career in the United States, and living in Florida, where his wife, Jeanette, was the first oboe of the Florida Orchestra. Shira and her husband, Don Weber, were hardworking rabbis with separate temples. Their three sons were now eight, six, and four.

As I look back now, the years when the children were young and growing were very special to me. I wasn't around as much as other fathers; of necesssity, I was more than slightly obsessed with my musical life. I didn't take my sons to their first baseball or football games, or my daughter to her first tea party or play with her and her dolls. But we did spend time together—there were graduations, bloody noses, tears, happy squeals, hand-in-hand walks from time to time. The fact of their being was, for me, the greatest joy I had.

In later years, when they were grown, there was nothing more happy for me than when I played with orchestras that my sons were conducting, or when I sat in the temple listening to my daughter give a deeply thoughtful and organized sermon or cantillate with a lovely, sweet soprano, singing perfectly in tune because she has such a good ear.

I've been a member of the audience listening to Michael conduct a concert and felt a shiver of pure joy and the pleasure of a quiet tear in seeing him as such a caring, powerfully communicative, professional musician. And I've watched David conduct a symphony orchestra or an opera performance and reveled in his joy in being a musician. He has a special affinity for voices. Shira and her husband, Don, are thoughtful, caring, and enormously attentive parents to my three grandsons, Noah, Ariel, and Eytan. The children share their mother's and father's rabbinical responsibilities and are at practically every service. In their home, they strictly observe Jewish traditions. The Webers also are caring in their community: Don is a volunteer ambulance driver, ready to throw on shoes and clothes, to dash out of the house to an emergency at the first sound of the beeper; Shira is caught up in community efforts, whether they involve women's rights, abortion rights, or the nature of political life in their community. And both of them share with their children the youngsters' participation in sports and games with their friends, down to and including carpooling. And when they really want to get away from it all, they board the little plane that Don flies quite professionally, and go off to wherever their desire takes them for that day. Shira and all three boys have shared this to the limit of the airplane, which can only hold three people at a time, the pilot included. But they have taken trips in all directions, landed, and had food in good restaurants near little airports; generally, they enjoy the freedom of the skies within a few hundred miles of their home in New Jersey. Not unexpectedly, all three boys have all kinds of airplane memorabilia, particularly Noah. From time to time, they have landed at Danbury, near our home in Connecticut, had lunch, and then flown home.

Michael continues his highly successful conducting life as general music director of the Radio Orchestra in Saarbrucken, Germany, where he works enormously hard and covers an immense repertoire; the very nature of the radio there requires him to learn and perform new and contemporary compositions constantly. His wife, Jeanette, is a wonderful musician on the oboe and is expanding her life as a solo performer in chamber music and solo concerts. And they are happily building their life together.

David's wife, Katta, is a gifted violinist, particularly in Baroque literature, which she knows and plays beautifully. The two of them have thoughtfully and happily presented me with my first two granddaughters: Sophia, who will be four years old in August of 1999, and Talia, who will be two years old in January of 2000. David is the successful and happy conductor of the Acadamie Européene de L'Art Lyrique in Aix-en-Provence. He's been very successful with chamber operas he has conducted there and throughout Europe.

VERA AND I were not the first couple who found themselves growing apart, sometimes imperceptibly, until the gap became so wide that it could no longer be bridged. I don't think either of us realized to what degree it was true that two strong personalities cannot exist in one house without clashes. For many years of our marriage we were a dysfunctional couple, our lives often rancorous with angry confrontations.

The children knew it, of course, but their world was so ordered and so comfortable that they didn't think anything needed to be changed. We were almost universally regarded as an ideal family. It was painfully, excruciatingly difficult to begin to recognize the irreconcilability of two paths going in different directions. Whatever happened from then on is completely private, and there is no point to adding to what I've already said.

EVER SINCE participating in the opening of the Kennedy Center for the Performing Arts in Washington, D.C. more than twenty-five years ago, I have performed there very often in various roles: as a soloist with the National Symphony Orchestra, in recital with piano, in performances in the trios, both with Leonard Rose and Eugene Istomin and later with Yo-Yo Ma and Manny Ax, and in piano quartets with Yo-Yo Ma, Manny Ax, and Jaime Laredo. In the office and at the social functions that always followed these concerts, I occasionally met a beautiful young lady named Linda Reynolds, who was working at the Kennedy Center.

As my marriage disintegrated and I requested a separation, I found myself increasingly drawn to Linda and, finally, dared to ask her out. The relationship, cautiously begun, became close. And suddenly I found out something that I really did not believe possible: that in my seventies, I could fall head-over-heels in love.

It was an extraordinary time of self-discovery. I began to revel in the joy and the art of happy living—feelings I thought I could never experience again.

I subsequently discovered that Linda was originally from Lumberton, North Carolina, the state where both sides of her family had settled in the late 1600s and early 1700s. It was from her that I learned that "Southern charm" was not just a cliché.

She's the only child of the late Honorable and Mrs. William D. Reynolds (he was an elected member of the state legislature). She idolized both of them. Her mother was responsible for her musical background: Mrs. Reynolds had been an extraordinary pianist, teacher of piano, organist, and choral conductor, an all-around musician and an alumna of, among other institutions, the Julliard School of Music. She was the cultural maven of her county and its environs. She founded and ran, pro bono, with the help of a small committee, a classical music series for about twenty-five years, until she became ill. It continues to this day. She and her husband were much loved in the community and, later, I even played a benefit in Mrs. Reynolds' memory in Lumberton. There I met charming, loving, and warm people.

Linda herself had been a very talented pianist, studying with university professors around North Carolina. But rather than going to a conservatory, she chose to attend Sweet Briar College, where she majored in music history and friends.

After college she moved to Washington, D.C., and worked at the John F. Kennedy Center for the Performing Arts, an institution that remains close to her heart today. As a result of her tenure there with the director of the Kennedy Center, then the president of the National Symphony, and finally with the general director of the Washington Opera, all three of whom happened to be my old Hurok friend Martin Feinstein, she learned not only about the production aspects of musical events but got to know many great artists and their managers as well. Therefore, she understood the kinds of lives musicians live. This was an added boon for me, aside from our shared love of music. And each other.

As the divorce proceedings became more and more difficult and seemingly interminable, Linda and I began to live openly in our Connecticut home. In 1995, we traveled together to France, Italy, Spain, Switzerland, and Sweden, and later to Singapore, Hong Kong, Tokyo, Shanghai, Beijing, and Jerusalem. I played concerts in all those cities, except Beijing and Jerusalem. Before going on the trip, I telephoned all the members of my family, Vera included, to tell them that Linda and I were going to travel around the world together so that they would not hear it from "friends." I introduced Linda everywhere as my fiancée, which was, in fact, quite true.

Soon after the divorce was granted, Linda and I were married. The ceremony took place on the afternoon of November 3, 1996, in our Connecticut home, in a small room facing the garden. All the people who worked in and around the house—cook, housekeeper, gardener, caretaker—were there as witnesses and guests, as were a few friends of Linda's from Washington and Atlanta and six friends of ours from New York. The ceremony, the sun-drenched day, the caviar, the champagne, and truly ecstatic friends made it all heavenly.

I must add that among the unexpected extra dimensions of my present life are Linda's happy, intelligent, and attractive friends. They visit often and light up our lives, and have joined with my old friends easily and wonderfully. Around them I feel as if I am their age! This unexpected gift was the best dowry. Linda, like me, likes good food, good wine, and is a Francophile. In addition to her innate intelligence, she has an outrageous, and sometimes wicked, sense of humor. *Quelle chance!*

She is also a most naturally charming and relaxed hostess. Now our home in Connecticut and our pied-à-terre in New York are filled with laughter and good conversation. The homes are beautiful, comfortable, and, most important, they smile. Life *can* be good!

The divorce shocked many people, particularly the children. They have made a huge and loving effort to bring their relationships with me ever closer—and I have happily reciprocated. I cannot say that they have accepted all the facets of my new life. Perhaps one day we will all share happiness together, enjoying theater, opera, concerts, meals, hot dogs, drinks, and giggles. And normal, happy conversations. Rose-colored glasses?

IN APRIL 1999, I traveled to Germany for the first time.

About ten years ago, while attending a conference to discuss the problems of orchestras worldwide, I met Mr. Franz Xaver Ohnesorg, the director of the Cologne Philharmonic Hall. He asked me whether I would come to Germany, and I demurred. Some years later, he asked me again, and again I said no.

For many reasons, at the beginning of 1998 I decided to go to Germany. Not to play, not even to bring along my violin, but simply to hear young people and to meet musicians there. After some discussions with the directors of both the Berlin and Vienna Philharmonic Orchestras, who insisted that playing concerts had to be part of the visits, a condition I could not accept, Lee Lamont and I thought of Mr. Ohnesorg, and she called him to discuss the possibility. Plans began to be made for the visit.

Eight months later, in December 1998, Judith Arron, the executive director of Carnegie Hall, had another attack of the cancer that had struck her eight years earlier, and died soon afterward. She was unquestionably one of the most innovative concert administrators in the world, and had felt strongly that Mr. Ohnesorg should be invited to join her and, eventually, become the new director of the hall. After her death, many candidates were given very serious consideration for the position. Finally, the chairman of the board, Sandy Weill, and I as president, supported by the executive committee, offered Mr. Ohnesorg the position, and he accepted. The announcement was made to the public in the second week of January 1999. Two months later, I flew to Germany.

I went with my eyes open, to look at today's Germany, not yesterday's. All the people we met were trying to find their way back to a sensible, healthy normality; they are not forgetting their past. They do not need an explanation of their history from anyone; they know it better than we think. The young people especially deserve to learn as much about their pre-1933 history as possible, but the history since 1933 must remain clear. With it all, I was left with a nagging worry that Germans not fall back into their habit of mindless routine. Rigid orderliness is an old German tradition, which others cannot deal with easily.

Linda and I saw many cities. We visited the Beethoven house, the Mendelssohn house. It was so moving to be near where Bach, Beethoven, Brahms, and Mendelssohn had lived, to touch their harpsichords and pianos, to stand near where they are buried. A very special pleasure was our visit in Leipzig to the home of my colleague Kurt Masur and his wife, Tomoko. But I did not return a different person musically. If anything, my lifelong ideas about music were confirmed. I am happy about all the meetings and the new friends we made. I am happy that I learned much I didn't know before—especially about the open attitude of the Germans toward themselves and their history. It was a good learning experience.

ONCE SOMEONE asked me to rank the ten greatest violinists in history. Omitting mention of my contemporaries, with the exception of Heifetz, whose greatness is unchallengeable, and omitting present-day performers who are all my friends, I listed: Nicolò Paganini (1782–1840), Antonio Vivaldi (1678–1741), Ludwig Spohr (1784–1859), Henri Vieuxtemps (1820–1881), Henri Wieniawski (1835–1880), Pablo de Sarasate (1844–1908), Joseph Joachim (1831–1907), Eugène Ysaÿe (1858–1931), Bronislaw Huberman (1882–1947), and Jascha Heifetz (1901–1987).

I knew I could not play the violin as well as Heifetz, Oistrakh, Milstein, or, today, Perlman or Zukerman. Or Anne-Sophie Mutter, Gidon Kremer, or Midori. I've always been self-conscious about the fact that I didn't have the necessary basic training and physical habits in violin playing. Perhaps that gave me the freedom to have the musical insights that are my strength and my pleasure, my reason for being. I don't think I've ever felt that I reached the true heart of any work. These days, when I take up a work that I've played for years, there is often a sense of fresh discovery about what I don't know. In recent years, I've had a dream: I would love to build a little conference center in the studio house of our Connecticut home, and sit there and have groups of young musicians in Japan and Moscow and Paris and London and Tel Aviv and Buenos Aires and Newark, New Jersey, and El Paso, Texas, and Bismarck, North Dakota, play for me, and then talk to them and to their teachers.

There were times, in the years between 1990 and 1997, when performances of mine were more variable than they should have been, and I was reminded of that on more than one occasion. I now have to face the fact that there are works I will never play again, because I do not have the massive physical freedom I had years ago. And even with the repertoire I still permit myself to play in public, I am beginning to wonder how long I should go on. I would much rather decide that for myself than have people tell me, "Isn't it time to quit?" How I wish I had twenty more years in my fingers, the hands of my younger colleagues—to give sound to all the knowledge and vision I have acquired about music. How I love to be onstage! How I love to play! And I must add my thanks to Robert McDonald, who for eight years has been a treasured musical partner and traveling companion. His quiet dignity, good sense of humor, and admirable musicianship continue to be of enormous value to me.

Certainly I continue to enjoy the sheer sensuous, personal, delectable opportunity of talking through music to others; if anything, my passion for that has increased. I want to go on playing, especially with young musicians. That would be a lovely way to begin my eighth decade in music.

I want to share my ideas and what I've learned about what is possible in music, share all that with younger performers and particularly with young teachers: how to search inside for what is achievable in music. There is no finite interpretation, no finite performance; there are only the infinite possibilities of beauty. And when the time comes, as it inevitably must, I will be happy to be onstage playing and have my life end with a fiddler's version of dying with one's boots on. Then I will consider my life to have been worthwhile, with a legacy I am proud to leave.

WHILE SPEAKING/WRITING this book I have mentioned many of the great musical figures who, collectively, were the single most influence in my musical life.

Here I must go back to my earliest years and Pierre Monteux. He was already world-famous when he came to San Francisco. A short, rotund—stout, really—generally smiling person who, as the French say, "lived well in his own skin." He was a complete master of the art of conducting, with a clear, graceful beat that had constant command of the orchestra and always shaped the phrases of the music being performed. His greatest gift, which taught me so much, was his ability to use his eyes and see where all the nearly one hundred musicians were at that moment in the music and to sense, instantly, if an individual musician was lost. Just before any instrumental entrance in the score, he would glance at the string, woodwind, or brass player, catch his eye, purse his lips, and make certain that the entrance of that person or group was precisely where it should be. Many years later, I coined a thumbnail description, saying "If I were going to sneeze two weeks later, he would have a handkerchief ready."

The next major conductor I met in those early years—1936, 1937—was Otto Klemperer, who was not only a giant physically (about six-foot-four), but also musically. Then, he was already recognized as being among the ten major conductors. That first time I played with him was somewhat of a minor problem—because of his height, he did not use a podium, but I, at five-foot-five, had to constantly look almost straight up to watch his beat and to meet his eyes, which gave me an enormous pain in my neck at the end of the Tchaikovsky concerto. In the ensuing years we played many times and I learned why he was considered one of the greatest exponents of middle-European musical culture at its best. From him I learned a great deal about phrasing in long lines.

Another musician whom I met in those early years was the great violinist Nathan Milstein. He was a friend of my teacher, Naoum Blinder, and, of course, I was introduced to him when he came to San Francisco to perform. He had a transcendental technique and natural musicality. Nothing he played, even the most outrageously difficult passage, seemed to take any effort. I always described him as the man who did not have fingers on his left hand but radar. An out-of-tune note never happened and any sound that he produced was unfailingly beautiful and absolutely correct musically. Over the years, he became a very close friend and he loved to spend time talking about music or painting or literature for the first twenty or thirty minutes of our being together. Then the violin would come out and he would play some solo Bach with laser clarity and, with a smile, show off ideas for his next devilishly difficult transcription. When I asked him once how he had developed his extraordinary facility, he said, quite seriously, "When I was growing up in Russia, it was difficult to get printed music, particularly between 1917 and 1924. But my sister, who was a pianist, had all the Chopin études and nocturnes. So I used them as exercises." Meaning, of course, that he learned to play piano thirds, sixths, scales, and arpeggios on the violin! Anyone can take a look at those scores and realize what an incredible training ground that was.

Another violinist, famous more in Europe than in the United States, was Arthur Grumiaux. He was a most elegant, wonderfully educated, and literate musician, with a profoundly classical approach musically and complete control of violin technique which made light of any difficulty. We became very good friends and I had the utmost respect and affection for him. I tried to help him establish a major career in the United States, but it was blocked by his wife, who had more control over his career than he, and did not understand the complete dif-ference in concert life between Europe and the United States. She demanded fees and attentions that were utterly unreasonable and so forestalled any real growth in his American career. He made memora-ble recordings, special treasures to this day, of Mozart and Beethoven sonatas, with Clara Haskil, a Swiss pianist whom I knew and admired.

She was a wispy woman with a light mound of gray hair that seemed to have been combed only occasionally. She stooped more than a bit, but was magical at the piano. She and Grumiaux made an ideal combination as they shared such musical depth and aristocratic happiness and insight. At one time, she and I made a tour of a few concerts in Switzerland and Italy, which I remember largely because of the clarion beauty of her sound, no matter which instrument in which city, and the dreadful time we had fighting Italian railroad passengers while going from town to town.

In those early days in San Francisco, between 1934 and 1939, I heard so many artists who, I realized many years later, left an unforgettable impression on my musical awareness. I can still remember, not the actual performance but the timbre of the voices of Giovanni Martinelli and Elisabeth Rethberg singing arias and duets in Verdi's *Otello.* The huge, commanding, golden power of Kirtsten Flagstad in Wagner operas, the honeyed warmth of Lotte Lehmann, both in opera and in recitals of *lieder,* where each word had its nuance and thrust according to the poetic meaning of the words.

I remember the overwhelming majesterial concept in an all-Beethoven piano sonata evening played by Sergei Rachmaninoff. The music roared, whispered, came flooding forth when necessary and then could bring you tenderly close. All of this in one recital. One did not listen to music but was bathed by it. I also remember hearing, unbelieving its clarity, beauty, and precision, the still-astonishing recording by Yehudi Menuhin of the Paganini violin concerto, which he made with Pierre Monteux in Paris when he was only thirteen or fourteen years old. And it was made in one take, one play-through, after which Monteux hugged him and Menuhin happily went back to his hotel. What extraordinary performances those early years produced! He also leaves a legacy of unstinting humanitarianism in his activities and devotion to those in need.

I remember, too, performances by Mischa Elman, who carefully caressed every note with a lustrous, honeyed sound, a richness of tone that was never treacly but instantly recognizable as his alone.

I performed regularly with Fritz Reiner in Pittsburgh, both at the Syria Mosque and later in wonderful Heinz Hall. He had the most incredible control and baton technique, a mastery that was recognized by all musicians who performed with him or heard him, and he exercised a legendary tyranny when it came to the musicians in his orchestra. One or two examples: I was riding with him in a taxi with Morton Gould, who asked him how he indicated the beginning of the right tempo in the third movement of the Mozart G Major Concerto for violin. Reiner looked at him over his half-rimmed glasses and said, "You simply give the upbeat this way, and that's the tempo." Gould asked, "But what do I do if they don't come in exactly in the right tempo?" Without skipping a beat, Reiner said, "Fire them." And he meant it. Once, during his long tenure as head of the Chicago Symphony Orchestra, we were playing the Prokofiev G Minor Concerto. There is a little bridge passage from one tempo to another that is played by the first cellist in the orchestra. For some reason, the cellist, who was also Hungarian, could not get the right change instantly. Reiner repeated it once or twice, and I could see him losing his temper, his face flushed and his eyes blazing. He was about to erupt and the whole orchestra was tense with fear. He stopped and said in a deadly quiet vioce, "Oh, we have a very romantic Hungarian here." In the dead silence, I looked at him and at the cellist and said "Which one?" Happily, it defused the moment. Reiner was the most wonderful colleague imaginable, completely controlling the orchestra at the very tip of the long baton he favored, thus creating the musical foundation which makes for really fine performances. Then the soloist is free to exchange ideas and instinctive phrases as one would in chamber music, playing with equal colleagues.

I was imposed as a soloist upon Sir Thomas Beecham in the early 1950s. My manager, Harold Holt, and I decided to limit my English appearances to one or two with a major conductor and orchestra in London only, in order to build a future all-England career. I remember playing a concert in Paris on a Sunday afternoon, and then having to fly to London for a first rehearsal of the Beethoven Violin Concerto with Sir Thomas and the Royal Philharmonic on Monday. One of London's unfortunately regular fogs occurred and my flight was delayed many hours so I had to go the following morning, on very little sleep, and rush to the rehearsal. I thought I played very badly and apologized to Sir Thomas, promising that I would do better the next day. He said, "Oh, don't worry, my boy. We'll work everything out tomorrow." For a major conductor to do what he did that night was for me a unique experience and a blessing. After all, the Beethoven concerto was known by everyone, certainly by the musicians in the orchestra, but Beecham took the score home that night and wrote in innumerable little indications from the beginning to the end, with instructions for all the strings, woodwinds, and brass. These were meticulously put in the next morning by the librarian before I came to the rehearsal. Then, one of the special experiences of my life: we were in a rehearsal hall, not the Festival Hall. Sir Thomas and the orchestra began the concerto. We played without a single interruption until we came to the end. All we did was look and listen and make music. At the end of that rehearsal, there was a dead silence and all of us, the musicians, Beecham, and I, all gave a sigh as if we had just come out of a special moment in time. Beecham and I became very close friends and played together many times, including my first recordings of the Brahms and Sibelius violin concerti in 1952.

Another musical moment that remains fixed in my memory: one summer at a festival in the tiny hill town of Menton on the French Riviera, Jean-Pierre Rampal and I went to hear a concert that was being given by Dietrich Fischer-Dieskau with Sviatislav Richter, the great Russian pianist, accompanying him in Schubert *lieder*. The concert took place in a little square on a high hill in front of a church. A grandstand had been built to accommodate the public. Fischer-Dieskau and Richter suddenly created a magical aura around those musical jewels, which was so breathtaking that I suddenly looked at Jean-Pierre and we were both crying. It is moments like this that we strive for and, as experienced listeners, treasure even more.

I WOULD also like to share three memorable moments from the years in Carnegie Hall that are very special to me.

The first was in 1976, when Dick Debs, then the devoted chairman, conspired with me to celebrate the eighty-fifth anniversary of the hall with a special gala. There were only about four months to pull this together, and booking world-famous artists is usually done approximately two years in advance. I remember getting on the phone and talking to a few musicians like Vladimir Horowitz and Leonard Bernstein, who lived in the New York area, and others who lived nearby, like Slava Rostropovich in Washington, D.C., and a few friends from overseas, such as Dietrich Fischer-Dieskau and Yehudi Menuhin. I asked them what they were doing on May 18, and, of course, to cancel anything they may have planned. And nobody, but nobody, said no. That not one person refused to come makes clear the importance of Carnegie Hall to every living musician.

The day before the performance, I sat in the middle of the main floor with Wanda Horowitz, the wife of Vladimir Horowitz, as well as the daughter of Arturo Toscanini. These two men probably had more to do with setting the standards of quality of performance in the twentieth century than any two other people one can think of. And of course their lives were intimately connected to Carnegie Hall for almost three quarters of the century.

As Wanda and I sat together listening to *lieder* being sung by Fischer-Dieskau, one of the greatest singing artists of our time, accompanied by Vladimir Horowitz, with Leonard Bernstein turning the pages and Mstislav Rostropovich leaning against the piano listening with complete concentration to the beauty that was pouring forth, I suddenly started to cry. This moment, I realized, explained why I had become so involved with Carnegie Hall and why everyone else had joined in. I looked at Wanda next to me, and she, too, was weeping openly. We held hands very tightly, and I still remember this as one of the single most rewarding moments of my life as a musician. The recording of the concert was aptly titled the *Concert of the Century*.

The second moment was in 1986, when the board, then chaired by the redoubtable and imaginative Jim Wolfensohn, decided to make the necessary repairs to the aging dowager of 57th Street. The ceiling was starting to come down, the air-conditioning and elevators had to be replaced, and there was much cleaning and repainting to be done, as well as changing the old seats, and, in general, trying to give a fresh look to the hall in its ninety-fifth year.

As we could not afford a very long period without activity or income, we put a six-month time limit on the entire reconstruction, something the engineers and work managers thought almost impossible. But we insisted, and a timetable was set up. I remember so clearly the day the first workmen came into the hall to begin tearing out the seats, pulling down old curtains and the supports over the proscenium and, in essence, baring the bones of the venerable hall. The work went on at a frantic pace, and we were able to locate the rare master craftsmen who could do the special plasterwork on the restored ceiling over the stage and the necessary iron-grille work throughout the building. I was so impressed by the quality and dedication of the workers that I thought the first sounds to be heard in the new hall should be at a special concert for all the men who had been working there.

We planned a gala reopening, but because we were subject to the actual finishing time of the project, we had only two months in which to finalize the date and begin to plan for those who might participate. Once again I reached out to friends: Leonard Bernstein and Zubin Mehta, old and friendly colleagues from the New York Philharmonic; Frank Sinatra, who had become a great friend and had told me of his love and respect for Carnegie Hall; the incomparable Marilyn Horne, who had appeared often on the Carnegie stage; my frequent and beloved collaborator Yo-Yo Ma; and, again, my local pianist friend, Vladimir Horowitz. All were on hand to reveal to the world the new hall in its gleaming majesty. The setting of the hall had finally come to match the breathtaking quality of the music on its stage. Today, with some revisions since the restorations, the sound of Carnegie is grander and more beautiful than ever.

The third unforgettable moment of my years at Carnegie Hall was the dedication of the main hall as the "Isaac Stern Auditorium." It was an idea that began with the executive committe and was then taken to the board as a special recognition of my years of devotion to the hall. I knew nothing of the precise plans, but having heard some whispers, I immediately excused myself from any of the meetings at which this was to be discussed. The board appreciated my desire not to know anything and warned me in advance when the subject would be coming up. The first time I heard about it was one day when I was on the car phone with one of the hall's secretaries, who said, "Oh, Mr. So-and-so isn't available. They're meeting to discuss the name of the auditorium in your honor."

That was in November 1996. The celebration, "Isaac Stern: A Carnegie Hall Tribute," was on January 28, 1997.

What occurred then was not to be believed. The entire main hall at Carnegie was transformed into an immense banquet room, and more than 1,500 guests were served a wonderful dinner. The hall was bedecked with flowers, and special drapes hung from the upper tiers all the way down to the stage level, on which there was a lectern and seven or eight chairs. At the head table with Linda and me were Mr. and Mrs. Gregory Peck, Brooke Astor, Kitty Carlisle Hart, Mr. and Mrs. Walter Scheuer, and Hillary Rodham Clinton. The performers were Sarah Chang, Sylvia McNair, Carlo Scibelli, Sanford Sylvan, Martin Katz, Jonathan Feldman, Grant Wenaus, and Marietta Simpson (unsurprisingly, the event was also a benefit for Carnegie). The sum raised at this event honoring me was an astonishing $15.3 million. As Sandy Weill, the hugely effective current chairman, announced the figure, Mrs. Clinton, sitting to my right, said, "Wow!" And she was correct: It was, I think, the largest amount ever raised at a single event. Obviously, much occurred that night that was touching, unforgettable, and most special. Among other things, I was presented with two albums containing letters from world leaders such as Bill Clinton, Jacques Chirac, and Nelson Mandela; and renowned artists like Cecilia Bartoli, Marilyn Horne, Maurizio Pollini, Leontyne Price, Robert Shaw, Beverly Sills, Sir Georg Solti, and John Williams, to name just a few.

The naming of the auditorium in perpetuity was something I had never sought or dreamed of. That it occurred as a voluntary gesture of goodwill made it even more moving and, of course, something I will cherish for the rest of my life.

BY THE time these lines are read in a book, I will have experienced a watershed event in my life and my career.

I have often said that I would like to cease major solo performances before everybody else wishes I would do so. Recently, I have experienced a rapid diminution in my physical abilities and have felt considerable personal unhappiness with my performances, more than some loyal and brave friends, most particularly my loving and supportive wife, Linda, would admit. And my children have been equally supportive, though lovingly critical, of anything less than concentrated efforts to do my best.

In the past three years, I have been troubled by arthritis in both hands. But much more painfully serious for me has been a steadily decreasing control of my bow arm. For decades, I have been known to possess one of the strongest and most flexible of bow arms, one that was capable of many different colors and that could speak from my ear and heart to the ears and sensibilities of my listeners. The bow arm is, after all, the voice box, the throat, the tongue, the speaking individuality of every performer. Bow control, bow speed, and vibrato are three of the elements that differentiate one player from everyone else. The greater the flexibility, the greater the range of emotion and thought that can be expressed.

My increasing difficulty in controlling the bow arm has led, in the last two years, to some unhappy and terrifying moments. At times I couldn't hold a bow with my fingers and would grab it with my fist. In one or two instances, it fell from my hands. Because of the pain in the right thumb and forefinger, I thought that this, too, was the result of the arthritis. But a very thorough neurological examination has revealed that I have the well-known carpal tunnel syndrome, a condition of the muscles and nerves of the hand that can afflict performers, athletes, and secretaries who engage in constant rigorous use of the fingers and hands. I've been told that the surgical procedure for this can result in the regeneration of both muscles and nerves, so that the hand can be restored to nearly its original strength. Should this happen, I will have regained the physical and musical control with which I can live proudly, and will be able to continue playing chamber music with friends and to give an occasional solo performance. By the time this book appears, I should have the answer. I hope to heaven and with all my heart that it will be in the affirmative.

Index

Illustration Credits

The photographs in this book are reproduced courtesy of the following:

A Note About the Writer

CHAIM POTOK was born and raised in New York City. His novel *The Chosen* was nominated for a National Book Award and won the Edward Lewis Wallant Award; *The Promise* was given the Athenaeum Prize; and *The Gift of Asher Lev* won the National Jewish Book Award. In 1997, he received the National Foundation for Jewish Culture Achievement Award; in 1999, his short story "Moon" was given the O. Henry Award. He lives in Pennsylvania.

A Note on the Type

This book was set in Minion, a typeface produced by the Adobe Corporation specifically for the Macintosh personal computer, and released in 1990. Designed by Robert Slimbach, Minion combines the classic characteristics of old-style faces with the full complement of weights required for modern typesetting.

Composed by Creative Graphics,
Allentown, Pennsylvania
Printed and bound by Quebecor Printing,
Fairfield, Pennsylvania
Designed by Anthea Lingeman

CPSIA information can be obtained at www.ICGtesting.com
228036LV00001B/27/A